I WILL SHOW YOU
HOW IT WAS

I WILL SHOW YOU
HOW IT WAS

THE STORY OF WARTIME KYIV

ILLIA PONOMARENKO

BLOOMSBURY PUBLISHING

NEW YORK · LONDON · OXFORD · NEW DELHI · SYDNEY

BLOOMSBURY PUBLISHING
Bloomsbury Publishing Inc.
1385 Broadway, New York, NY 10018, USA

BLOOMSBURY, BLOOMSBURY PUBLISHING, and the Diana logo
are trademarks of Bloomsbury Publishing Plc

First published in the United States 2024

Bloomsbury Publishing Plc does not have any control over, or responsibility for,
any third-party websites referred to or in this book. All internet addresses given in this
book were correct at the time of going to press. The author and publisher regret
any inconvenience caused if addresses have changed or sites have ceased to exist, but
can accept no responsibility for any such changes.

ISBN: HB: 978-1-63973-387-3; EBOOK: 978-1-63973-388-0

LIBRARY OF CONGRESS CATALOGING-IN-PUBLICATION DATA IS AVAILABLE

2 4 6 8 10 9 7 5 3 1

Typeset by Westchester Publishing Services
Printed and bound in the U.S.A.

To find out more about our authors and books visit www.bloomsbury.com and
sign up for our newsletters.

Bloomsbury books may be purchased for business or promotional use. For information
on bulk purchases please contact Macmillan Corporate and Premium Sales Department at
specialmarkets@macmillan.com.

To Maks Levin, our colleague and friend
who gave his life in the name of journalism during the Battle of Kyiv

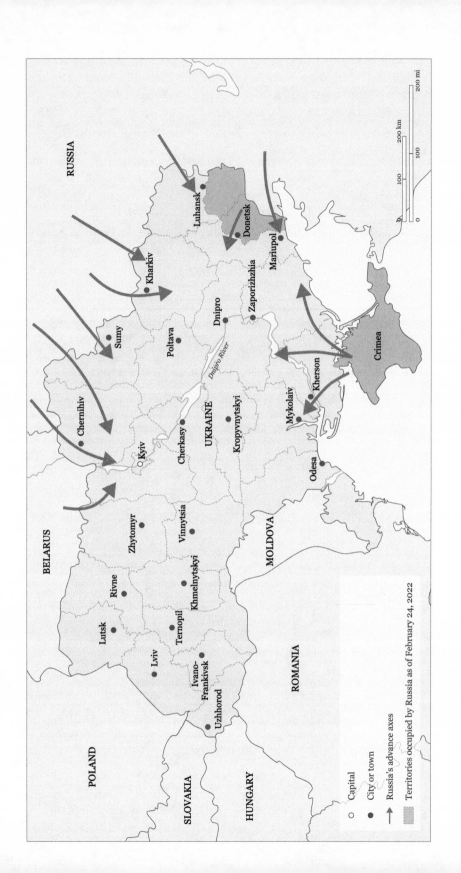

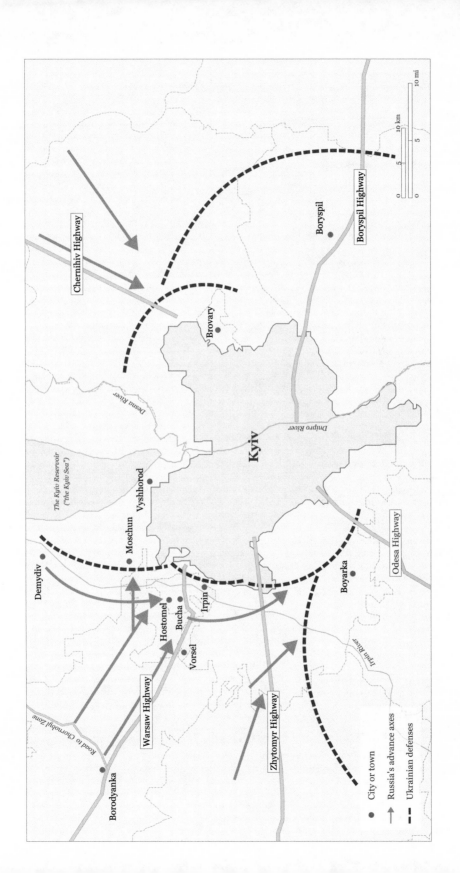

ONE

S lowly we go.

The lonesome highway runs through pinewoods somewhere east of Kyiv.

Spring is finally proving itself. Nature is waking from the long cold, and the sunshine is awesome. This seems to be the year's first dry and warm day, as if a dark force has suddenly lost its grip and the world is set free again.

Last year's grass is still gray and brown. But those meadows by the riverside close to the town of Rusaniv are fresh and beautiful in any season.

The H-07 Highway is empty.

And we walk loosely, stopping briefly at abandoned townhouses and at the jumbles of concrete blocks dumped on the road. We proceed as short buzzes from shoulder-mounted radio sets instruct us to.

We, a handful of reporters, Ukrainians and foreigners, once again, and as we have throughout our careers, have gladly abandoned all common sense.

We follow a Ukrainian combat team.

The helmets, the olive-green armored vests, the tourniquets, the AK-74M rifles slung over shoulders, the blue tape wrapped around upper arms, the knives, the MultiCam-colored gloves, the ammo magazines fully loaded.

Sleeve patches bear the image of a skull on a black-and-red heraldic shield. Also, the motto: "Ukraine or Death."

I've spent a lot of time with the 72nd Mechanized Infantry Brigade in the war's previous years. Deployed in Donbas since 2014, the brigade is known as one of the toughest, most aggressive, most battle-tested Ukrainian formations.

It was they who managed to break through the death trap at Izvaryne in August 2014. It was they who gave Russian-led militants a hard time during the Battle of Avdiivka in early 2017.

With these guys, I survived the most dangerous two hours of my life during a fierce Russian mortar attack at Avdiivka's battlefield position Promzona in May 2017. Once upon a time, in a brief improvised ceremony on the suddenly quiet front lines, I was invited to take a vodka shot with the brigade's top commander and several leading officers to commemorate their fallen.

We still mourn the painful loss of twenty-three-year-old Major Andriy Kyzylo, call sign "Orel" (Eagle), of the 72nd. His assault team managed to take an enemy platoon strongpoint south of Avdiivka in late January 2017. The young officer, along with several of his men, was killed amid fierce (and eventually unsuccessful) enemy counterattacks.

The brigade had taken up position at the Butovka coal mine. I shared hot tea with soldiers in the snow and cold. We loitered amid the sooty ruins, trying to stay warm. That was my first war zone deployment as a defense reporter with *Kyiv Post*, then the largest English-language publication in Ukraine.

Andriy Kyzylo's close friend Andriy Verkhoglyad was part of the assault team. He found it hard to come to terms with his commander's death. We remained in touch in the years after on Facebook and elsewhere. In 2018, I put him forward for the *Kyiv Post*'s 30 Under 30, the annual award for successful young Ukrainians.

And I secretly shed tears mixed with iced whiskey when the audience gave Verkhoglyad a standing ovation at the award ceremony at the Kyiv Hilton in 2018.

This smiling blond guy, a favorite of war photographers, the twenty-seven-year-old decorated battalion leader, reunited with his late friend in a clash with Wagner mercenaries near Svitlodarsk in June 2022.

Now streets in Kyiv are named after each of the guys.

So many memories, so many names.

Now it's the Battle of Kyiv 2022. And I am with my brigade again.

Russian lines run down the road in the town of Peremoga a couple of kilometers away.

A soldier hugging his rifle waves to us.

"All right, boys and girls, here we go."

The road suddenly ends at a heap of crushed concrete and twisted rebar. This is what remains of the local bridge over the Trubizh River, one of many leading to Kyiv. It has been destroyed. What's left of the two-lane platform helplessly bites the water sluggishly flowing beneath. There's a ridiculously large swath of TM-62Ms, anti-tank land mines, spreading from both sides of the road.

Also, two dead bodies on the roadside next to a pile of concrete rubble.

Russians.

It's their dirty swamp-colored fatigues and the frayed remains of red sleeve ribbons. Their pale bellies are bloated. Postmortem paralysis has shackled their fingers.

The cadavers lie with arms up to their shoulders. Ukrainian troops thoughtfully covered the dead men's faces with their own fatigue jackets to protect our tender civilian feelings.

I shove my hands beneath my sweaty armored vest to feel a bit more secure. And I force myself to move closer. I am not a fan of looking at the dead, I will tell you.

"Well, hello there, you fucks," I whisper.

Yeah, I know. That's not a very good example of sticking to the BBC standards. But hey, cut me some slack. Over the previous twenty-two days, I have seen things I could never have imagined.

I saw the whole nation, everything my generation loved and cared for, standing just a step away from annihilation. I saw the sky light up and heard sirens scream.

I saw people fleeing fire and death, many nearly barefoot, in shock and terror.

I saw giant plumes of smoke rising from the battlefields of Bucha. I heard the razing whistle of incoming shells. I couldn't go to bed without hearing Ukrainian artillery pounding Russian positions close to my neighborhood in Kyiv.

Two soldiers carrying shovels pass by from our rear.

The Trubizh is not a wide river, but the current has undercut its banks in places. In the deep hollow of one such cut, Ukrainian emergency response workers, all dressed in black uniforms with green reflective tape, carefully dig into the moist soil.

"You guys be careful." The wind brings their voices.

"Remove the layers bit by bit."

Every spade bite unearths something in the damp soil. Tatters of frayed cloth, boot bottoms, clumps of earth mixed with clotted blood, pockets of foaming fluids. Then, blackened fingers barely distinguishable from the dirt of their internment.

The subtle smell of death slowly fills the dark pit.

The workers act as if it's nothing.

"All right, get those stretchers and lashings. We got another one almost ready."

The local townsfolk of Rusaniv buried several Russian soldiers in this pit.

They were all killed several days ago in a Ukrainian ambush as they tried to seize the river crossing and ensure their further advance toward Kyiv.

Emergency response workers tie the rotting bodies, covered with black dirt, to stretchers and trail them one by one to the river.

Then they ferry them to the other side on a small rubber boat.

A 4x4 truck is waiting next to the broken bridge. Now, in a sick irony of fate, the aggressor's dead soldiers are being given a chance to somewhat redeem themselves.

Six dead Russians, via civilian mediators, are to be handed back to the enemy—in exchange for two living Ukrainian soldiers held in captivity.

War is different here and there. Some Russians don't give a damn. Their dead are left where they fell on the battlefield. In some cases, Ukrainian command finds it hard to get Russia interested in retrieving scores of body bags from storage refrigerators.

In other cases, commanders at the local level make deals to halt hostilities for a minute so both sides can recover their fallen.

The small town of Rusaniv is barely significant.

But it was established as far back as the 980s A.D., about the time Prince Volodymyr the Great officially introduced Christianity in the Kyivan Rus. One of the Trubizh River's sweeping bends harbored a substantial fort, one of many that used to defend the medieval kingdom.

Ironically enough, the invaders of the twenty-first century will never make it past this long-forgotten barrier.

Farther down the road, the charred remains of a destroyed Russian T-90. Five or six knocked-out BMP-2s marked "O" also lie scattered on the riverside.

Another ambush.

One of the charred vehicles still has that disgusting sweetish smell of burned canned food. Track traces on the ground show the machine had rampaged like a doomed beast desperately growling for life.

Ashes, frayed tatters of fatigues, medicals, soiled paper-towel rolls, dirty plastic bags, everything splayed all around, as if these things burst out of the monster's eviscerated belly.

"It is hard to identify the Russians killed at this spot. According to Ukrainian troops, none of them had any official identifying documents during the attack."

That's the reporter Andriy Tsapliyenko waltzing around with his cameraman. This guy was my hero when I was a kid. In the last twenty years or so, he has been one of the biggest stars of Ukraine's TV news, appearing every night with reports from every single possible conflict on the planet, from Afghanistan to Liberia, Iraq, Congo . . . and then Ukraine.

In my family, Tsapliyenko had been a synonym for "a TV reporter in a war zone." Now we're kind of in the same boat.

"In my hands, I hold banking cards that used to belong to one of them," Tsapliyenko continues. "They read 'Aleksandr Gagarin.'"

Those Russians died nameless. No dog tags around their necks, no passports in their pockets. The 72nd troops believe their commanders took their IDs away from them before the ill-fated assault.

Piles of charred garbage dumped onto the ground next to the beheaded BMPs appear to contain an assortment of interesting things, like cheap canned fish products from Ukrainian supermarkets. Something tells me they did not buy this Ukrainian-made food with hard cash.

A couple of pictures for a story, maybe a video on my iPhone . . . and it's time to go.

The 72nd troops are calling. We've been sticking out in this open place under the Russians' nose for way too long now.

As I leave the battlefield, a Ukrainian emergency response worker drags another body tied to a stretcher.

The dead Russian soldier's face is unnaturally pitch-black from the moist dirt and decomposition. He is the last to leave their awful pit. During moments like that, I offer thanks to the universe that it's not me doing this job.

It's still very silent—the short cease-fire to exchange the dead for the living between Russia and Ukraine is being carefully observed.

I crawl back to the other side via the bridge's remains, grasping at sharp concrete debris. Try to not tumble into the cold river when you're cocooned in fourth-class British-made armor!

"Hey dudes, check this out," a soldier calls out to us reporters. He holds a Russian vehicle communications helmet he found somewhere. "To hell with them fuckers!"

He throws the headset into the river, and the thing sinks out of sight.

I walk back to an abandoned house at the town's end, where warfighters peacefully smoke in the garden by the road.

One of them bites his cigarette and puts Russian sleeve patches out on a wooden table.

"The latest items in our collection, gentlemen."

Russian insignia collected from the dead.

Two patches show a monochromic coat of arms—the imperial two-headed eagle—and a logo of some combat unit: two crisscrossed rifles put against a sword hanging from above and belted with ribbons.

THE ARMED FORCES OF RUSSIA

How nice is that, huh?

There's also a name on a tab: "Lubsandabayev B.N."

Taking a picture again on my iPhone.

Who knows. There might be a story behind this name that suddenly popped up from the dirt and ashes.

. . . That was on March 18, 2022.

The fiery turning point of the Battle of Kyiv.

Russian invasion forces stood just east and west of Ukraine's capital, trying to break into Kyiv. Or at least suffocate the half-abandoned city in a relentless siege.

More than three weeks after the invasion day of February 24, they had advanced to within kilometers of the city boundaries, desolating our suburbs and setting nights alight with the glow of fire and smoke.

But on that riverside at Rusaniv, the sun was shining for us all.

There was an unspoken feeling of confidence and pride in everyone's eyes.

Long gone was the talk of taking Kyiv within three days, in a blissful shock-and-awe strike, the triumph of Russia's imperial might.

The invading Russian forces had bogged down in fierce fighting.

They were exhausted. They had absolutely screwed up their logistics. They sustained heavy losses. They could no longer move forward.

It was becoming clearer that Kyiv would be saved.

The blitzkrieg plan that looked so good on paper and in TV propaganda suddenly hit a wall.

The initial shock had gone. Dead Russian paratroopers were scattered in the ruined streets of Hostomel, and the woodland roads of Kyiv countryside became a giant graveyard of armored columns.

The battle was far from over, and the entire nation was bleeding.

But they were not going to get Kyiv.

We could feel that.

And we, a handful of mediocre Ukrainian reporters from different media outlets, were on our way home to Kyiv in a Ford pickup truck, feeling elated as never before on that sunny day.

We were where we belonged, witnessing and reporting history in the making.

The Battle of Kyiv was indeed one of the most tragic—and the most bizarre—events in modern history. It was the opening act of the biggest European bloodbath since 1945, and one of the most shamelessly trumped-up, absurd, and unnecessary wars the world had ever seen.

One man obsessed with his ego had simply declared a neighboring nation "Nazi" and disdainfully decided on its fate.

Kyiv, the symbolic sanctuary of the ancient East Slavic world and the center of Ukraine's revolutionary fight for independence, was the ultimate prize.

And truth be told, at the darkest moments of February and March 2022, the Russians were indeed close to getting that.

We were just moments away from bidding farewell to our home and our way of life, and could only hope that our defeated nation in chains would continue a guerrilla war for freedom.

Yet, as half of the world's media was burying Ukraine alive, as half of the West was faintheartedly thinking how to again adapt to a new reality in Europe, Ukraine managed to fiercely fight back—and prevail.

After more than a month of brutal fighting, Russia eventually gave up on Kyiv and left by April 2022.

Outnumbered and outgunned, Ukraine sustained the most critical blow. And unexpectedly delivered Russia the greatest and the most defining defeat of this war. It spelled a stunning end to the Kremlin's megalomaniac plans of a quick and easy conquest of a forty-million-person nation.

Ukraine did it alone, by itself, still with very little defense aid from the West. And that uneven victory altered the course of European history.

It dealt a devastating gut punch to the rise of the revanchist Russia hungry to devour and dominate Eastern Europe again. A very large part of the Kremlin military might stockpiled for decades destroyed in the woods and roads of northern Ukraine.

A human-made miracle right in front of our eyes, in the streets and neighborhoods we lived in and loved.

The Battle of Kyiv and what preceded it were a tragic story of shameless lies declared in front of the entire world intended to disguise a delusional lust for power. And of the imprudence and half-heartedness of so many decision-makers in Ukraine and the West.

It was about inconceivably senseless loss of life, the roar of thousands of artillery guns shaking the earth, the smell of fire and mass graves, horrific atrocities, and machines of armor with their crews inside glowing red-hot next to roadside malls and flower shops—something we thought was simply impossible in our time and place.

And it was about countless soldiers fighting until the bitter end to save the nation's capital. And air force pilots going out for nearly suicidal missions against overwhelming Russian forces in the sky. And about ordinary people taking up rifles for the first time in their lives to meet invaders in a hopeless fight in their own streets.

So many millions of men and women, from high-ranking officials to regular folks like us, making the moral choice of not giving in to the dark—but doing what was right, no matter what.

How did we come to this place, in our age of Netflix, AI chatbots, and food-delivery apps?

I'll do my very best to show how it was from inside the proud ancient city of Kyiv, Vladimir Putin's greatest desire he tried and failed to lay his hands on.

But first—let's go to a place far more pleasant than a Russian soldier's grave.

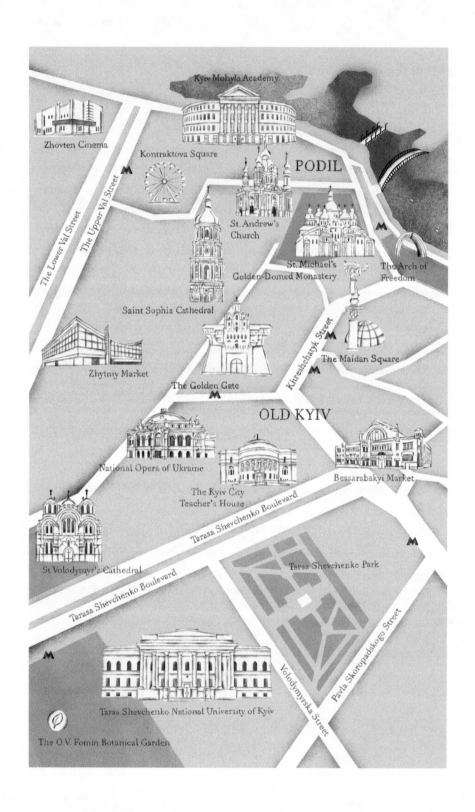

Trukhaniv Island

The Verkhovna Rada

The Mariinsky Palace

Dnipro River

The Chimaeras House

THE GOVERNMENT
QUARTER

The Presidential Office

The Kyiv Pechersk Lavra

The Motherland Statue

PECHERSK

The Kyiv Fortress

The Olympiysky Stadium

Maria Zankovetska Park

The Hryshko National
Botanical Garden

Velyka Vasylkivska Street

The Baikove Cemetery

TWO

S ue me, but I say Kyiv is one of the world's best places for the winter holidays.

In Ukraine, we officially have two Christmas days a year—December 25 and then January 7, under the Eastern Orthodox tradition.

The Christmas season "officially" begins near December 19, Saint Nicholas Day, when in many families, parents place gifts under their kids' pillows to be discovered in the morning. (In 2023, they switched Saint Nicholas Day to December 6—which in fact means the official Christmastime craze in Ukraine is supposed to begin two weeks earlier!)

That's a fine tradition even in Donbas, though the region is far less religious than, say, western Ukraine.

Around that day, crowds gather at Sofiivska Square in the old city to witness the opening ceremony for the nation's main Christmas tree. Every year, there are so many people sipping champagne, kissing one another, singing, and taking selfies that it's sometimes hard to break through the crowd to a comfortable spot in the square.

But, of course, the real craze begins as early as November, sometimes even before Black Friday. Zillions of shops decorate their windows, Christmas-related ads and posters are everywhere, TV channels outdo themselves broadcasting the Coca-Cola train commercials, and supermarket chains go nuts trying to sell as many decorations, candles, and tangerines as possible.

Several districts of Kyiv block off traffic and kick-start month-long Christmas fairs. On Khreshchatyk Street and between the Mykhailivska and the Sofiivska squares in the upper city, Christmas vendors sell every sort of street food and drink imaginable. There's also a giant stage next to the New Year's tree with live music practically 24/7.

The same goes for Taras Shevchenko Park, which becomes a sort of forest of lights where people go crazy singing karaoke. In Podil, there's always a skating rink and a ski slalom for kids. No one cares if winter this year is too warm and snowless. There must be a skating rink next to the observation wheel on Kontraktova Square.

When Volodymyr Zelensky took office, he opened Bankova Street in the government quarter for pedestrians. Yes, of course, the square right in front of the Presidential Office became a place for yet another winter fair with a pretty decent skating rink.

Normally, the season is considered over by January 19, Epiphany Day. But I swear, in 2022, some of the most stubborn coffee shops continued playing Frank Sinatra's Christmas hits up to damn near the Russian invasion day in late February.

It feels like the world starts spinning around nothing but the holiday. And despite the omnipresent references to Christianity, it's almost completely secular. In Kyiv and many other cities, they installed the central Christmas tree even during the wartime winter, for crying out loud!

And of course, there's New Year's Day—which means that between December 31 and January 2, the whole nation pours into a frenzied spree of shopping, cooking, binge-drinking, watching *Die Hard* and *Home Alone*, and then recovering from hangovers and the pain of getting back to work.

Back in the day, we also had a thing for rewatching old Soviet movies we all know by heart.

But in the wake of what has happened to us all in 2022, I guess that is over.

So here I am. It's December 17, 2021, the high peak of the Christmas season. From the distance of months, those days now seem such a happy time. Life was good. The city was full of light, and it was breathing fun and business.

That December was mostly about icy rains. Nothing like our childhood memories full of snow. The pains of global climate change, I guess.

But I was feeling warm and cozy—because, once again, I'd found shelter from the cold at the Ziferblat, a co-working place in the Golden Gate area. You just come in, take a vintage alarm clock at the counter, do whatever you want inside, for however long you want, and then pay for the time as you leave.

Back in those days, we at the *Kyiv Independent*, a brand-new media outlet of our own creation, did not even have an editorial office,

In our first weeks, we had no money. But we quickly got going on a website and a newsletter. Without an office, we knocked about and held editorial meetings at cafes or co-working spaces or wrote our stories from home. This was the "nomadic period" of our business venture, when stories were born wherever we could sit down and place a laptop on our knees.

I grab a big cup of coffee and flop down on a comfy sofa next to a Christmas tree and a friendly gathering enjoying their Monopoly game a bit too loudly.

The *Kyiv Independent* needs a story.

Something rather weird has happened beyond this tiny world of soft piano music and holiday lights.

"Kremlin drafts pacts to limit Western influence in post-Soviet countries," I type, drafting a working headline on my laptop.

"Amid the ongoing security crisis, Moscow has suggested a grand agreement with the West that de facto aims to reinstate its Cold War time exclusive sphere of influence in Eastern Europe and also prevent Ukraine from ever joining NATO," I write.

"After voicing a series of public demands and holding negotiations with Western leaders, the Russian foreign affairs ministry published two draft pacts on Dec. 17, offering to sign one with the United States and the other one with NATO.

"The Kremlin's move came following months of tensions that skyrocketed when Moscow amassed nearly 100,000 troops surrounding

Ukraine in November. Western and Ukrainian intelligence assess Russia's actions as a threat of an all-out invasion of Ukraine."

Amid ongoing rumors, Russia's foreign ministry published the draft pacts on its website.

Two days before publication, the document was handed over to United States Assistant Secretary of State Karen Donfried.

And that was one hell of a read.

As if it had just won a major regional war, Russia was literally and openly trying to impose a new order in Europe.

First, a "draft treaty" for NATO.

Or, to be more precise, a set of demands substantiated by nothing but the Kremlin's demonstrative and provocative overconfidence. In black and white, Moscow simply demanded that NATO terminate all military activities and buildup within a Russian comfort zone.

The boundaries of this comfort zone were very loosely outlined, reaching far beyond Russia's internationally recognized borders. And it stated that both sides must avoid situations that might be deemed "national security threats."

Moreover—and this was the most brazen bullet point—Moscow insisted that member states that had joined the NATO alliance after May 27, 1997, must now withdraw all military capabilities throughout Europe except for those that had already been deployed prior to that day.

This was presumably referencing the Founding Act on Mutual Relations, Cooperation and Security, a road map for NATO–Russia cooperation signed nearly twenty-five years earlier. Basically, what they were demanding was that NATO's key military allies, such as the United States, the United Kingdom, and France, get out of all former Warsaw Pact nations

And of course, NATO was supposed to formally disavow accepting any new member states, specifically Ukraine. And to not carry out any military activities, such as joint military exercises, in Eastern Europe, the Caucasian region, or Central Asia.

Moreover, Moscow said both sides must define a certain broad zone within which there could be no military drills and maneuvers at a level higher than that of a combined arms brigade.

But hey—as a gesture of peace and a nod to the Cuban Missile Crisis of 1962, Moscow suggested that a Cold War–style hotline be established to ensure direct communication between NATO and the Kremlin.

The pact also said Russia and NATO must not deploy ground-based, short- and medium-range missile systems in areas from which they would be capable of striking the other side.

Second: the list of demands to the United States.

These largely duplicated the "draft treaty" with NATO. Presenting the United States as the real puppet master behind the alliance, Moscow demanded that Washington formally promise not to accept any new NATO member states, specifically the nations that used to be part of the Soviet Union.

Also, the United States was supposed to forget about any new military bases in former Soviet states that had not already joined NATO (yes, Ukraine and Georgia), and they were not to use their military infrastructure for any military activities, or even have any bilateral military cooperation.

The "draft treaty" again said Russia and the United States must abstain from activities that could be considered "threats to national security." The right to veto any activity Russia didn't like applied to large and vaguely defined swaths of the globe—in other words, wherever the Kremlin saw fit at a moment.

Both sides were to abstain from deploying strategic bombers or warships in any area beyond their respective national borders, where they might be capable of striking each other's territories.

For some reason, the United States Air Force Global Strike Command and the United States Navy were to severely curtail their presence and activities around the world, especially in Europe and Asia, and even Alaska. This would of course make room for the far weaker Russian Air Force and Navy, granting them dominance in the post-Soviet region.

Something similar was to happen to all United States nuclear weapons deployed beyond American soil—they all must be dismantled and sent home. That included an estimated two hundred air-dropped nuclear bombs still stored in Germany, Italy, Turkey, and Belgium, the

Cold War remnants. Tellingly, this did not include nuke-carrying submarines plying the ocean, of which Russia has many.

Russia, for its part, was to give nothing in return. For decades, it hadn't had any nuclear weapons deployed beyond its national borders, except for ocean submarines, part of its much-vaunted global nuclear triad.

The message was: Get out of what we now declare our exclusive influence zone.

And we don't care that it's not 1953 anymore. And we are not even close to being in a position or have the right to issue such demands. And in the world of 2021, such a pact would mean ditching decades of post–Cold War history and ignoring the will of multiple nations that have joined NATO or were hoping to do so.

The Kremlin presented the situation as if NATO and the United States, suddenly, owed it a new Yalta Conference, at which they were supposed to partition Europe, again.

Get out of our way to all-out revanchism, especially when it comes to Ukraine, or else.

Of course, that was a knowingly impossible ultimatum.

As former United States ambassador to Russia Michael McFaul very correctly stated at the time, Russia was simply issuing bold, unilateral demands. It did not suggest its own withdrawal from Transnistria, or Abkhazia and South Ossetia, or Crimea and East Ukraine.

It did not promise to withdraw its nuclear-carrying Iskander missile systems from Kaliningrad Oblast that were pointing at the heart of Europe. And it did not promise to stop its assassinations or cease supporting antidemocratic forces in the West or the wayward regime of Aleksandr Lukashenko of Belarus.

And it was concentrating a one-hundred-thousand-strong invasion force against Ukraine. For the second time in 2021.

Was it trying to extort new concessions from the West?

Or, as the *Wall Street Journal* said then, was it possible that the Kremlin never intended to pursue any negotiations and that it might simply be setting up a grand casus belli if these absurd demands were not met?

The West was trying to stay diplomatic and careful, as usual.

"Jen Psaki, the White House spokesperson, reportedly confirmed United States officials had been informed on the suggested pacts and were to discuss them with the European allies.

"'There will be no talks on European security without our European allies and partners,' Psaki said.

"We will not compromise the key principles on which European security is built, including that all countries have the right to decide their own future and foreign policy, free from outside interference.

"However, she said there was no reason to believe that the United States and Russia would not be able to find a common ground and reach a security agreement the way the two powers used to in the previous decades."

All right, the article is done. Sent to an editor.

Now it's time to stretch my legs and raise a glass at the nearest Drunken Cherry. It's a chain originally from Lviv that serves nothing but a very special hot cherry bounce that tastes especially great in winter. Yes, foreigners living in Ukraine, I'm looking at you and I know you love it.

Also, why not just take a walk?

This city is something special.

It's about everything it has seen in well over twelve hundred years of its history. It's a mixture of god-awful Soviet panel buildings, traces of its ancient glory as the capital of Kyivan Rus, the Stalinist gravitas, the Russian Empire, and the insane mayhem of commercial development of our times.

According to a myth, Andrew the Apostle, on his journey to spread the word of Jesus, once came to a place by a wide river. He erected a cross on a hill where today towers St. Andrew's Church overlooking the Podil. And he said that one day, a great and sacred city would rise in the land.

Those hills by the Dnipro have harbored settlements since approximately the fall of the Roman Empire. But centuries later, Vikings ruling the Slavic tribes made Kyiv their capital, "the mother of Rus cities."

Kyiv has risen to preeminent glory and then been kicked to the bottom of the heap. It has been the coveted prize of princes, tsars, khans, and dictators. It has been burned to ashes several times and has completely changed its face over the centuries.

It has been the heart of the Slavic kingdom stretching from the White Sea to the Black Sea, and it has been reduced to an insignificant crossroads that had to wait seven hundred years to rise again.

Kyiv is "the New Jerusalem," home to thousand-year-old monumental cathedrals and monasteries, where Eastern Christianity was introduced.

He who ruled Kyiv was the ruler of the kingdom.

The hills overlooking the Podil and the Dnipro riverside, with all the remains of the ancient walls and defensive ditches, are where so many things from history textbooks actually happened. In the world of eastern Slavic nations, Kyiv is just like Rome to Western Europe—the place where it all began.

No wonder Vladimir Putin wanted Kyiv for his twenty-first-century imperialistic spree. Moscow spent centuries monopolizing the legacy of Kyivan Rus and even religiously positioning itself over the sanctuaries of Kyiv, but nope. The ancient capital would prove its mettle.

Kyiv is a weird place in many ways.

Today it's also a mixture of everything that Ukraine is. In its streets, you can hear Russian pronounced in a specific eastern Ukrainian manner. And lots of western Ukrainian accents and dialects. Also, lots of English speakers.

Folks from all corners of Ukraine come and settle in Kyiv for education, a career, and a better tomorrow. Over the last decade or so, it has become a melting pot of those originally from Dnipro and from Donbas, or Kherson, or the little towns of West Ukraine.

Once upon a time, we at the *Kyiv Post* realized that except for a couple of guys everyone else working there wasn't actually from Kyiv.

A city of migrants in hot pursuit of freedom, and happiness.

I was among those many when, in May 2016, I came to Kyiv by train with something like $100 in my pocket and a backpack. This city is about starting from scratch and making your way. Renting a cheap apartment in the suburbs and then taking a million steps forward.

So many of us newcomers eventually ended up settling down in new homes in Kyiv satellites like Irpin, Bucha, Sofiivska Borschahivka, or Hostomel, contributing to the messy local real estate market.

In the war of 2022, those quiet suburbs helped save this city.

Kyiv is about countless hipster coffee shops and century-old parks. It's a mixture of all cultures possible, where a folksy Ukrainian establishment stands next to a shawarma kiosk and a top-notch Crimean Tatar restaurant, then next to a famous Chinese one, as well as a good Indian place.

In Kyiv, we probably have more Georgian restaurants than Tbilisi does.

When it comes to bars and pubs, or pizza or sushi places, I state with complete certainty that we Kyivans are spoiled. There are so many of them, and almost all are very good, at every level, from generic football boozers to sophisticated cafe theaters or theme bars for fans of vinyl records.

Yes, you're right, tons of other cities are also good at this. But what's special about Kyiv is that going out is much more affordable and pleasurable. In my travels abroad, in bars and restaurants, I often catch myself thinking that with such service, these establishments would have few patrons in Kyiv.

The proud city has given birth to so many famous people. As you walk the streets, you can see countless memorial plaques showing their faces.

In that building on Baseina Street, the future prime minister of Israel Golda Meir was born. If you walk past the city garden in front of the Cabinet of Ministers, you'll see a statue of a man sitting on a bench and contemplating something extremely emotional at the entrance to the Dynamo Stadium.

That's after Valeriy Lobanovskyi, the world soccer legend. A barely noticeable house in the Andriivskyi Descent was home to Mikhail Bulgakov, the author of *The Master and Margarita*.

The city has its problems with Soviet-era infrastructure, crazy traffic, and god-awful flea markets next to subway stations. But you know what? You end up loving this easygoing mess of life questionably managed by a tongue-tied former boxing champion. Our beloved mayor, Vitali Klitschko.

I roll myself into a coat and walk out on Volodymyrska Street again. Friday night is in full swing. Lots of laughing groups of two or three walk here and there on the slippery icy pavement (damn it, Klitschko!), sipping hot mulled wine from paper cups.

"It's the most wonderful time of the year . . ." Yes, that's true.

Volodymyrska is quite possibly one of the world's oldest continuously populated streets. It's been around for at least a thousand years, serving as the medieval city's main lane. Here you can find one of Kyiv's finest miracles—the Golden Gate.

Now it's a huge arc of stone and timber, a replica of what used to be the main entrance into the ancient city. Several decades before the First Crusade, Grand Prince Yaroslav the Wise ordered the construction of a new city wall to defend the growing capital.

The Golden Gate, inspired by the defenses of Constantinople, was crowned with a chapel so that a traveler would know he or she was entering a Christian capital.

The Wall of Yaroslav stretched from the Golden Gate to what is now Maidan Square, then up north to St. Michael's Golden-Domed Monastery, and then it ran west along the Peizazhna Walkway to Lviv Square.

If you pay a bit at the Golden Gate, you can see the remains of the original walls inside the dome. And if you feel a bit brazen, you can take a bottle of champagne and go up to the observation balconies and see a fantastic view of Old Kyiv. (It's a great spot for a first date, I swear!)

If you look north, there is Saint Sophia Cathedral, one of the most sacred centers of Eastern Christianity, established by Prince Yaroslav at the spot where he once defeated an army of Turkic nomads.

What lies a bit to the north are the hills by the river where Slavic tribes quarried the first building stones of what later became Kyiv.

And all around this ancient place, you'll find ornate nineteenth-century buildings full of hipster coffee shops and secret novelties. If you know where to make a turn on Reitarska Street, you'll enter the Yard of Crows. Yes, actual crows living in a big cage in the backyard.

Or you'll come across a four-hundred-year-old linden next to the remains of ancient pagan sanctuaries. Or a small statue of Panteleimon, a Persian cat that used to live at a restaurant next to the Golden Gate. According to legend, the poor animal died in a fire many years ago. But its spirit is enshrined in the bronze monument that welcomes everyone in that corner.

Just next to the Golden Gate, there is a small garden square. In the summertime, it's great to have a coffee on a bench underneath garden tents and listen to the street musicians that perform across from a bunch of ice cream kiosks and the Prince Yaroslav Monument.

I hear them singing Nirvana and Chris Isaak, even in the wintertime. Do I get this wrong, or is singing in the cold not good for one's voice? No idea.

But nonetheless, that's another special thing about Kyiv. Our street musicians, be they singers, guitar players, pianists, or drummers, are exceptionally good.

And now this beauty floats in the sea of Christmas lights. And crowds of happy people roam about, laughing and chatting.

At the Golden Gate's Drunken Cherry, a glass of hot delicate brandy is as good as it gets in such weather and at such a time.

Yet another Friday night comes as visitors sipping cherry drinks rumble in the crimson light of the venue's giant chandelier made of all manner of drinking glasses.

Just randomly checking news from behind my standing table:

"Estonian defense minister: 'NATO rolling over for Russian demands would be a disaster for European security.'"

Nah, whatever.

Everything's going to be all right, as always.

Life is good, no matter what the world's movers and shakers are up to.

THREE

If only we could see the heavy storm gathering over our heads.

From where we are now, it's clear that the December ultimatum was a major turning point in the transition to war.

The decision to prepare for a full-fledged invasion of Ukraine had in fact already been made. But Russian diplomacy (and the chorus of propaganda that is its soundtrack) was in the midst of a boisterous, highly scripted drama. The story was familiar: Russia was under attack; still, as the victimized innocent party, it would offer the vicious, trigger-happy West a chance to redeem itself and reach peace.

We in Ukraine didn't pay this too much attention.

The country was still living life as usual. Social media was more interested in arguing about which COVID-19 vaccine brand was most fashionable (I was on the Moderna team!) than concerned with yet another absurd public stunt by the Kremlin.

The ultimatum was merely another headline next to endless corruption scandals and quarantine restrictions.

In our defense, we had our reasons.

For months in 2021, this "security crisis" shamelessly fabricated by Kremlin media was so in your face and so drama-queeny that it was hard to take seriously.

Over the previous eight years, we'd become acclimated to living in a toxic media environment, with hateful propagandistic stink always wafting from the east.

Yes, ever since we ousted the corrupt Russian-backed autocrat Viktor Yanukovych in 2014, we had been "the Western puppet," the "fascist failed state," the "traitors of Russia." Russian TV propaganda had been obsessed with Ukraine for so long that we'd become used to the stench.

The Kremlin has always been about intimidation, haughty grandstanding, and cheap demagogy. It had made sleazy criminal slang the language of its public diplomacy. Acting like a low-life street thug squeezing money from the hood had become its go-to political strategy.

It was also simply convenient to continue a safe and comfortable war of words with the West. This picked-out-of-nose confrontation had long ago taken the form of constant hand-wringing about "the risk of nuclear holocaust"—as if the conjured mushroom cloud provided cover for the oligarchs as they pocketed billions from oil and gas transfers to Europe and binge-bought luxury apartments in Miami Beach.

So even in mid-December 2022, it felt pretty okay to see Moscow issuing absurd demands to NATO and the United States. It was totally unsurprising that the Kremlin would continue whining about how "the West does not respect Russia's fair security concerns" in its relentless TV propaganda.

The Kremlin had been selling this "besieged fortress" narrative to its population for years, if not decades. Knowingly far-fetched confrontational anti-Western propaganda is among the main pillars of the Kremlin rule in Russia. The new ultimatum fit the same old blah-blah pattern, many believed.

Moreover, as one might recall, this was the second major security crisis we'd seen in 2021.

The first one broke out suddenly only months before, in April.

The local low-intensity war in Donbas had continued for nearly a decade, but the hottest battles of Russia's intrusion were left behind in 2014 and 2015. The 450-kilometer front line mostly stabilized after the Battle of Debaltseve of February 2015 and the formalization of the subsequent phony "general cease-fire."

We journalists continued writing obituaries for between 80 and 130 Ukrainian soldiers killed in Donbas every year. Mostly the deaths were the result of sporadic clashes with Russian-led militants, or sniper fire, or land mines, or rare scouting missions. Sometimes, there were localized splashes of hostilities, like the fight for Avdiivka in early 2017.

But the active war was put on hold and generally frozen. And as years passed, the war slipped into somnolence. Up until the last months of 2021, there were weeks in which daily communiqués from the Ukrainian military reported few if any "cease-fire violations."

This war never really wanted to be fought—unless orders were given from on high.

The situation in Donbas moved off the general public's radar. This uneventful, endless bore in the country's far east became the rarefied concern of a rather small community of activists, veterans, and journalists.

The occupied countryside that lay just a fifteen-minute drive from the front line lived its own life. Donbas and Crimea, as well as other military news stories, popped up mostly only during our noisy election campaigns.

Those that followed the situation routinely anguished over the "forgotten war in the middle of Europe" as it slipped from the world's spotlight.

There was endless idle talk about the Minsk accords year after year.

In case you're unaware, the Minsk accords are, simply speaking, two treaties that Russia made Ukraine sign after heavy defeats in Donbas in late 2014 and 2015. Of course, this period also saw Russia's annexation of Crimea, another sore point.

Formally, the treaties were road maps toward ending the "internal conflict" in Donbas. This was supposed to grant very broad autonomy for Russian-controlled breakaway "republics" in Donetsk and Luhansk and also to lead to free and fair, internationally monitored local elections in the occupied zone.

As always, the devil was lurking in the details. The "broad autonomy" here meant that the "republics" were to be in fact completely independent from Kyiv, with their own independent militaries, and the right to veto any Ukrainian foreign policy moves (such as the rapprochement with NATO and the EU, naturally).

Of course, injecting these Kremlin-controlled enclaves back into Ukraine under Russian terms would have meant a slipknot around Ukraine's neck. And, as we strongly believed, a time bomb planted in our midst and a threat to our future as an independent nation free from Russia's suffocating influence.

From the moment the signature ink dried, Ukraine had been trying to come unscrewed from the damning treaty and to keep the smoldering war in Donbas at bay.

Thus, the never-ending soap opera of Minsk talks went on and on.

The negotiation group continued to hold its meetings, regularly proclaiming yet another cease-fire to commence by Christmastime, by harvest season, by Easter, or by the beginning of the school year. I think I lost count at twenty attempts to impose a truce that sooner or later failed.

The monitoring mission of OSCE (Organization for Security and Co-operation in Europe) continued to report advanced Russian military hardware in Donbas, as well as truck convoys coming from Russia on a regular basis. But Moscow framed the whole thing as a "civil war" lead by "popular militia defending Donbas against Ukrainian nationalistic death squads."

Everyone knew that Russia controlled the entire situation. Ukraine kept shouting about that, and many in Western media, for the sake of balanced objectivity, obliged by calling the Russian collaborators "rebels" and "separatists."

By 2022, we had lost some four thousand combatants in the eight years since the conflict began in 2014. According to the UN, the total death toll reached over thirteen thousand, including civilians and Russian-led militants.

Even in the Ukrainian-controlled part of Donbas, it became a new normal.

Everyone got used to the fact that Donetsk and Luhansk were now poverty-stricken enclaves ruled by criminal gangs, Russian money, and the law of the gun. Luhansk had admittedly always been pretty depressed.

But Donetsk, which had seen spectacular progress before 2014, was trapped in a timeless gray void.

The old separation line ran some twenty kilometers from my hometown, Volnovakha. The town used to be a railway hub of twenty-five thousand situated equidistant between Donetsk and Mariupol.

Nothing of military significance had happened there in a long while. For years after 2014 and 2015, life was more or less okay. The place had even seen some significant local development.

Many of my fellow countryfolk crossed the front line in both directions as if it were an international border. Others used to make forays from the occupied territories to Volnovakha to cash out Ukrainian pensions and buy Ukrainian products in local supermarkets.

Enterprising minivan owners made good money transporting people in both directions. The best drivers had their own pulls "on the other side." At extra cost, they'd take you across an entry point without the extra hassle of ID checks and trunk searches.

Many who fled Donetsk in 2014 had established new lives in Kyiv and elsewhere, including Russia.

It was obvious that Ukraine would never get around to breaking the front and retaking Donetsk and Luhansk. That would entail insane urban fighting, with inevitable Russian intervention. A massive civilian death toll with such a bold move would mean the immediate withdrawal of Western support and a crushing military defeat.

Everyone in Ukraine remembered the Ilovaisk disaster of August 2014, when advancing Ukrainian forces were trapped and slaughtered by regular Russian units.

It was also more than clear to the Ukrainian leadership. So, for years, the very idealistic concept of a "peaceful reintegration" of occupied territories had been enshrined in law.

And as time moved forward and the war became less intense, the death toll fell accordingly. Between 2018 and 2021, the UN recorded 381 civilian deaths on both sides of the front line. The annual civilian death toll dropped from 162 in 2018 to 44 in 2021, and these casualties were largely due to unexploded ordnance rather than armed clashes.

It seemed clear the Russian-led intrusion in East Ukraine had already sputtered out as an active armed conflict. We expected that the war's outcome, good or bad for Ukraine, would be decided in fierce diplomatic battles rather than on actual battlefields.

And we believed that the Kremlin was just fine with this status quo.

The Russian incursion had not prompted a complete Ukrainian collapse or the accession of Ukraine's Russian-speaking southeastern regions. And yet this endless "no war, no peace" situation dealt Ukraine a nonhealing wound that prevented it from any actual movement toward NATO and the EU.

The Kremlin had no real responsibilities in the occupied territory in the east. Proxy occupation didn't cost that much (an estimated $5 billion a year). If their intent was to stymie Ukraine's westerly aspirations, this was a pretty good deal. And the West seemed to generally prefer the stalemate over a new war.

And sooner or later, the West, in the name of continuing business as usual with Moscow, might eventually give up and force Kyiv into implementing the Minsk accords on Russian terms. That's what we feared in 2019 as a bevy of journalists were invited to the Presidential Office so that Zelensky could explain the "Steinmeier Formula."

This "formula" was a plan for implementing the Minsk treaty suggested by the German foreign minister at the time, Frank-Walter Steinmeier, who later became Germany's president.

The plan envisaged the following: a total cease-fire in Donbas, then local elections under Ukrainian legislation in the Russian-controlled part of the region, followed immediately by permanent "special territorial status" if OSCE declares the elections free and fair.

However, here's the question: Do we have those elections before or after the Kremlin withdraws its regular forces and militants and lets Ukraine reestablish control of its state border between Russia and Donbas?

Of course, the Russian answer was no military withdrawal, no Ukrainian presence in the region and at the state border, and bogus elections to legalize the occupied zone as a foreign-controlled enclave in Ukraine's body.

This was unacceptable to Ukraine.

Even though the Zelensky administration favored making small steps through painful concessions and negotiations in the hope of finding an acceptable peace settlement—such as approving the Steinmeier Formula in October 2019—there was an understanding that this was pie in the sky and that eventually the military would be called upon.

We needed to strengthen our armed forces, and we needed allies.

No one wanted the disaster of 2014 repeated.

We in Ukraine were beating our heads against the wall advocating for defense reforms and military development under best Western practices. The pace of that reform could be described as "two steps forward, one step back."

And for years, we Ukrainian journalists kept traipsing to NATO HQ in Brussels only to eye-roll again as Jens Stoltenberg reiterated that "NATO keeps the door open" and "Ukraine will be a member state, but not now."

Of course, absolutely everyone knew that was not going to happen—because of Russia. This agonizing monotony had dragged on since I was a schoolboy in the 2000s.

And it seemed like this could last for an indefinitely long time.

And then, on March 29, 2021, four Ukrainian troops were killed by snipers. It happened near the town of Shumy, close to occupied Horlivka.

We'd had dozens of incidents like that in previous years. But the Ukrainian press quite naturally called this an escalation. After weeks and months of almost complete quiet, the sensitivity threshold was pretty low.

The Minsk negotiations group was automatically activated. Zelensky requested another Normandy Format talk. The foreign affairs ministry called on the world to react. But the world's attention was elsewhere, and yet another deadly clash in Donbas was instantly drowned in the stormy sea of headlines about COVID-19 and that giant tanker blocking the Suez Canal.

Then, on March 30, Ukraine's top general, Ruslan Khomchak, presented a report to the Verkhovna Rada, the Ukrainian parliament, saying Russia had concentrated twenty-eight battalion tactical groups (BTGs) in Donbas, Crimea, and areas bordering East Ukraine.

Moreover, according to the general, Russia was expected to deploy twenty-five more BTGs in the near future, which posed a threat to Ukraine's "military security." Russians were reportedly preparing for the Zapad 2021, the strategic drills due to take place in September in cooperation with Belarus.

Okay, maybe not breaking news just yet.

But then things started really going off the rails.

On April 1, Russia's foreign minister, Sergey Lavrov, claimed on TV that the "confrontation between Russia and the West has reached rock bottom." Still, he hoped that "adult people understand the risks of fomenting tensions."

Apparently, what Russia was doing all those years before was nothing but rainbows and rosy unicorns. And the West was fabricating false claims about Russian intentions all of a sudden.

According to the Kremlin mouth Dmitry Peskov, Russia was fully entitled to move its military forces within its own territory, and the movement posed no threat to Ukraine. Just a day later, however, he accused Ukraine of "provocations" and said "the situation in Donbas is very frightening."

He did not disclose how this "situation" was any different from any given period between 2015 and 2021.

What was unfolding was a pattern that would be used again by the Kremlin in early 2022. An escalation of very graphic and inflammatory rhetoric in the media with very little connection to events on the ground.

On March 30, Russia declined a Ukrainian request to declare yet another "Easter cease-fire." Sporadic clashes continued, with at least ten Ukrainian soldiers killed by April 8. Russia and its proxy forces accused Ukraine of killing a child with a drone strike. But OSCE on the spot found no evidence of a Ukrainian role.

Nonetheless, Russian propaganda outlets began aggressively pushing the narrative of a "Ukrainian offensive" to commit genocide in Donbas.

On April 8, a Kremlin administration deputy head in charge of Ukraine said that if Ukraine committed a "Srebrenica," Russia would have to stand for the defense of Donbas, and that would be the end of Ukraine.

Yes, Ukraine, which stood still for years unable to realistically retake the region, suddenly decided to unfold a war of aggression. Just when Russia had concentrated a very large military force within and near its borders.

What a coincidence, huh?

By April 8, according to the White House, Russia had amassed the largest military presence in the region since 2014. Ukraine's general Khomchak appealed to the voice of reason, saying on April 9 that Ukraine had never even contemplated any "general offensive action" and that Russia was using intimidation for its own ends.

But the train of narrative couldn't be stopped. By April 11, Dmitry Peskov was saying that a "civil war" in Ukraine "might resume soon," and that Russia was merely protecting its own security and that it would not shy away from "defending the Russian-speaking population of the southeast."

Russia's national security council chairman, Nikolai Patrushev, one of the Kremlin's key war criminals, went as far as to say that "while flirting with the new United States administration, Kyiv is ready to plunge the country into war, despite the country's deteriorating economic situation."

According to Patrushev, Ukraine could use "United States-backed provocations and terror attacks" as a cause for going to war.

The next day, Russia very dramatically closed the Kerch Strait for Ukrainian military vessels for the next six months.

I remember walking around Kyiv during those days. It struck me as a bit bizarre that most people in the streets seemed unconcerned. In the Kyiv subway, in supermarkets, in the parks, people were minding their own business, not paying much attention to what was in the news.

". . . the Russian military has deployed Iskander ballistic missile systems to Voronezh, a city 175 kilometers northeast of the Ukrainian border . . ."

At the time, some of my friends used to shoot me messages like, "Hey, do you think we should be worried?" I would toggle between my slightly irrational feelings and my voice of reason for a moment and then text back: "Nah. It's going to be all right. They are bluffing."

Our chances did not look great if the worst was really to come.

Numbers were only growing day by day.

In mid-April, the director of Ukraine's military intelligence said Russians had some eighty-nine thousand troops poised against Ukraine. The Pentagon later said Russia had mustered more than it had in 2014, and it was unclear if it was just for drills. On April 20, the EU estimated that there were some one hundred thousand troops concentrated.

Satellite pictures published by Maxar Technologies showed swaths of newly arrived jet fighters, armor, and field hospitals in Crimea and Voronezh.

As of 2020, our country had a 250,000-strong armed forces, plus several tens of thousands with the National Guard, some 800 tanks, 1,100 lighter armored vehicles, some 1,800 artillery pieces, some 125 capable aircraft, some 300 rather obsolete air defense systems. And basically no navy.

This is quite a force, but defending a country as big as Ukraine against Russia, with its massive air power and missile stockpiles? I don't know.

And then from left field, on April 16, the Kyiv city administration published an online map of air raid shelters and other places one could find cover in the event of Russian bombing. Basements, underground parking, street underpasses. Just like that.

That was the first time the words "air raid shelter" appeared in the life of present generations in Kyiv.

"Oh, fuck, this is not good, not good" was all I could think as I wrote a news item on the story.

In Russian criminal slang, there's the word "*bykovaniye*." It's when someone is inadequately aggressive and bullish, usually in an attempt to extort something from someone.

In one of its articles from that time, Ukraine's top media outlet *Ukrainska Pravda* very accurately called what Russia was doing "the escalation of *bykovaniye*."

Russia had concentrated a military force of one hundred thousand against a neighboring country, parts of which it had occupied. It issued threats of elimination under pretexts that existed only in its state propaganda narrative, pretending to have the high moral ground of a defender.

And it shamelessly portrayed itself as an innocent victim of a Western-led grand conspiracy that might entail a nuclear holocaust.

At the peak moment, on April 22, Vladimir Putin delivered a state-of-the-union-like speech to the Russian parliament, saying that "unfriendly steps toward Russia are ongoing."

"We're acting at the limit of our restraint," Putin said.

"We often don't bother to respond to unfriendly steps or even to overt rudeness . . . We want friendly relations with all international actors, including those with whom, politely speaking, we do not always agree.

"We do not want to burn all bridges. But he who interprets our good intentions as indifference or weakness and wants to ultimately burn or blow those bridges up must know that the Russian response will be asymmetric, rapid, and tough.

"Masterminds behind any provocations threatening our core security interests will seriously regret their action . . . But I hope no one will cross any red lines in respect to Russia. And it is up to us to decide where those red lines are in every particular case."

In other words, "Do as we please and as we say, or else."

The Russian president did not specify what sort of rudeness or unfriendly actions Russia had faced to feel so bitter about the world. Maybe that was Angela Merkel and Emmanuel Macron begging him not to attack Ukraine. Or Joe Biden having a phone conversation with him and inviting him for a summit in a third country to ease tensions via diplomacy.

Russian street thug diplomacy at its finest.

And you know what?

The day after those phone calls, Russia's defense minister Sergei Shoigu announced that drills in Crimea were over and that Russian military units were to get back to their bases. Over the next few days, a few cautionary voices maintained that we could truly chill out only when we saw Russia de-escalate.

But by May 1, this absolutely controlled, made-up-out-of-thin-air crisis was over. Tensions calmed down in a snap. And Russian media space experienced instant amnesia about all the threats of "provocations" that had been so desperately acute just days earlier.

Putin flexed his muscles for a while. His TV propaganda machine showed the Russian people what a tough guy he was and how dearly they needed him in power as the Western enemy was preparing for war again.

Moreover, Putin got Biden for a historic summit in June.

Unsurprisingly, the high-profile meeting in Geneva resulted in basically nothing but very general statements on how there can be no winners in a nuclear war and how both powers would therefore seek reduced tensions.

But Putin was unabashedly enjoying himself again. He probably even imagined himself as none other than Leonid Brezhnev deciding on the world's fate next to Richard Nixon at the height of the Soviet might in 1972.

And—what a miracle—the front line of Donbas calmed right down with the end of the April crisis.

In May, I had a deployment with Ukraine's 10th Mountain Infantry in Zhovanka, close to occupied Horlivka in Donbas.

And what I saw was again the same boring routine in a place where time stands still.

Soldiers as usual were dashing through wood-reenforced trench lines knuckle-deep in the mud and rain. Almost complete silence as fighters served their four-hour duty at machine guns, keeping an eye on the horizon. Most were not even wearing body armor. They cleaned their weapons, stroked their dugout cats, sipped coffee, and smoked a lot of cigarettes.

No wonder most of the global media lost interest. Nothing new was happening. The Ukrainian military could not advance or leave. So it had to stay in this *Groundhog Day* while the endless standoff went nowhere.

Life was running as usual.

In late summer 2021, I finally succumbed to my friends' persuasion and took a vacation (yes, I can't live without work, now denounce me).

My university friend and roommate Ivan (he'll play a very important role in the events to come!) and I hit the road on a two-week car trip around Ukraine.

We had some decent Dunkel beer in Lviv and saw the majesty of the Carpathian Mountains. We went as far west as Chop—the small train station that is the final frontier before the EU border.

Then there were the beaches of Odesa invaded by myriads of hideous jellyfish, and the Antonivsky Bridge across the Dnipro River in Kherson. We enjoyed the wineries of Koblevo on the Black Sea coastline, with me drinking wine straight from the bottle and shouting from the passenger seat at bad drivers on our way.

We passed the fields of giant wind turbines at the rosy lake Sivash just north of Crimea.

And then Mariupol, the place we'd spent years in as students.

The city by the Azov Sea in 2021 looked much, much better than it had six years earlier when I left it. The streets were miraculously smooth and clean. Lots of open lawns and street artwork. Nothing like I remember from my university years when I used to kick garbage piles at the bus station waiting for my ride home on Fridays.

New coffee shops, restaurant chains, and food courts that Mariupol never had before. New bike lanes and boutiques. What used to be just a long and dirty concrete breakwater prying into the sea was now a very good-looking, wood-decked pier with yachts and boats moored at its sides.

New yellow-and-white buses rushed to and fro from glassed-in bus stops marked with little anchors. Even the giant of Azovstal steel mill seemed to be producing less of the chemical stink and soot that used to descend on our windowsills every night.

Mariupol, once a depressed Soviet rust belt monster with a god-awful ecological legacy, was turning into a comfortable and quiet regional European city. With its cocktail bars, parks, and sushi places by the seaside, it was on the verge of becoming the finest recreational center of East Ukraine.

Nolan Peterson, an American war reporter living in Ukraine, once said the Mariupol seaside reminded him of Florida. Give this city some time, maybe install a couple of fake palms, and there you go.

Ivan and I decided to stay in town for a few days to see old friends and relatives. At one point I ventured out on a long walk across the city, to see all those places of old.

Hey, there's our old student dorm near Bakhchivadzhi Market. A renovated nine-story Soviet-style house, where we had so many all-night-long drinking parties.

Once upon a time, a big after-party following a national-level academic competition hosted by our university ended in a massive scuffle in the middle of the night. That was our gathering versus the university comedy club also celebrating something one floor up. The party was kind of spoiled; the dorm manager was close to calling the police. But political science nerds from all corners of Ukraine were fascinated by that little adventure.

Oh, we had a lot of fun and melodramatic love stories there.

Also, there's the old bookstore I worked at to earn my apartment rent after I was eventually kicked out of the dorm. Down the Peace Avenue, there's this singing fountain in Drama Theater Square, where I used to bring girls on dates.

Seeing this, I felt a sort of wistful regret for leaving Mariupol for another life in the capital city. Maybe I should return to where it all began.

And I snapped an unusual number of photos. Freedom Square (more commonly known as "The 1,000 Little Things") used to be an ugly patch of broken concrete pavement with an even uglier Vladimir Lenin statue hanging over it.

But then it became a nice place of musical fountains and a grandstand, with twenty-five white dove figurines installed in a circle to symbolize twenty-five Ukrainian regions united in peace.

On that day, the square shined gold for me in the sunset.

Unknowingly, it was my last goodbye to Mariupol as we knew it.

Six months later, all these places would perish in the fire of war.

And just near that square, Azov Regiment soldiers would frantically ambush Russian tanks amid charred ruins. Right on the street leading to what used to be my university dorm. Then they would retreat to the bowels of the hulking steel mill, which soon became a warren of death.

It's hard to say why exactly the Kremlin resolved to do what it did in 2022, against all expectations.

They certainly believed that Ukraine would be easy prey and the world would show little reaction. It is obvious that they greatly overestimated themselves and greatly underestimated Ukraine.

Or, maybe because during his grotesque hyper-isolation during COVID-19, the aging dictator obsessed with pseudo-historical conspiracy theories underwent a mental degradation. And maybe he decided to leave a megalomanic footprint in history as the reestablisher of the Russian Empire in the twenty-first century.

Maybe Putin and his inner circle wanted to outdo the triumph of the Crimean annexation of 2014 and easily make the capital of the Ancient Rus fall into their hands.

They had spent years and billions on the propaganda of hatred, revanchism, territorial grabs, and confrontation with the West while more than 12 percent of Russians did not have toilets in their homes.

One way or another, the bunch of old KGB bureaucrats sitting on the mountain of petrodollars, full of themselves, amid increasingly notorious economic stagnation and a steady decline of Putin's popularity, and in anticipation of the general election in 2024, adhered to their most effective instrument of retaining power—a victorious little war.

FOUR

November 8, 2021, was just one of those Mondays when you come to the office thinking you'd prefer a couple of hours of sleep over yet another morning meeting.

Nonetheless, I arrived at the *Kyiv Post* editorial office on Zhylyanska Street even earlier than usual. I was on duty to post yet another COVID-19 statistics update.

So, I was lazily yawning, sipping my coffee, and occasionally saying hi to other early bird guys before they fell asleep at their desks. I was supposed to post the thing before the ten A.M. morning meeting, but meh.

When the work was almost done, just minutes before the powwow, I noticed that something was wrong with the website. It wasn't responding when I tried to save the article's draft on the dashboard. Just not working at all.

For crying out loud, please tell our admin this website is lagging again.

Anyway, the meeting started.

Chief editor Brian Bonner, our grumpy American boss in his early sixties, took the floor in front of us. He looked down, his hands deep in his pockets, nodded a little, and shuffled about.

"I have to tell you that this is our last editorial meeting."

What?

"I have been given an order to shut this newspaper down. There will be no website, no stories, no printed edition. We are all fired as of today. And we must leave the premises."

How do you like that for an upbeat start of the week, huh?

Syrian-born Odesa development tycoon Adnan Kivan had decided to kill the *Kyiv Post*, which was Ukraine's top English-language publication. We'd had a series of conflicts with the publisher as he repeatedly tried to interfere with our editorial independence and hiring policy, something he publicly vowed to respect when he purchased the newspaper in 2018.

He tried to push his people on us, from his TV channel in Odesa, which was mostly busy praising the owner and serving his agenda, something we mostly learned from Facebook. And Kivan was openly bitter about us criticizing Ukrainian authorities in our stories.

Brian was ready to go to the mat to save the sweet little child he'd spent like twelve years of his life shepherding. At the same time, we journalists were absolutely pissed about the owner's infringements. There were days when we thought Brian had defected to the other side as he made trips to Odesa to meet with the publisher.

But Brian was on our side all the time. There was no room for compromise for a newspaper whose survival rested on credibility and the trust of its readership. A final, last-ditch Sunday trip to Odesa resulted in what Brian had to tell us that morning.

There was dead silence in the room.

Remember me telling you about that newspaper website glitch? That wasn't a glitch. We were just silently stripped of our access to the website.

Immediately after the meeting, Kivan's press service announced publicly that the *Kyiv Post* was only "temporarily halting its work" and that it would be "transformed into a new media platform not only in English, but also in Russian, Ukrainian, and Arabic, with quality print and video content."

Moreover, they said the *Kyiv Post* team would be "strengthened by the best journalists from the United States, Canada, and Europe."

The newsroom crew tried to save the newspaper. For twenty-six years, countless journalists had worked their butts off to uphold the *Kyiv Post*'s high reputation. They called Kivan and tried to persuade him to let us keep the brand, if he was so sick of owning the newspaper, or let us find a willing buyer.

The tycoon said no. Twice. After an emotional meeting, we decided to go John Wick on the situation. We rolled out a statement on Facebook saying that Kivan had taken his revenge and purged a newsroom that did not want to obey and serve his interests.

There was a hell of a scandal in Ukraine, with foreign embassies issuing statements of concern. The situation got so absurd that at some point Kivan told us no one had actually been fired, and whoever wanted to stay could stay, but Brian was out and there would be a new chief editor.

We, of course, showed a middle finger, threw the last party at the office, and walked away. Not a single writer decided to stay. Hand on heart, speaking for myself, absolutely no regrets.

Brian was so devastated that he quit journalism after forty years in the business.

And here we were, some thirty guys and girls in our twenties and early thirties, from across the world—Ukrainians, Americans, Brits, a Russian, a person, a French person. All booted from a job we had devoted countless sleepless nights to.

Any ideas?

For years, we'd spent so much time together in the same room that we all were friends. And beyond that, we hung out after-hours, celebrated birthdays and holidays together, crashed on one another's couches during breakups. In interviews we gave during the *Kyiv Post* scandal, we jokingly called the office "a family-style newsroom."

We decided to stay together. If we couldn't save *Kyiv Post*, we'd at least try to save its spirit and values.

Three days after that awesome morning meeting, we established the *Kyiv Independent*, a brand-new English-language media outlet from Ukraine and about Ukraine.

We had no budget and no sponsors. Everything was to be established from scratch. But right from the start we had huge public support in Ukraine and beyond—people hugely appreciated our attitude.

We launched a fundraising campaign on Patreon and GoFundMe, which gave us our start. We decided that we'd had enough of being dependent on just one moneybag who thought he could tell us what to do.

We figured we'd be better off backed by the support of our readers and our community. But that's easier said than done. In Ukraine, the very concept of an independent media outlet financed by its audience was severely underdeveloped. Other media startups had found it hard to scrounge up more than a few dozen followers on Patreon.

And the media advertising market in Ukraine is almost nonexistent. But if you have nothing left to lose, why not try to do something nearly impossible and truly remarkable?

Many businesses and lawyers offered us help pro bono in what we were attempting. We had our first noisy meetings in Kyiv coffee shops or online from our homes via Zoom. At some point the owner of Beeworking, a chain of co-working spaces in Kyiv, shot me a message saying we could work in one of his places (seriously, thank you for this, man).

So, we banged out our first *Kyiv Independent* stories sitting in a tiny room with just six chairs in Podil. But hey, we could use the place's coffee machine and have as many free cookies as we liked!

And right from the start, when we didn't even have a website, we had to jump into covering yet another regional war crisis.

Yes, when it rains, it inevitably pours down in torrents.

On October 30, yet another story by the *Washington Post* said Russia had resumed concentrating large military forces against Ukraine.

And as Michael Kofman, a revered military expert, was saying, this was not a drill.

Here we go again.

As we learned from additional reporting in the *Washington Post* later in the war, United States intelligence notified President Biden of a looming Russian invasion as early as October 2021. Right from the get-go the United States had everything—from satellite pictures to sources from within Russian power circles.

The White House decided to do a number of things: talk to allies to make sure America was not alone in the deterrence, let Russia know there would be consequences for any aggression, and, if eventually necessary, be ready to provide Ukraine with weapons to fight.

As early as October 31, President Biden's security adviser Jake Sullivan held a briefing during which he said there had been talks with NATO allies regarding the situation. As far as we understand, what the White House had to say did not leave many allies that impressed, and it's hard to blame them.

At that point, knowing the Kremlin's habit of extortion and intimidation, on display for the second time that year alone, it was difficult for most to accept that Moscow was indeed preparing a major European war.

Quite expectedly, beginning in November, NATO's Jens Stoltenberg asserted a dozen times NATO forces would not fight for Ukraine in the case of a full-scale Russian invasion, although it would support Kyiv.

Ukraine was the least impressed.

Right up until the beginning of February 2022, many in Zelensky's administration would be quite skeptical regarding the possibility of war, and they were quite open about this in conversations with us journalists.

On November 1, Ukraine's Ministry of Defense debunked the assertions, saying that according to the latest intelligence, there was no Russian buildup at Ukraine's borders. It even asserted that the media reports were "most likely a psychological destabilization operation," planted by Russia itself. What Russia was doing on the ground was "in fact, planned movements following the end of military exercises."

Ukraine's National Security and Defense Council secretary Oleksiy Danilov, in his own style, emotionally dismissed the media reports as "disinformation." He was not even moved by the fresh satellite pictures of Russian bases overflowing with newly deployed hardware published by *Politico*.

In early November, CIA chief William J. Burns flew to Moscow. Obviously, to talk to the Kremlin and see what they were up to. After that, there was less bravado in Ukrainian high cabinet circles. Ukrainian military intelligence service chief General Kyrylo Budanov was among those who were publicly taking the threat more seriously.

In mid-November, Budanov laid out his intelligence: Russians had some 114,000 personnel positioned against Ukraine, including 92,000 ground units. Following its September drills with Belarus, Russia had very brazenly deployed scores of armored vehicles and missile systems near Ukraine's border. And according to Budanov, that meant either preparations for a large-scale war or an attempt to ratchet up psychological pressure.

The United States insisted that the situation was more serious than the April war crisis. We know from Ukrainian officials that the United States warnings were not very detailed, even though the Americans were saying that there was a high probability the invasion could be expected in winter 2022.

The Conflict Intelligence Team (CIT), a respected online investigations group that would leave its mark in the history of Russia's war, reported in late November that Russia was concentrating an "alarming" amount of military power.

In addition to the 4th Tank Division deployed in November, Russia had also deployed units with the 1st Tank Army, as well as units with the 49th and 58th armies.

That was already comparable with the April crisis figures. The most notable buildup was seen at the Pogonovo base near Voronezh. Russia was concentrating its forces in the western and southern military districts bordering Ukraine.

The Institute for the Study of War (ISW), yet another paramount entity in this war, in mid-December claimed there were "good reasons to question Putin's seriousness" despite obvious evidence of military preparations. Russia was probably capable of limited operations, like an escalation in Donbas, with very questionable practical results.

But going as bold as the scale of the Afghan War of 1979–89?

The ISW said the most likely explanation was that Russia was trying "to panic the West into abandoning important principles and accepting Russian actions that would severely damage Western interests and security but would be less dangerous than the massive threat Putin is presenting to Ukraine."

With all this saber-rattling, Putin was already getting traction from his extortion. He made the West say it would not defend Ukraine by force. The Kremlin received public and repeated guarantees there'd be no direct involvement.

And it wouldn't stop there.

Putin would make the West ask for diplomacy and peace. The entire West, including the president of the United States, will spend months literally trying to talk Putin out of war via countless phone calls, summits, calls for compromise, and the acknowledgement of Putin's interests.

He'd make Western diplomacy look weak and prone to vast concessions for the sake of avoiding the war at all costs.

The West would come on bended knee and beg for peace.

And all Putin was to offer in return was to not invade Ukraine—as simple as that.

Obviously, in hindsight, Russia ignored all the warnings and initiatives put forth in the media and behind closed doors. In the months following the April crisis, it never stopped laying the groundwork for invasion, most notably ideologically.

We in Ukraine admittedly paid little attention to the article "On the Historical Unity of Russians and Ukrainians" published in July on behalf of Putin. Many perceived this 5,500-word doorstopper as just another act of monkey business by a half-mad dictator known to fixate on vulgar pseudo-historic conspiracy theories.

The article stated all the most common dogmas of Russian chauvinism familiar to anyone living in post-Soviet nations. Russians, Ukrainians, and Belarusians have been the same people since time immemorial (of course, Russians are the senior among the three). And then the grandeur of the old kingdom was lost, and ever since, other powers have spent centuries sowing a feud among the brotherly peoples.

As a result of a global conspiracy, Ukraine and its language and culture were artificially created in the nineteenth century to tear it from the breast of Greater Russia. And in 2014, in reaction to the just war in Crimea, the West made Ukraine the antipode to Russia, and Moscow was not going to tolerate this.

Meanwhile, of course, Russia was the bird of peace that has always wanted to live amicably with Ukraine and the rest of the world. But now Ukraine didn't want to implement the Minsk accords and didn't want Donbas back. Somewhere in the essay's many pages: "Kyiv's anti-Russian policies present the risk that Ukraine could lose its statehood."

Full of revanchism, imperial grievances, and threats, the screed shocked many in the West. But, in fact, the undereducated KGB bureaucrat in charge of a nuclear arsenal was only regurgitating what's been around for decades among marginal Russian ultranationalists.

We'd heard it all before and didn't recognize it as the repurposed ideological rationale for the biggest European war of aggression since World War II.

After so many years of being buffeted by the Kremlin's never-ending hate propaganda storm, we essentially failed to take the maniac's words seriously enough.

We had to learn a sad lesson: Do not underestimate the lunacy of aged dictators. There's no hidden agenda. They are no 3D chess grand masters whose plans are unfathomable to simple mortals.

There's no rationality or pros and cons.

Years and decades spent in a restricted bubble among those who can't say no inevitably launches a strongman into a galaxy far, far away from the real world we live in. And in that faraway galaxy the most idiotic propaganda so zealously nurtured for years is the only air they breathe, and it eventually becomes their reality.

Sometimes, they really mean the insane shit they postulate.

And the very system of loyalty and nonresistance that they have built for years around themselves leaves them unchallenged in their madness. And the argument of "well, he's not just alone on the throne to decide on everything, he's just a face representing an entire clique" may just not work.

The entire clique of those besotted with unlimited power can be a bunch of delusional Kool-Aid drinkers ready to set the world afire for their petty whims.

Back in the days of 2021, we were giving way too much credit to Vladimir Putin and his system as supposedly rational and forward-thinking.

But that's my sad hindsight from the distance of time.

Most probably, the April crisis was just the war's dress rehearsal. Seeing the reaction to that feint, the Kremlin likely concluded that the West would be ready to concede to almost anything to prevent the worst, or that, in the event of war, it would chicken out the way it had with Crimea in 2014.

That the West is weak, corrupt, spoiled, spineless, and that it believes in nothing but its own comfort. That it's been a long time since the West abandoned its values, that it will easily roll over and throw a forty-million-person nation under the bus for the sake of a false sense of security.

And as all this was going down in late 2021, and as the intel grew ever more ominous, the ranks of the appeasers continued to swell.

Dozens of "senior national security experts" (who by just pure coincidence were often related to the Kremlin's Valdai Club) were bombarding the media with the idea of just giving Russia what it wants.

"Negotiate Peace with Russia to Prevent War over Ukraine." "The West's Weapons Won't Make Any Difference to Ukraine." "Diplomacy Isn't Appeasement." "Will the West Ignore Russia's Ukraine Redlines?"

A lot had to happen to break through this cacophonous echo chamber.

And not only in the West, but also in Ukraine.

In many ways, Ukraine survived thanks to a million big and little miracles, and not a few extremely belated decisions that were not supposed to happen at all.

To begin with, it's about names.

General Valeriy Zaluzhny was appointed by Zelensky as the commander in chief of the armed forces in summer 2021. I remember the wave of joyful surprise that rolled through our defense community: "Woooooow, are you kidding us?"

General Zaluzhny wasn't known to the public then. But he was popular in the military. He was among the very few sound and even talented senior career officers who by some miracle managed to remain in the ranks despite decades of bitter despair and neglectfulness that reigned in the Ukrainian military before 2014.

Moreover, he was among senior commanders who gained their real battlefield experience in Donbas and worked to reform and modernize the Ukrainian military after the setback of 2014. Zaluzhny became a general in wartime, unlike many others who were in fact bureaucrats promoted due to years in service and extensive connections.

I remember Taras Chmut, a retired marine and later the head of Ukraine's remarkable military charity foundation Come Back Alive telling everyone that Zaluzhny was the right man in the right place and that we were unbelievably lucky to have him.

Zaluzhny gained nationwide prominence for the first time in October 2021. There was an incident in Donbas, not far from my hometown, near the village of Hranitne.

Militants shelled artillery on Ukrainian positions and killed a soldier. Zaluzhny gave a personal order to kill, and a Bayraktar TB2 targeted and destroyed a Russian D-30 piece. This was the Turkish-made drone system's combat debut in Ukraine—and Zaluzhny for the first time showed his temper.

Ukrainian social media was ecstatic. "Whoa, the new general has got balls!"

The Ukrainian military over the years had had its share of bitter humiliation as the Ministry of Defense forbade soldiers from returning fire without a say-so from above (to avoid provoking Russia, yeah). This always resulted in outbursts of indignation in the media and beyond.

Along with Zaluzhny, other new battlefield commanders were promoted, too. General Oleksandr Syrsky (by the way, he's ethnic Russian born in Vladimir Oblast) was in charge of the ground forces. General Sergiy Shaptala, the former leader of the 128th Mountain

Infantry, was the Chief of General Staff. They both came from the purgatory of the Battle of Debaltseve of 2015.

Then there's the defense minister.

Oleksiy Reznikov was appointed in November 2021, as part of Zelensky's big shuffle in the government—I think my last article for the *Kyiv Post* covered the change.

Once upon a time in early 2020, Zelensky did a stupid thing and dismissed then–defense minister Andriy Zagorodniuk. Zagorodniuk was a top manager from the drilling business, the first purely civilian, "NATO-style" defense minister and the opposite of the old post–Soviet military establishment.

Media and anti-corruption watchdogs liked him and called his defense reform plan a promising start. But Zelensky sacked Zagorodniuk after just six months in office, without giving him a chance to show any results. Rumors had it that the defense minister lost the job because of his opposition to the "mutual withdrawal of forces" initiative in Donbas promoted by Zelensky's chief of staff Andriy Yermak.

But Zagorodniuk told me there was never any conflict between him and Yermak. Zelensky, in his own manner, simply decided that the armed forces need a defense minister who had "military experience."

To many in Ukraine, the concept of civilian oversight over the military was a shocking notion. How could a white-collar guy be in charge of the Defense Ministry when what was needed was a chest-of-medals military general?

So Zelensky appointed Andriy Taran, a sixty-five-year-old retired lieutenant general and long-time military diplomat.

And good lord, that was a mess.

The ministry immediately backslid decades in time. It became mired in endless wars of words with criticizing journalists on social media. Minister Taran did not talk to the media, did not issue any reports to the parliament.

The ministry struggled to sign the necessary contracts to complete annual procurement programs on missiles, munitions, fuel, and vehicles for the military. Many top-priority programs, such as the Neptune missile system, were bitterly underfinanced, and the ministry failed to spend its budget allocations in time in 2020 and 2021.

Programs to introduce legislative reforms, such as the inception of the Territorial Defense Forces, or new military regulations fully synchronized with NATO practices, or military housing programs, failed or saw little or no progress under Taran.

Taran's deputy for defense procurement Igor Khalimon was forcibly suspended from office after a criminal inquiry. But Taran did not want to leave his old buddy behind and reappointed Khalimon as his "advisor" on procurement issues.

On top of that, we in Ukraine had a wonderful year and a half when the country's defense minister and the top commander of armed forces couldn't be in the same room.

Minister Andriy Taran and General Ruslan Khomchak hated each other's guts so much that many important processes in the sector were simply paralyzed.

Ukraine's defense minister and top general sued each other over who had the final say on the use of air force aircraft for commercial transportation services. The distinction between the authority of a defense minister and the head of the armed forces are largely unclear, so there was absolute chaos.

Two post-Soviet generals were chest-beating, butting their heads, and trying to prove who was the real big daddy in the army.

And that's only a year before Russia's full-scale invasion.

At the end of the day, even Zelensky's parliament's faction admitted that "we need an effective manager to implement drastic changes in the Defense Ministry." (Oh, you don't say!) And Taran resigned "on medical grounds."

You shouldn't worry about him—one of this country's worst defense ministers was severely punished by being appointed as ambassador to Slovenia.

When Reznikov, a civilian minister, stepped into the position in November 2021, he brought some sanity into this mess. And it was good that Reznikov and General Zaluzhny immediately demonstrated good working chemistry.

The year 2021 also saw the fall of Arsen Avakov—the almighty minister of the interior, the unsinkable strongman who had been concentrating more and more power into his hands ever since 2014.

Well, there's no such thing as indispensable kingmakers when real democracy finally works—the deeply unpopular and seemingly invincible Avakov was dethroned and replaced with the much more moderate, civilized, and technocratic minister Denis Monastyrsky.

When it comes to the Main Directorate for Intelligence, the military intelligence body, we had Kyrylo Budanov—a young general in his thirties with very real combat experience. When the worst comes, we'll recognize him as one of the most accurate prognosticators of the storm few listened to.

One way or another, be it due to American warnings or just dumb luck, Ukraine ended up with strong and capable defense and security leadership teams on the eve of Russia's grand war. One only regrets that so many things weren't done much earlier and so much time was wasted.

In this list, Zelensky's childhood friend and SBU security service head Ivan Bakanov ended up exiled because of what happened as Russia invaded. The SBU was simply riddled with multiple cases of high treason and collaboration with Russia, so amid public pressure, Zelensky eventually booted his long-time associate.

Speaking of Zelensky . . . By the end of 2021, his presidency was, if not falling into a nosedive, then not in the best shape.

Nothing really surprising here. Zelensky, just like any president of the previous fifteen years, had had his share of huge and small scandals. Such as the one when Ukraine's security services failed to seize a bunch of Wagner mercenaries traveling from Belarus to Turkey, reportedly due to interference from the presidential administration.

And Zelensky's popularity before 2022 was constantly nosediving with time. Again, that was very typical for Ukrainian presidents (except for Russian-backed mafia boss Viktor Yanukovych), who typically got elected on waves of dissatisfaction with their predecessors and then failed to meet inflated popular hopes.

By the end of 2021, Zelensky's approval rating hovered near 24 percent. Yet, he was still the country's most popular face—because the rest were even worse.

Zelensky in Ukraine has always been "that comedian guy" who ran a popular show ridiculing the country's movers and shakers. The platform brought a kind of solidarity with regular people sick of politicians and their intrigues. He and his team appeared on TV screens in homes across Ukraine, on New Year's Eve and Women's Day, with his fringe jokes about politics, family issues, and the traffic police.

It just happened to be that by 2019 people were deadly sick of Petro Poroshenko, his opaque, underhanded dealings, his irrepressible itch for self-promotion, and his personality cult aggressively enforced via Facebook bots.

And Zelensky saw a once-in-a-lifetime opportunity to toss his own hat into the ring.

A comedian challenging a powerful oligarch, the most buffoonish presidential race in the country's history. The opponents were accusing each other of stooging for Moscow, posting videos needling each other in the middle of the night, demanding that they both give urine samples for a drug test (because Poroshenko's team peddled stories that Zelensky was a cocaine junkie).

Who needs Netflix when one can run through the jungle of Ukrainian politics?

The grand moment came when the two clashed in a fierce debate at the Olympiysky Stadium in Kyiv in front of twenty thousand supporters and millions watching the spectacle live on TV.

We, the team of journalists, were sitting in our then—editorial office on Pushkinska Street, putting our legs up on desks, popping open beers, and shouting as Zelensky and Poroshenko tried to K.O. each other with insults and punchy phrases.

That was the moment of absolute triumph of wild democracy in this country.

Even several Russian anti-Kremlin TV channels aired the debate with Russian translation. In the absence of any political life or free speech in their own country, they had to peep over the fence and envy the neighbors.

And here we go—Zelensky wins by a landslide. A groundbreaking 74 percent of voters backing the comedian. Zelensky won almost everywhere, including Donbas, except for a number of constituencies in West Ukraine.

Many in the West tend to believe that Ukrainians massively voted for Zelensky because they saw him as a continuation of his most famous movie character, Vasiliy Goloborodko, the simple history teacher turned president.

While this is certainly not entirely wrong, there's more to it than that: A vast majority of Ukrainians knew Zelensky long before the Netflix show. And many voted for Zelensky as Zelensky—the guy "on our side" who had spent years ridiculing the system and who wasn't an "experienced real (read, corrupt) politician." He was a regular fed-up citizen who promised to clean house top to bottom.

The start was promising. A new president, young and full of energy, he smiles, jumps out of his motorcade in front of the parliament under the shining sun. He shakes hands with the cheering crowds at the Verkhovna Rada.

He stands in front of the nation's parliament. He says from now on, everyone is a president. And everyone in the government will be working hard for this country. Otherwise: "What you can do is get a piece of paper, a pen, and resign." He comes with an agenda of finding a way to a just peace in Donbas via diplomacy.

And as it often happens in Ukraine, the hero of the day quickly loses his luster.

I met Zelensky on quite a few occasions before 2022. Over time, it was becoming more obvious, at least to me, that Zelensky really enjoyed *being a president*. But he wasn't much of a fan of *working as a president*.

I remember the day of October 1, 2019, when Russian media suddenly announced that the trilateral group of Russia, Ukraine, and OSCE had reached an agreement on the Steinmeier Formula—the road map to implement the Minsk accords.

The move triggered mass protests in Ukraine ("No surrender to Russia!"). So, the Presidential Office summoned a short-notice briefing at Bankova Street so Zelensky could offer his explanations.

He hastily answered our questions on the main issue. And then they gave the mic to an American journalist in the room (I don't really remember who he represented, but it was definitely a huge outlet).

It was still during the heat of the Ukraine-Trump scandal, when the forty-fifth United States president allegedly withheld defense aid until Zelensky agreed to help him find dirt on Joe Biden. So naturally, American journalists wanted an extensive comment from Zelensky.

He did make a short remark on the issue and then abruptly said the briefing was over: He didn't have time for more.

"But Mr. President . . . ," the Americans cried out.

For want of a better response, Zelensky simply replied in broken English: "Do you have any children?"

You should have seen the American journo's face at that moment.

I mean, dude.

We don't care if you suddenly decided to go home. You are the president of a country resisting a proxy war with Russia. And today is a milestone that may mean a lot for the future. And it's like five P.M.

Zelensky's personal vanity project was a splendid show, but then the dull work had to begin. A lot of things were going wrong with this attitude prevalent in the Bankova.

Judging from things we saw and heard, Zelensky wasn't that involved or interested in military affairs or defense reforms. And amid this reluctance, many behind him were pulling out opaque schemes, creating new bureaucratic monsters such as the sadly remembered Ministry for Strategic Industries.

In the first half of Zelensky's term, a running joke went that there were only two things Ukraine still lacked: a new big ministry for the manufacturing of warm socks and also another governmental commission for the cultivation of tomatoes.

Ministers, heads of agencies, and prosecutors walked in and out in chaotic reshuffles that demonstrated no tangible long-term plans. People right under Zelensky's nose in the administration and the parliament were gaining huge informal influence on key decisions in the country.

And there was always this guy, the favorite one, like Zelensky's first chief of staff Andriy Bogdan, always standing behind the president's shoulder and whispering in his ear.

A scandal follows another scandal.

Many people felt that Zelensky was weak and not serious enough for the job. Numbers speak for themselves. According to a poll from early December 2021, 51.6 percent of Ukrainians did not believe Zelensky would be capable of defending this country in case of Russia's full-scale aggression.

I must say that the Ukrainian defense community also discussed this issue. We used to chuckle as Zelensky visited the trenches of Donbas before 2022, with all those clumsy ill-fitting helmets and body vests over his office shirts.

What if the worst really comes and we don't have a supreme commander in chief?

But.

The *Fallout* game creators were right: War never changes.

But there should be a second line: War makes people reveal their true selves. It puts them in a situation where everyone must make a tough moral choice.

On February 24, 2022, this had to happen to all of us. Neither Zelensky, nor politicians of the West, nor opinion leaders, nor regular dudes in the street like me were allowed to be an exception.

Meanwhile, the storm continued to gather.

And to be honest, we had little understanding of what we were supposed to do with the torrent of dark omens and predictions coming from every corner.

In early December, United States intelligence made it loud and clear. Russia was preparing an invasion with the involvement of up to 175,000 troops in early 2022. The intelligence on the upcoming war was so detailed and compelling that as early as December 2021 even European skeptics, such as Germany, changed their minds, according to the *Financial Times*.

And numbers were growing every week. By late December, Russia had concentrated 122,000 troops within a two-hundred-kilometer zone along Ukraine's border.

CIT again monitored the deployment of even more antiaircraft missile systems, as well as units from Siberia, Ural, and the Northern Fleet, along with masses of tanks and self-propelled artillery pieces. The concentration of Russian military power against Ukraine had now long surpassed the April crisis figures.

Germany's *Bild* in December published the first of the "scary maps" (as we called them), saying that Russia aimed to seize two thirds of Ukraine's territory, including Kyiv. The arrows of Russia's axes of attack were pointing to Kharkiv, Odesa, Dnipro, Poltava, Nikopol.

And speaking of the diplomacy that so many high-minded intellectuals wanted so much: There was a whole lot of diplomacy—until almost virtually the last hour.

In the last weeks of 2021, Biden and Putin alone had two direct conversations, on December 7 and 30. Both calls resulted in nothing—other than Putin telling the United States president that nothing was going to happen.

If you want my opinion, as seen from the distance of time, all the Western diplomatic efforts were doomed from the start.

No matter what the West or Kyiv would say or suggest as a compromise or a concession, no matter how many more useless summits and talks there could be, the outcome was preordained.

The word "diplomacy" could have no meaning other than "surrender Ukraine."

And all that time, the Kremlin was staging a gigantic shit show. It was playing the victim of a global smear campaign and the dove of peace.

Maria Zakharova, the Russian foreign ministry spokeswoman, on December 4, 2021:

> The United States is carrying out a special operation to escalate the situation in Ukraine and shift the responsibility onto Russia. The operation's essence is about provocations near Russian borders, along with accusatory rhetoric toward Moscow. Nothing new—it's classic Western tactics. The only stunning thing is the scale of boldness and lying.

Yeah, indeed. I'm deliberately sticking to mostly publicly voiced statements to demonstrate the infuriating barefacedness of Russian lies just weeks before the shit really hit the fan.

Putin's mouth Dmitry Peskov on November 28 called the United States intelligence statements "hysteria" escalated by "Anglo-Saxons" (an integral part of the Kremlin's newspeak slurs):

> Russia has never prepared, is not preparing, and will never prepare any invasion. Russia is an absolutely peaceful nation that is interested in good relations with its neighbors.

Also, Peskov, on Christmas Day 2021, just a month and a half before the invasion:

> Russia has never been the first to attack anyone.

Just a day before that, Maxar Technologies and Reuters published fresh satellite pictures showing hundreds of newly arrived Russian tanks and artillery pieces in Crimea and along Ukraine's northeast border.

General Valeriy Gerasimov, the chief of Russia's General Staff, speaking on December 9, 2021:

> The redeployment of units as part of military training process is a routine practice for any nation's armed forces. The military activity is carried out within Russia's national territory and does not require

any notifications. The information regarding an alleged Russian invasion of Ukraine spread by media is a lie.

On the same day, Russia again declined a Ukrainian proposal to announce a "Christmastime cease-fire" in Donbas.

And all the while, the Kremlin, in the best tradition of totalitarian doublethink, did not hesitate to send barely veiled threats of war.

One of the most fundamental problems of this period was that Western leaders, when it came to relations with Russia, were not dealing with equal peers on the Russian side.

They were not facing legitimate politicians and representatives of the nation that might have certain legitimate security concerns, who acted in good faith, and with whom there could be space for misunderstanding, diplomacy, compromises, win–win deals, etc., etc.

All this time, the West was dealing with the mafia.

The mafia that had a giant nuclear arsenal in its possession. And, as a mafia, it used nothing but its typical instruments: intimidation, extortion, assassination, bribery, violence.

Hence, the world's greatest seller of fear was openly and aggressively sending a message: Do as we tell you or face World War III. And the rhetoric in state-run media was so absurdly overacted that it was still hard to take seriously in Ukraine.

Russia's deputy foreign minister Aleksandr Grushko, while commenting on the December ultimatum to the United States and NATO:

> [The West] now has two ways—either take what we have put on the table seriously, or face a military technical alternative.

That was in fact the first time Russia upped the ante to direct threats leveled at the West. And the Kremlin was putting it as melodramatically and demonstratively as possible.

For instance, in late December, Russia's Lavrov did not hesitate to remark that the December ultimatum was to "mitigate threats in the European theater . . . hopefully, not the theater of action."

I remember our unified reaction to these words: "Oh, fuck your face! What kind of war with NATO are you even talking about? Your own daughter has lived most of her life in New York City."

But this was mostly all happening in the news, not in the streets.

Ukraine continued living a very normal life.

We all used to get into work at nine A.M., work our butts off all day, then proceed to spend nights in the neighborhood bars of Podil—I'll make sure to take a walk with you through this magical heart of Kyiv, the place of our finest pubs and by coincidence where our office was located. I promise, really, but let's wait for less anxious times for that stroll.

I remember many Western journalists interviewing us for stories and they always asked how the popular mood was in Kyiv.

And I had little to reply other than: "Well . . . that's not really what people are talking about waiting on their orders at McDonald's."

At the state's higher echelons, top officials were also definitely divided.

General Budanov was saying Ukraine's military would not be able to repel a full-scale invasion without large Western defense aid. And yet, in any case, with or without assistance, he was confident Ukrainian soldiers and officers would fight until the bitter end.

Facing the worst, the government would have to simply crack open weapon dumps and hand out firearms to regular people so they could fight for themselves and their families.

Our foreign minister, Oleksiy Kuleba, predicted that if the West eventually decided to appease Russia at the expense of Ukraine, the country would fight anyway. With everything it had at hand.

And at the same time, Oleksiy Danilov, Ukraine's National Security and Defense Council secretary, said on December 30, 2021:

> As of today, we don't see a huge danger at our borders. We're not seeing an overt Russian aggression threat . . . the domestic destabilization of our country remains Russia's top priority. The situation is under control. Moreover, this is one of information attack against our nation, when they try to intimidate us. Our specialists say Russia isn't physically capable of a larger invasion.

Sounds a bit more comforting, doesn't it?

You cherry-pick the facts and statements you want to be true. You prefer Danilov's "nah, it's just a psyop" over a picture of untrained civilians with Molotovs trying to ambush a Russian armored column amid the ruins.

Some part of you wants to buy this.

Everything is going to be all right. We've already seen Russians bluffing and saber-rattling for propaganda and concessions. We know what they're up to.

It was in early January shortly after the end of the New Year's Day season. Pouring cold rain in Kyiv was followed by heavy snowfall.

So as always happens in Ukraine, the capital city and half of the country's highways turned into one giant traffic jam.

But I had to catch up with my girlfriend, Natalia, who was trying to get back to Kyiv after a weekend with her parents in West Ukraine. Gotta give her a hand with her bags and everything else in such nasty weather—it wouldn't hurt to buttress my reputation as a caring boyfriend.

Waiting for several hours at a McDonald's next to the Kyiv central bus station, I sipped coffee and watched *Don't Look Up*. I'm sure you remember that big hit on Netflix. Leo DiCaprio and Jennifer Lawrence running around on my iPad's screen, trying to warn the world of an upcoming doomsday, as the world plays reckless and comfortably denialist.

Also, the latest news:

Bloomberg: UKRAINE'S ARMY IS UNDERFUNDED, OUTGUNNED AND NOT READY TO STOP A RUSSIAN INVASION

CNN: FAMILIES OF RUSSIAN DIPLOMATS TO LEAVE KYIV AND LVIV

Don't. Look. Up.

FIVE

E arly January was rather calm.

All attention switched to Kazakhstan, which became the stage for a short-lived massive anti-government protest. The everlasting "leader of the nation" Nursultan Nazarbayev was quickly dethroned and banished by his own former henchmen.

Russia, along with its satellites with the Collective Security Treaty Organization (CSTO), openly supported the palace coup. They sent in their troops as "peacekeepers" to support "Kazakhstan's effort to restore law and order."

To us, that was not a good sign. The Kremlin got a chance to demonstrate the projection of its power and its elite airborne forces on the go. Russia's satellites Armenia, Kyrgyzstan, Tajikistan, and Belarus showed their readiness to actively support the sovereign's foreign military ventures.

Potentially, this meant the Kremlin could have an "international coalition" and involve its "allies" against Ukraine, politically or militarily.

Nonetheless, there was an absolute consensus on the need for the most resolute reaction possible. Calls for common sense and prudence wouldn't help. The Kremlin is spreading panic porn and shamelessly exploiting the West's fear of war. In this game of who blinks first, Russia needs to be forced to back down.

Otherwise, there would be no end to the moronic demands of "you make humiliating concessions, or we will destroy Ukraine."

We did not even know for sure if we could expect any substantial aid from the West if things got really bad.

We were quite confident in the usual suspects—the United States, Britain, Poland, the Baltic nations. But in general, the West was more than divided. For months, the EU couldn't even decide whether it should disconnect Russia from SWIFT if the Kremlin did a crazy little thing like a full-scale war of aggression in Europe.

On January 6, I was invited to hushed meeting with Josep Borrell, the EU high representative on foreign affairs. We sat down in a tiny conference room at the InterContinental Hotel in downtown Kyiv. And I must say I and other Ukrainian journalists in the room were absolutely pissed off.

"We have to avoid a war," Borrell told us. "And one of the ways to prevent war is to spell out the possible consequences. And certainly if there's aggression against Ukraine, there will be a strong response from Europe, mobilizing all our capacities to make Russia pay a high price. Not just sanctions on individuals, also [measures] affecting [the Russian] economy."

I couldn't help but ask: What price will Russia pay if they invade? How exactly are you going to punish Russia? Are you going to force Putin to watch the final season of *Game of Thrones*?

Don't you think when the EU is so diplomatically polite and vague about the "consequences" that the Kremlin only perceives this as the lack of resolve and weakness? They are openly spitting in our faces, and we're trying to talk them out of the invasion by talking nice, sweet, and inoffensive?

The EU top diplomat shrugged in response.

"You can be sure that for those interested, the ones who will be affected, [these suggested measures] are not vague," he told me.

Another reporter asked whether Borrell believed it was time to impose preemptive sanctions to show the EU was not going to tolerate what Russia was doing to Ukraine.

Borrell's entourage in the room chuckled at the question.

We left the hotel in disarray. The EU remains the same. Over-bureaucratized, too high in the clouds, too soft, not ready to break out of its comfort zone. A month later in early February, Borrell went on to Moscow, only to have a disastrous meeting with Lavrov. The Russian minister was openly ridiculing and humiliating United Europe, and all the EU's top diplomat could do was smile awkwardly.

Like I said, a notorious street thug does not appreciate being nice, diplomatic, and solution-oriented. He acknowledges nothing but your ability to fight back.

Things were not looking good in this regard at all. This escapist logic of bowing down to Russia's growing appetite and trying to be nice (only to avoid trouble for a moment) was clearly prevailing.

French president Emmanuel Macron, for instance, was calling on fellow EU leaders to work together and draw up "a new security deal with Russia" that would be based on "a frank dialogue with Moscow."

Here's the example of what sort of frank dialogue Russia was ready to have.

Sergey Ryabkov, Russia's deputy foreign minister, in an interview with TASS on January 9, 2022:

NATO must pack its shit and get out to the boundaries of 1997.

I'm not exaggerating, this was exactly what he said. By 2022, indoctrination had become so integral to Russia that even top public diplomats essentially morphed into state propaganda bots.

Russian officials were throwing in any possible mere claims that would feel juicy in the media and help create an environment of a looming world war—in which Russia would surely be a victim of aggression.

On January 27, Russia's foreign ministry nonproliferation department head Vladimir Yermakov crawled out of the woods and claimed in an interview with TASS that NATO planned exercises using B61 nuclear gravity bombs in a simulated conflict against Russia.

However, in all of this, I'm not ruling out the very weird possibility that many of them, potentially even Lavrov and Peskov, hadn't been informed that the Ukraine invasion was actually going to happen. It's very likely (and subsequent media inquiries give every reason to believe so) that only a very restricted number of top-level Russian officials and oligarchs knew—the rest were just safely following the party line, as always.

In an authoritarian, top-down, closed, and inherently paranoid system the weird can be everyday normal.

They were probably thinking that this was yet another *"bykovaniye"* campaign and not for real. And thus they didn't need to watch their language and remember who they were jumping on. And many, such as this Mr. Tough Guy Ryabkov probably sensed an opportunity to come up big time with the bosses—and bolster their career prospects.

Dmitry Peskov, in an interview with CNN published on January 15, 2021:

> We're observing NATO's gradual encroachment in Ukraine's territory with its infrastructure, instructors, stockpiles of defensive and offensive weapons, the training of Ukrainian military service members and so on.

Moreover, according to Peskov, events had brought Moscow and the alliance to a "red line," and Russia "could not tolerate this anymore." And yet Russia had no intentions to do anything about, for instance, its own missile systems in Kaliningrad—"because this is Russian territory."

Please remind me then why Ukraine, a sovereign independent nation, was supposed to do anything about any weapons on its own territory?

Peskov never specified what sort of particular "NATO infrastructure" and "offensive and defensive weapons" the Kremlin felt threatened by in Ukraine. Was this about a handful of American, British, and Canadian instructors providing tactical and medical training to Ukrainian soldiers near Lviv at the request of Ukraine in response to Russia's eight-year war in Donbas?

Or maybe it was about the planned construction of two small Ukrainian naval bases in Ochakiv and Berdyansk? The United Kingdom in 2021 approved a 1.7 billion pound sterling loan for ten years so Ukraine (a country that has basically no navy) could build coastline infrastructure and buy eight missile boats and two used British minesweepers at some point in the future.

Was that the sort of military threat mighty Mother Russia was so afraid of?

And why exactly was Russia feeling so direly threatened that it had to amass over one hundred thousand troops and issue aggressive all-or-nothing ultimatums to the West?

If you go back to interviews of the time, Russian officials were as vague as possible about what the all the fuss was about—other than Ukraine's potential NATO membership, that Moscow "can't stand anymore."

It had been fourteen years since the Bucharest Summit of 2008, when Ukraine and Georgia, against expectations, did not get their membership action plans. Of course, because of the "Don't Provoke Russia" position supported particularly by Germany and France. NATO in public switched to saying that Ukraine would someday be a NATO member—but first it had to work on its democracy.

And this continued on, and on, and on, from the time yours truly had been knee-high to a grasshopper.

And it was no secret that, basically, NATO membership wasn't going to happen any time soon—because of Russia. As a result, Russia had a clear path for its 2014 invasion, and we paid a heavy price for the years of fake neutrality that served no one but the expansionist regime in the east.

Even president Biden, in his speech on January 20, 2021, for the umpteenth time softly admitted that Ukraine was "not very likely to join NATO" based on how much work Kyiv had to do in terms of democracy and "a few other things going on there," as well as on the question of whether allies would vote to bring Ukraine in.

But the Kremlin meanwhile continued throwing hopelessly ambiguous allegations of "NATO's military absorption of Ukraine's territory" and the "gravely deteriorated security situation in Europe" because of "the NATO and United States attempt to undermine Russian security."

The Kremlin never published any satellite pictures of the hordes of NATO divisions preparing to invade Russia. Or of any NATO bases in Ukraine. Or of anything else in Ukraine and beyond that might pose an existential threat to the world's leading nuclear power.

Back then, we had several dozen FGM-148 Javelin systems (which, by the way, were moved to Donbas to deter a potential Russian armored breakthrough). We were also preparing to acquire several used Island-class patrol boats provided by the United States—and we considered ourselves lucky.

Guess when Western-provided weapons started flowing in really huge numbers. Yes, after Russia eventually invaded and we spent months begging for weapons as our cities were being turned into dust.

It wouldn't take long for events on the ground to show how truly afraid the Kremlin was of "the NATO encroachment" and its "military infrastructure" in Ukraine.

Journalism, meanwhile, had much more than words to show.

On January 11, CIT analyzed videos showing Russia redeploying Iskander-M ballistic missile systems from East Asia to Ukraine. Rob Lee of the Department of War Studies at King's College London detected between four and five Iskander-M brigades "fairly close to Ukraine." The *New York Times* reported that Russia had deployed attack helicopters close to Ukraine, yet another bad sign.

In the age of smartphones in every pocket, it's impossible to hide anything completely. Almost every day, there were new videos of trains carrying masses of vehicles and equipment from all corners of Russia. Much of the footage was being geolocated at railway points and confirmed as moving west.

Confused and worried relatives of Russian service members were leaving comments on TikTok and elsewhere, sharing rumors.

Spetsnaz units from Khabarovsk, heavy rocket artillery and motorized infantry brigades from Amur Oblast, Pacific Ocean marines from Vladivostok. Military police units. Hundreds of contracted service members at a time. All were allegedly moving to Belarus or to "the Ukrainian border" for periods of between two and nine months, and even longer.

Some commentators were reassured their men were being sent six thousand kilometers from home for nothing but "exercises." But others were worried that it was "something else."

What should we take from this?

It seemed quite bizarre that Russians were spending enormous resources to redeploy major forces from the other side of the world to Europe—just for drills with Belarus. One would rather expect Russia's Eastern Military District to have exercises at home, as normally happens.

But then again, since when had the Kremlin started counting money when it came to political escapades? The Russian officials claimed this was being done to test their transportation infrastructure's capability to ensure the rapid redeployment of large military forces for nearly ten thousand kilometers.

The Allied Resolve 2022 drills in Belarus were planned to take place between February 10 and 20. Rather unusually for the Kremlin's pompous playbook, there wasn't much public information put out about the exercises. Neither the quantity of troops nor the script was made public.

According to Telegram tales from that time, the simulation was about four nations committing a perfidious invasion of Belarus. The imaginary states of Nyaris, Pomoria, and Klopia were to attack the free and proud Belarus under the wise rule of Aleksandr Lukashenko from the north. And Dnieprovia (yeah, that's Ukraine) was to attack from the south.

But the valiant united force of Russia and Belarus was to repel the treacherous attack and score a glorious victory that would shine through ages, of course.

As early as January 18, Russian forces were gradually arriving in Belarus.

And United States Secretary of State Antony Blinken was implacable: The invasion could start at short notice. And the CIA chief in mid-January was already in Kyiv to see Zelensky.

Okay, let's have a look at the map.

According to the *New York Times*, from early January, Russia had nearly one hundred thousand troops near and in Ukraine. Some thirty-two thousand collaborationist forces troops were active in occupied Donetsk and Luhansk, and there were nearly twenty thousand Russian regular troops in Rostov Oblast, close to the border with occupied Donbas.

A large concentration of Russian forces at the well-known training centers of Pogonovo (Voronezh Oblast) and Soloti (Belgorod Oblast) could potentially threaten northern Luhansk Oblast and Kharkiv.

Even larger groups near Klintsy and Pochep (Russia's Bryansk Oblast), as well as Yelnya (Smolensk Oblast), could potentially be a threat to Sumy, Chernihiv, and eventually Kyiv—especially now that Russian forces were also moving to Belarus for drills (or "drills").

We believed the Kremlin would have nearly thirty thousand troops in Belarus in February.

If they stay at Belarus's southern border with Ukraine, they could pose a threat to west Kyiv, or Zhytomyr, or Rivne, or Lutsk. But Polesia—the giant strip along the Ukrainian-Belarusian border—is a land of woods and swamps, and it had very few large roads an attacking force could use to advance south into the deep of Ukraine.

Another very large concentration was also seen in occupied Crimea, of course.

Ukraine was being surrounded from four main directions—north, northeast, east, south. What was this all about?

If this was about a full-scale invasion, then the mission was to seize most, if not the whole of Ukraine, including Lviv (which sounds as crazy as it gets). They would almost for sure try to break into Ukraine's continental south, closer to Kherson. And then they'd move as fast as possible northeast toward Zaporizhia and Dnipro.

At the same time, the Belgorod group could rush into Ukraine to block and bypass Kharkiv and to move farther toward Dnipro. The two Russian axes—the north and the south—could meet up somewhere near Pavlograd east of Dnipro.

The bulk of Ukraine's military force would then be isolated in a giant pocket in Donbas.

Militia forces and Russian regulars would engage Ukrainian forces all along the old front line of Donbas—Mariupol, Volnovakha, Avdiivka, Luhansk Oblast.

Almost certainly, Russians would also attack Kyiv from the east and from the west, taking advantage of their posting in Belarus if Lukashenko obeys. And maybe, in a large amphibious operation, they could try to gain a foothold somewhere on the Black Sea coastline, and then engage Odesa, Mykolaiv, Kherson, enter the Transnistria, and then move north toward Kyiv . . .

Russians would definitely enjoy supremacy in the air and in the sea. There would be a merciless torrent of missiles.

But—there are also a lot of questions here. I know you've heard me ask them before, but let's rehearse them again and hope the Kremlin is listening in.

We're talking about a full-fledged invasion of a forty-million-person nation the size of France. Russians had nearly 100,000 troops and, according to Western media, it could have up to a total of 175,000— that would include all branches and components, like logistics and the navy. Does that feel like enough for a strategic operation that could realistically expect the occupation of most of Ukraine?

Do Russians expect to seize large metropolitan areas like Zaporizhia, Dnipro, let alone Kharkiv, Odesa, or Kyiv, with their defenses and extremely complicated terrain? Ukraine is a big country, and it's divided in half by a wide river, the mighty Dnipro. And there are very few large bridge crossings.

A shock-and-awe operation could potentially defeat Ukrainian armed forces. The Ukrainian military would disperse, with its organized remains withdrawing to West Ukraine.

And then what? Do Russians have enough resources to ensure the effective occupation of vast expanses of very unfriendly land stretching some seven hundred kilometers from the north to the south and at least eight hundred kilometers from the east to the west?

And the occupation would inevitably face a resistance movement organized and led by the remains of Ukraine's regular military and paramilitary forces. By 2022, we had at least several tens of thousands of retired service members with vast combat experience gained in Donbas.

Besides, in the worst days of 2014, when the Ukrainian regular military was disorganized, ordinary Ukrainians demonstrated the ability and motivation to massively self-mobilize and form paramilitary formations—the legendary volunteer battalions. Those guys, many of them yesterday's taxi drivers and programmers, fought like hell wearing nothing but fatigues from the nearest hunting shop and old sneakers—you have my word on that.

The Russians would have to impose a brutal occupation regime, which would make it even more unpopular. And it's very doubtful that they'd be able to rustle up enough local collaborationists to govern and police the occupied territories.

And without widespread support and effective control, any puppet government in Kyiv (and elsewhere) installed at the point of Russian bayonets wouldn't last a day. We're not even talking now about things like international backlash, massive humanitarian disasters and refugee crises, or Russia's own losses.

At the end of the day, it seemed pretty obvious that Russia would almost certainly drown in a long, barely predictable, dirty war it just wouldn't be able to win.

And it wasn't carrying out any mobilization efforts behind the lines, it wasn't forming strategic reserves or an appropriate logistics system, it wasn't mobilizing its economy or deploying a large grid of military hospitals for such a large war.

A limited operation? Maybe.

Russia might have enough forces to open a new front against Ukraine, or try to capture a certain region, like Kharkiv, or Mariupol, or the whole of Ukraine's south between Crimea and occupied Donbas.

But why? What's the point? What's the prize? Is this just for the sake of Putin's sick ego, his misguided play to stay in power? Ukraine will certainly offer fierce and organized resistance, there will be (at least some sort of) international reaction.

Russia could try to seize Mariupol or even the rest of Donbas. But what would that give the Kremlin except losses and more trouble? Russia has more than enough barely profitable coal mines and steelworks in its own depressed regions. The tumor of occupied Donbas served its purpose well as it was. It was never even supposed to be anything economically or politically sustainable.

Capturing Kharkiv? Maybe, but why bother to ask for more trouble from the West if Donetsk and Luhansk are already giving Russians what they want?

Any ideological reasons? But the Kremlin does not really believe in anything but money and staying in power for as long as physically possible. They don't really care about Donbas, or "The Russian World," or anything of the sort. They attacked Ukraine and seized Crimea in 2014 because they felt it was dangerous to have a successful, prosperous European Ukraine in front of the Russian people's eyes.

And they did that in the most careful way possible so the West could plausibly feel comfortable closing its eyes and settling on the fragile status quo. A land corridor between Russia and occupied Crimea? A grand war in Europe seems a price a bit too high for solving the peninsula's freshwater issues.

And the Kremlin was being so defiant and ostentatious about its military buildup and so theatrical about this "immediate war threat from Ukraine and the West" that one just couldn't help but feel the stink.

Moreover, Moscow had more than enough and far subtler and safer tools for projecting power against Ukraine. Cyberattacks, political provocations, efforts to destabilize and demoralize the country from within.

No, they can't be serious.

It just made no sense.

They just couldn't be that delusional and stupid.

They are fucking with us, and they feel they can go unpunished. We have to show them that we're not someone to mess with.

Diplomacy behind closed doors continued in Geneva and beyond.

Quite predictably, NATO declined Russia's knowingly impossible ultimatum.

NATO secretary general Jens Stoltenberg on January 10:

> We made it very clear that we will not make compromises regarding any European nation's right to choose its own way, including regarding security treaties. So the non-infringement of this principle is fundamental.

But, as Stoltenberg noted a bit earlier in an interview with the *Financial Times*, the alliance was ready to work and mitigate Russian concerns, such as steps "on arms control, on efforts to try to have more transparency on military activity, exercises, and also on lines of communications."

Maybe that's just me being simple, but I think if you have "grave security concerns" and your suspected war adversary says it's ready to cooperate and show you everything it has, that's at least a way to go. Well, unless you have something else in mind.

I think around mid-January, all contacts with Russia effectively stalled.

Apparatchiks in Moscow were demanding that the West give them an official written no (show us how you really, really, really decline our demands on paper!). And they were saying it publicly that there was no point in new talks anytime soon—without NATO "wrapping up its infrastructure and getting back to the boundaries of 1997."

At that moment, much of what we're discussing now was still mostly food for thought for concerned journalists and experts.

The Wild West of Ukrainian Facebook was as blatant and unforgiving as always: Macron is a weak weirdo, Germans are only waiting to sell us out for their beloved Russian gas, Zelensky is a clown and a coward, and Putin may put his tanks up his ass.

Also—#UkrainiansWillResist.

But that's the Wild West of Ukrainian Facebook. Ordinary Ukrainians continued living a very normal life.

I even dare say that for most ordinary Ukrainians, this period was rather about something that we called "Vova's Thousand Hryvnyas."

Once upon a time, Zelensky decided to go bold and support the COVID-19 vaccination campaign in the country. The rollout started pretty late and was messy, and many were still feeling nah.

So, here's the idea—everyone who had gotten two jabs was entitled to one thousand hryvnyas. To access this windfall, you use the Diia app on your smartphone and apply for the program. The app already knows you already have an electronic vaccination certificate.

Then you must get a special account from your bank (also online via any banking app) into which your money will magically appear. Done! You could spend the cash on certain things like cinema tickets or the gym.

Surprisingly, most of the money allocated by the government was spent on books. Yours truly, for instance, treated himself to two beautiful editions of George Orwell's *1984* in English and Russian. Bookstore owners and theaters couldn't have been happier after the long COVID famine.

But then this started to change.

On January 14, you wake up in the morning and scroll through morning headlines, sipping coffee and combating sleep with your iPhone in hand. A swipe of the thumb:

MASSIVE CYBERATTACK AGAINST THE UKRAINIAN GOVERNMENT

Ukraine's foreign affairs ministry website on its home page showed a black screen with the following text in Russian, Ukrainian, and broken Polish:

> Ukrainian! All your personal data has been downloaded to a public network. All data on your computer has been erased, and recovery is impossible. All information regarding you is now public. Be

afraid and expect the worst. This is retaliation for your past, your present, and your future. For Volyn, OUN UPA, Polesia, and the historic lands.

Many government websites just stopped responding that day. Polish media immediately reacted, saying that the Polish version was not written by a native speaker.

Be afraid and expect the worst.

It felt a bit dizzying.

Was this done by a group of rogue shit faces in a garage pretending to be Polish? Or by a foreign power trying to sow panic and fear?

I think on that day, the Ukrainian nation started truly feeling that something very wrong was going on.

SIX

I hate it when it's freezing in Boryspil.

And especially when it's freezing and one has to wait at Ukraine's flagship airport east of Kyiv. And not reclining comfortably in the business lounge sipping a $10 Americano, but roaming all around the Terminal F building, or even just near the runway—for many hours.

On January 25, a bunch of Kyiv reporters were invited to complete the exciting trip across the city's two main river bridges, in the thick of the morning rush hour. The prize: a chance to see some history in the making.

So, there was a lot of waiting.

The airplane was supposed to arrive at twelve P.M. Then suddenly everybody got a message from the United States embassy—the arrival was postponed until two P.M. Then to three forty-three P.M. Then to four P.M. Finally we were informed that journalists would be allowed to come and see the miracle at six P.M.

This kind of reminded me of December 27, 2017, when we spent something like twelve hours on a Boryspil ramp waiting for a Ukrainian Air Force Ilyushin Il-76. As many as seventy-three Ukrainian soldiers and civilian captives were set to return home following the first large prisoner swap with Russia in years.

We were singing and dancing in the frost to keep our bodies warm, sipping hot tea and chewing sandwiches brought by thoughtful volunteers. The crowd of the released prisoners' relatives had no choice but to join us in our time-killing antics in the night.

Finally, well after midnight, the airplane arrived. Petro Poroshenko, for some reason wearing camo fatigues and a new ground forces beret, decided to arrange a full-fledged publicity show.

The plane had taxied to the terminal, the freed captives had disembarked onto the tarmac. But then everybody had to wait for the Poroshenko people to line up the long absent fathers, uncles, and brothers behind Poroshenko's back, so the triumphant president could personally lead them into the hands of their loved ones, in front of a myriad of cameras.

The same place, the same frosty evening five years later . . . Finally, a Boeing 747 marked NATIONAL in giant blue letters docked at Terminal F. A forklift unloaded pallets one after the other onto the ground.

First, crates of black plastic containers with rounded edges. Javelins. Then loads of olive cylindrical tubes. SMAW-Ds, the bunker killers. Then piles of boxes filled with something that was hard to recognize in the poor light.

> . . . as we have already noted, this is the third shipment of United States military aid that has arrived in Ukraine over the last few days. Earlier, the United Kingdom sent over two thousand anti-tank portable systems to Ukraine amid Russian war threats and stalled negotiations with the Kremlin . . .

That's a guy from Suspilne TV, his lips already blue with cold, giving a live broadcast on YouTube from the scene.

Yep, that was definitely worth the pain.

A historic air bridge between Ukraine and the West was finally open for business.

American birdies full of weapons arrived every two or three days. British Royal Air Force's Boeing C-17 Globemaster first arrived on January 17.

I know many people in Britain get angry when someone even mentions the name of Boris Johnson. But to us in Ukraine, this weird dude with a crop of wispy blond hair became very close to a national hero.

BoJo may be loathed by many at home, but here in Ukraine, he has streets named after him. Yes, he was experiencing his own personal Churchill moment, and this flamboyant yeller was saying things that so many soulless, computerlike red-tapers ceased to feel long ago—democracy, the fight for freedom, values, a battle of David versus Goliath.

Weirdly enough, this extravagant character running around and calling for the stubborn support of Ukraine at any price appeared to be in the right place and time to play a special role in modern history. There always needs to be a weirdo standing for going the hard way instead of simply striking an easy deal with the devil.

Our social media proclaimed him a fellow Ukrainian Boris Johnsoniuk. Confectioner's shops in Kyiv's Podil created a special white cream pastry after him.

The decision voiced by defense secretary Ben Wallace in the chamber of green seats was a whiff of fresh air and hope for us.

Next Generation Anti-Tank Weapon: The acronym "NLAW" entered our life and invaded our minds, giving a go to thousands of newly hatched anti-tank warfare experts on Facebook.

When the first NLAW batch arrived, Ukrainian social media detonated: "God Save the Queen!" Her Majesty started her reign with no one but Winston Churchill coming to her chamber for weekly conversations.

And in the dawn of her life, Britain was the first to break through the wall of hesitation and start immediately sending weapons to a victim of yet another massive European war of aggression.

The age of the Javelin on the throne was gone, and Ukraine got a new holy grail. It didn't take long for the Ukrainian military to start posting videos on YouTube with detailed guidelines on how anyone could use them.

First, check if the weapon looks intact and appears to have no visible fractures. Make sure the sight and the firing mechanism are not damaged, too. Then, install the battery and push it down until you can hear a click.

Assess the tactical environment and choose between the two modes of detonator arming distance—either twenty meters or one hundred meters. Then switch the tumbler to select between overfly top attack (OTA) and direct attack (DA) modes.

Put the weapon on your shoulder and hold it by the grips in the front part. Use the foldaway bar if necessary. Switch both safety locks off. Activate the predicted line of sight system and track the target for two or three seconds. Aim at the Russian tank's turret if you're using the OTA mode, or at the hull's center if using the DA.

Push the launch button. Drop the thing and change your position immediately.

Oh boy, if only we had known then what role those tubes of fire would play in the lives of forty million people as they faced down an invading army.

The airlift ground on.

Britain, America, the Baltic nations, Poland . . . Javelins, SMAW-Ds, NLAWs, Stingers. Every arrival is like a little Christmas, which Ukraine's defense minister reports on Twitter.

We are not alone. We still have friends by our side.

We genuinely thought this was going to be a strong signal to the Kremlin.

Yes, the West is divided. But there are nations that are not going to sit idly by and are already helping Ukraine with advanced weapons. The message was more than clear—do not go in. Ukraine will have thousands of modern tank killers with which to greet Russian armored convoys.

Meanwhile, Germany's defense minister Christine Lambrecht on January 24:

> We must do everything possible to de-escalate. Arms supplies are
> useless at the moment.

Yeah, sure. A month before a full-scale war in Europe, arms supplies to a wound-be victim of aggression made no sense at all. Here's what was really making sense—preventing other nations, like Estonia, from sending German-made weapons to Ukraine. Also, expressing concerns and calling on "both sides to de-escalate."

From the distance of time, I still find it hard to understand what prevailed in these people's minds. Was it outstanding naivete, or bureaucratic faintheartedness, or a haughty desire to just feed us to the Russians "for a greater good?"

The Russian buildup continued. There wasn't a week without fresh satellite pictures from Maxar showing new Russian units deployed to bases near Ukrainian borders.

And as talks with the West stalled, Russia again started turning up the volume on the narrative of "Ukraine waging a genocide in Donbas."

On January 19, Russia's Communist Party (KPRF) filed an "address" calling on Putin to grant official recognition to the "Donetsk People's Republic" ("DNR") and the "Luhansk People's Republic" ("LNR"), the breakaway enclaves occupied and fully controlled by Russia.

In 2014, the letter said, the secession from Ukraine was supported in "referendums" by 89 percent and 96 percent of the "DNR" and the "LNR" populations, respectively. Ever since, according to Russian communists, the two "republics" had established themselves as "fully legitimate states having all democratic institutions."

And for years, "new Ukrainian authorities" had been waging a "policy of genocide" toward the people of Donbas and constantly undermining a peace process:

> All along the contact line, again, there are multiple cease-fire violations recorded. Artillery shells destroy the civilian population's homes, schools, other infrastructure facilities. Ukraine seizes settlements between the contact lines where, in particular, Russian citizens reside.

For eight years, the letter said, the people of Donbas had been living under Ukrainian shelling with ten thousand killed, fifty thousand wounded, and more than 3.9 million having fled the region to Ukraine or Russia.

Therefore, to help protect the people of Donbas from the Ukrainian "policy of genocide," Russian communists suggested that Putin recognize the "republics" as independent nations and immediately initiate "negotiations" in cooperation with Russia, including agreements on "security issues."

The letter referred to the UN and the OSCE, but it somehow failed to mention that both monitors present elsewhere in Donbas were not reporting any significant uptick of hostilities or violence against civilians.

The letter also somehow failed to mention the critical backstory: how Russian subversives led by Igor Girkin and other warlords unleashed the regional war in 2014 and, with support from the Russian regular military, forcefully occupied Donetsk and Luhansk and waged their war on Ukraine from densely populated urban areas.

It did not mention the fact that, according to the UN, 88 percent of civilian deaths in the region occurred in the heat of hostilities in 2014 and early 2015. That's including the 298 killed in the Russian downing of an MH17 passenger jet. Also, the fact that between 40 and 50 percent were killed by land mines or unexploded ordnance.

Moreover, according to OSCE, between 20 percent and 35 percent of civilians were killed in "DNR" and "LNR" attacks on Ukrainian-controlled territory.

Russian communists for some reason decided not to explain the fact that cities like Slovyansk, Kramatorsk, Mariupol, Sievierodonetsk, and Lysychansk returned to normal, peaceful lives after Russian warlords were defeated and expelled by Ukraine. The cities of Ukrainian-controlled Donbas lived on, did their self-governance under Ukraine's decentralization reforms, and elected their mayors, many of whom happened to be local Russian sympathizers.

They did not mention that there had been no "genocide" or "ethnic cleansing" in Ukrainian-controlled cities, how Mariupol became the fastest-developing city in eastern Ukraine—or how after years as "republics," Russian-dominated Donetsk and Luhansk turned into economically depressed, criminalized black holes.

In late 2021, even Russian-led militants of the "DNR" reported a total of seven civilian deaths over the past year, without specifying how many were killed due to Ukrainian armed violence and how many were killed in unexploded ordnance incidents.

That was before the "Ukraine's eight-year genocide of Donbas" was introduced as a key pro-war propaganda talking point.

As often happens in Russia, such parliamentary "addresses" filed especially by the KPRF are used to test public reaction, including abroad. The January 19 address was no different.

At this point, this particular parliamentary razzle dazzle seems to have been too much even for the Kremlin.

As Ukraine's foreign minister Oleksiy Kuleba commented, the "recognition" of occupied Donbas would mean Russia's complete withdrawal from the Minsk accords. Or, in other words, the Kremlin was to lose the slipknot it had been tying around Ukraine's neck for years.

But if you think about this as intimidation, this makes much more sense.

By the way—speaking of Russia having absolutely nothing to do with the complete control of the "breakaway republics" and the "Donbas rebels": I remember a very funny incident back in December 2021, when a reporter noticed that a local court in Russia's Rostov-on-Don sentenced a clerk to five and a half years in prison.

This clerk ran a local company responsible for food supplies for the Russian military. The guy tried to mediate a bribe worth almost 1 million rubles to Russia's Southern Military District's epidemiological service.

The service officer demanded monthly bribes for ensuring unrestricted access to food supplies for Russian regular military formations deployed to . . . yes, "Donetsk People's Republic and the Luhansk People's Republic territory" in 2018 and 2019. According to the verdict, Russian formations served "regular tours of duty" in occupied Ukraine.

The case's protocol even described how the Russians pulled it off. At the border with occupied Ukraine, Russian trucks dropped their license plates and papers and then proceeded to their destination points where they were checked by Russian military officers and guarded by "the host party."

The convict's company was supposed to transfer thirteen hundred tons of food twice a month. According to estimates by Radio Liberty, this was enough to provide nutrition to some twenty-six thousand troops.

The document immediately disappeared from the court's website. And Kremlin mouth Peskov called it a "mistake." But we in Ukraine had a good laugh at the fuckup.

Of course, for all those years, it was no secret that Russia had complete control of occupied Donbas. We knew how much Russia spent to keep the enclaves afloat, who among Russian generals were in charge by rotation, and how "the 1st and the 2nd army corps" were integrated into Russia's Southern Military District command structure.

Seeing Russian apologists in the West practicing the most frantic forms of mental gymnastics to present this as an "internal Ukrainian conflict" is a special sort of exotic fun.

Especially if one is a Donbas native and saw how this dirty and villainous war was unleashed with one's own eyes.

Nonetheless, the war propaganda train just couldn't be stopped.

On January 24, the state-owned Russia-1 TV channel issued an "interview" with top "DNR" collaborator Denis Pushilin, in which he asserted that the Ukrainian military was preparing an offensive in Donbas.

According to Pushilin, Ukraine was deploying Javelins, tanks, artillery, and rocket systems, as well as bringing in "foreign journalists" and "instructors from the USA and Britain." These latter were "almost openly taking pictures of themselves near combat positions and posting them on the internet."

Sergey Lavrov on January 21, following yet another useless meeting with United States secretary Blinken:

> We're not ruling it out that this hysteria is being bolstered by our Western colleagues to cover for Kyiv's total sabotage of the Minsk Accords, if not to provoke the use of force in Donbas.

I was becoming fond of all these miraculous coincidences. Again, just like in April, as Russia had concentrated the biggest military force in the region since the fall of the Soviet Union and was openly threatening a war, Ukraine and the West suddenly decided to launch a massacre.

Senior Russian diplomat Konstantin Gavrilov following arms-control talks in Vienna on January 23:

> Everything has been made clear, voiced, and warned. We're not going to tolerate it when our citizens are under attack . . . Only dogs bark. The wolf bites, and that's it. As our chief of general staff said, Russia can respond to any provocations. And it will not let anyone hurt, let alone kill, its citizens.

This tough hombre did not specify what sort of "provocations" would trigger a response. The Kremlin would know it when it saw it.

It seemed just another absurdist spin to maintain Russia's everyday state propaganda agenda. But it was just the beginning.

The real abyss of war-thirsty insanity was yet to come.

There was a bit of an odd sentiment on Bankova Street.

Late on January 19, Zelensky issued a televised address to the nation.

He said the media was full of reports of an upcoming war with Russia, that the invasion could begin at any moment. But what's new about that, he asked. Ukraine has been fighting Russia's military encroachments since 2014, and the risk of a major escalation had always been around.

What's different this time around, he said, is that there is much more turmoil. And Russia is capitalizing on this, playing on fears to make everyone anxious and to undermine Ukraine's economy and business environment.

In this situation, he continued, everybody should chill out and calm down. The media should stop helping Russia spread hysteria, and Ukraine's partners should be saying more not about what Russia is going to do but how they will respond if Russia invades.

Ukraine does not want war. But it is preparing, and it is not afraid, and it has faith because it has honor and pride. And it has partners whose support is stronger than ever before.

What should you do? Just one thing. Stay calm, keep your head cool. Be sure of your strengths, of our military, of our Ukraine. Do not hype yourself up. React with wisdom instead of emotions. Use your head, not your heart. Do not shout that all is lost, but remember that everything is under control. Do not be anxious all the time about what's going to happen tomorrow.

I'll tell you: On January 22, we'll celebrate Ukraine's Unity Day. We will launch the Zaporizhia Bridge. In a year, we'll complete the longest highway between Uzhgorod and Luhansk. We'll be as always building roads, bridges, schools, arenas, carriages, airplanes, tanks. We'll get most of our population vaccinated.

In April, we'll celebrate Easter. In May, as always, there will be the sun, weekends, shashlik, the Victory Day. And then summertime, and we'll be passing exams, joining universities, planning vacations, pottering about the garden, getting married, having weddings . . . And then the autumn. I hope we'll be cheering our national soccer team in Qatar.

And then the winter, and we'll be preparing for the New Year's Day. And as always, on December 31, we'll sit down to tables with our families. And I am sure that in the New Year's address, I'll speak to you: "Dear Ukrainians! See? I told you. Good for you! We did not panic or succumb to provocations. We were calm, strong, and we're celebrating the New Year with no panic, no fear, and hopefully, with no viruses. And, as I sincerely believe, with no war.

For the love of God, man. You don't want to know what you'll have to tell us at the end of the year 2022.

The address caused quite a stir.

There was nothing even closely resembling panic shopping, let alone mayhem in the streets. But there was a sense of discomfort slowly creeping into many minds.

And many were not happy with "The Shashlik Speech." Zelensky is trying to smooth-talk us through the situation. He's selling us fairy-tales of summertime fun while Russians are getting their tanks warmed up. Many became increasingly sure Zelensky was weak and a denialist, and that he was still doing nothing.

As of late January, 53 percent of Ukrainians believed Zelensky would not be able to defend Ukraine.

People reacted in very different ways.

Some were sending everybody they knew images saying something like, "Pray for peace! There's still time."

Others were engaged in Ukraine's national sport of those days—emergency bags. Oh god, we had our fair share of holy wars on Facebook over whose wartime survival kit was more wisely/smartly arranged.

Do you know what you should have at hand in case of a full-scale invasion by the world's biggest nuclear power?

Here's your recommended list from the Kyiv city government:

Use a high-quality backpack with the volume of at least twenty-five metric liters. Make copies of all your most important documents like your ID, your driver's license, papers confirming your real estate and vehicle ownership. Hold all papers in a polyethylene bag within quick reach. Add your credit cards and cash. Also, take several pictures of your loved ones.

Put in your area's printed map and make arrangements regarding a certain place where you can meet with your loved ones. You may face a lack of communications in wartime. Prepare a small radio set and spare batteries. Also, a flashlight, matches, a lighter, a multitool pocketknife, a waterproof compass, and a watch.

You may be exposed in the open with no shelter as a result of an attack. Put in several large plastic garbage bags, a roll of packing tape, and some twenty meters of synthetic cord—you might have to construct an improvised tent.

Prioritize the basic set of seasonal clothes, warm socks, underwear, comfortable and reliable footwear.

Also, put in condoms—you might use them as tourniquets to stop bleeding or as waterproof bags for matches. Put in basic hygiene items and a first aid medical kit.

You may find yourself falling short of access to food. Put in flatware, food supplies, and fresh water that will help you survive for several days. Prioritize compact, long-lasting, and high-energy products like dark chocolate, tinned meat and fish, crackers, instant soups.

Some preferred posting pictures of their weapons safes: "Now here's my fucking wartime emergency kit!"

Of course, Zelensky's administration wanted to calm the population and prevent panic and a societal collapse. This was the last thing our fragile economy needed, even though public morale was high and stable, and the whole country continued life as usual.

In January, around the Orthodox Christmastime, Zelensky took a very ostentatious vacation and posted videos on Instagram from the ski resort of Bukovel in the Carpathian Mountains.

No wonder so many in the United States were angry about the "it's all right, stop the hysteria" campaign.

On January 23, the United Kingdom's foreign minister, Liz Truss, asserted they had intelligence on a potential puppet leader Russia wanted to install in Ukraine following the military occupation. The British said the Kremlin was considering Yevgen Muraiev—a pro-Russian former member of parliament and the owner of the minor cable TV channel NASH.

In Ukraine, this couldn't help but trigger a wave of Homeric laughter.

Like, seriously? Muraiev was indeed a Russian bootlicker, formerly part of Yanukovych's Party of Regions. But he was a political outlier, his name mostly known only to journalists and experts and his political party hardly scratched a popularity rating of 4–5 percent.

You should really consider someone a bit more serious if you want to install a collaborator in charge of a forty-million-person nation under occupation.

The alleged list of Russian candidates included long-forgotten names from the time just before the EuroMaidan—the revolution of late 2013 and early 2014 that ousted pro-Russian Yanukovych and reaffirmed Ukraine's national course toward EU membership.

That's Nikolay Azarov (Yanukovych's prime minister), Andriy Kliuyev (Yanukovych's chief of staff), Sergey Arbuzov (the guy who briefly replaced Azarov in 2014 and then fled with the whole gang), and Vladimir Sivkovich (who on earth is that?).

I mean, the person who made this list in Russia had no clue about present-day Ukraine and what it has become after the EuroMaidan.

Or was Russia deliberately feeding British intelligence absolute horseshit to make the West believe the Kremlin had a long-term plan for Ukraine's occupation?

This just couldn't be for real. Russians just can't be *that* delusional about Ukraine.

Or could they? Now, from the distance of time, I'll not be surprised if it's ever confirmed they seriously contemplated those stooges as worthy candidates to rule over the enslaved postwar Ukraine. The Kremlin got so much else wrong, why not this, too? I'd come to see these missteps not as a bug but a feature of a system based on lies from top to bottom.

Meanwhile, one by one, day after day, foreign embassies announced they were initiating evacuations from Kyiv.

First families, then nonessential staff. Then senior diplomats. Consular services terminated until further notice.

The United Kingdom, then the United States, Canada, Israel, and so on. All citizens are strongly advised to leave Ukraine. Then the recommendations switched to "as soon as possible" and then to "leave Ukraine immediately."

All Ukraine's foreign affairs office could really do was issue a bitter statement for the media saying that the departure of foreign missions was "premature."

11 Bankova Street . . . the Presidential Office. The Ukrainian White House.

We sit at a giant round table in the chamber of white and gold like King Arthur's knights or something.

We all know one another, but no one really feels like talking much.

We look at one another in silence, lazily drawing in our notebooks. We are some twenty journalists representing Ukraine's top media outlets.

We have all been secretly invited to come and talk. No records, no notes, nothing of what will be voiced in this room can appear in print or on the country's laptop screens—that's the rule.

"Well, hello there!"

Andriy Yermak, the presidential administration head, busts through the door, accompanied by his press aide.

"So great to see everyone, especially my favorite gotcha questioners!" he says, smiling, and throws a thick stack of papers on the table.

Yermak just recently turned fifty.

He's heavily built, short-haired, and unshaven. All dressed in coyote tan pants and tactical jacket, just like his boss in a room next door.

Yermak is the one who is sometimes jokingly called "the real president of Ukraine."

Formally, he's Zelensky's chief of staff. But, in fact, he's the country's number two. Over his two years in office, he has managed to concentrate very serious power and steer a lot of key decision-making processes into his own hands.

That includes attempts to work out a solution with Russia on Donbas, prisoner swaps, and direct contacts with key people in the West. The

"Normandy talks" of Russia, Ukraine, Germany, and France—that's his remit, too.

He's someone the media calls a gray cardinal, the guy always standing behind Zelensky wherever the president goes.

Here's the thing about Zelensky: He's into favoritism. This often involves someone from Zelensky's media empire in Ukraine: his fixers, or his childhood friends he's stayed in touch with and brought into the business. Yermak is a lawyer and a movie producer.

And of course, Yermak comes with his own long tail of colorful controversies.

As we gathered in the Presidential Office, there were still fresh memories of a gigantic scandal involving Ukrainian secret services and their alleged failure to arrest a band of Russian Wagner mercenaries during a flight between Belarus and Turkey.

Ukrainian media directly accused Yermak of having torpedoed the action to appease the Kremlin ahead of possible peace talks. Wagnergate, as we called it, was a massive political earthquake. And up to this day we're not any closer to learning if high treason at the Presidential Office had indeed taken place.

Nonetheless, Yermak managed to survive all the drama and retained his position.

Now the storm of war is gathering . . . and this office has a lot to answer for.

We ask questions one by one, in the order we sit at the round table.

"Andriy Borysovych, what do you really make of those Russian drills in Belarus? I mean, this all feels hinky, don't you think?"

That's the journalist Sonya Koshkina of the *Livyi Bereg* publication.

Yermak tosses his head.

"We still believe the Russians are doing this to apply political pressure," he says.

"Moscow is going off the rails, that's for sure, going way too far this time around. But here's the thing—we must not help them. All the doom talk, all the turmoil will only bring us to a place where Russia won't have to lift a finger to destabilize us.

"They'd love to get us without a hand's turn if we degrade to the point of social collapse and mass hysteria. So let's stay sober, let's all get real and think about what we say and what we write to the public."

Journalists at the table exchange glances.

Some appear relieved at having their expectations confirmed that there won't be a big war.

Some get their eyes rolled up—now here's the mastermind behind Zelensky overtly downplaying the threat and embarrassing the West.

"I want you to understand one thing," Yermak continues. "We're all adults here. And this administration has everything under control. We see everything, we hear everything. We have Kyrylo [the military intelligence chief general, Budanov], he's one of the world's best people in the field. In any case, we continue to aggressively develop our military. Strong economy, stability, and growth are our strength. Can you name another country that talks about reforms at such a time, and implements them? That's us."

Okay. But why are the Americans doing this? What they say and how they insist on the invasion's high probability is unprecedented. We've never seen things so intense.

"See, guys, it's really complicated," Yermak says, spreading his hands over the desk.

"Folks in the West aren't used to the constant threat of war we've lived with for years. The Canadians are now talking about getting their diplomats' families home. They're worried about what happened in Afghanistan in August. And they really, really don't want that mess again.

"So they're like: 'We're better off thinking about leaving Ukraine now. We don't want to face criticism if Russia really attacks and we're not ready to get our people out.'

"I'm telling you again, we are preparing for all contingencies. And let me just say, a while ago, Hillary Clinton called me and said she admired our evacuation mission in Kabul. Our military intelligence guys rescued seven hundred people from the airport, you remember."

We, the journos in the room, continue pressing the official. It's not every day that Western embassies talk about war and evacuate their diplomatic staff, right?

"We believe the threat level is not that great," Yermak says, looking as confident as one could in his position. "We tell them all: 'Guys, let's coordinate our steps, otherwise it sends a really bad signal to the public.' I'd also say that in many cases there's a human factor. In the United States Department of State, some people have a hair trigger. They do stuff and then back down, all the time."

But what about Russians withdrawing their families from Kyiv and Lviv?

"To the best of our knowledge, this is not happening."

Journalists exchange glances again. Who's telling tales then, CNN or Yermak?

All right, moving on. The United States—did the Americans demand that you offer the Russians any concessions? Western media talk about this.

Yes or no?

"One hundred percent no." Yermak does not hesitate for a second. "And I want to finally take all these speculations off the table because it's sickening. Right now, we have unprecedented support from our Western partners. That's including intelligence data on Russians. Biden directly said he'd do everything within his power for us."

Yermak grabs his iPhone from the table and starts shaking it in front of us.

"Jake Sullivan and I talk regularly, and the chemistry is good. I'm telling you, this guy is the world's best national security expert, and our discussions are serious and substantive.

"One of the things I've learned is that we must be stubborn. We need concrete steps, not conversations and expressions of concern. You believe Russians are going to invade and you want to help? Here's what you can do for us.

"Many in the West are unhappy with our rhetoric regarding NATO. No, we're not dropping our membership bid because Russians are angry. Many don't like this. France and Germany are pointing fingers at each other about who's really against Ukraine in NATO.

"But we want concrete steps, and I'm telling you this—we will not be pleased if we're not invited to the Madrid meeting this summer."

Oh, those innocent days of February 2022, when our topmost concern was whether the West would have the guts to include us in the upcoming NATO summit in June, despite Russian threats.

But back to the possibility of war: Western democracies all say they are determined to introduce punishing sanctions on Russia?

"Yes, they all say this." Yermak nods. "But we really need more than that. Now. If Russians really come in, the strongest sanctions are going to mean nothing."

We lean back in our seats and rub our necks. Half of the room is clearly not optimistic. Especially when it comes to the issue of Western resolve. Will they actually do something substantial if the worst comes?

It's my turn to ask a question.

It will be the last question. For some reason, I always end up getting a seat just to the left of Yermak, at the very end of the question circle.

So, isn't it easier for the West to just make us implement the Minsk accords the way Russia sees it "to avoid war"?

What do we do if that happens?

I really want to know. I don't see what would prevent Brussels and Washington from simply telling us: "Fuck off and roll over, it's not our problem, you signed that Minsk paper, and we want business as usual with Russia."

"Look, people." Yermak sighs and starts off on a long speech.

"As a lawyer, I can tell you I'd never have signed the Minsk accords. I'd personally like to strangle the guy who wrote the thing and ordered it signed. But we're forced to move that way because there's a Ukrainian signature from 2014.

"Here's what we're doing—we've involved the world's best legal counsel and have found a range of loopholes we can use in our favor based on international law—the special constitutional status for Donbas, the control of the border with Russia. We have the Steinmeier Formula approved. Which means the Minsk can be implemented only when OSCE recognizes elections in Donbas as free and fair. The Russians have to accept this, otherwise they must abandon the Steinmeier Formula."

I do my very best to conceal a silent grunt of laughter. Does anyone really think Russia gives a damn about all these sophisticated legal nuances?

Yermak throws a stack of legal documents on the desk. He's noticeably emotional and switches from Ukrainian to Russian.

"We have found answers in international law about how to ride this out. And we are well-prepared for diplomatic discussions. And you know, Poroshenko, who ordered the Minsk to be signed—he can put his lectures on our red lines for Russia up his ass!"

On February 9, Yermak had another powwow with us explaining his detailed plan for finding a way around the Minsk disaster.

In a bitter irony of fate, in just several days, the long-standing issue will fix itself—in a way. The eight-year-long Minsk Process will vanish in a haze forever in just one stroke of Vladimir Putin's pen and the first incursions of Russian forces.

I leave the Presidential Office with a deeply uncomfortable feeling.

Yep, the country's number two talks sweet. But are we buying this? Yes, if you simply want to.

And at the same time . . . it's all becoming really worrisome.

Our famous TV news stars pour out of the Office and walk toward their Land Cruisers.

The Bankova is a bit empty in the winter afternoon sun.

But there's still a Christmas village right outside the Presidential Office windows. A tall Christmas tree, a small, improvised shop serving hot dogs, a spinning ride, a skating rink decorated with angel figurines.

For crying out loud, Zelensky. It's February. Enough already.

Anyway, after such an intense press gaggle, why not a walk in the winter sunset?

The *Kyiv Independent* office in Podil is a forty-minute walk away. Amid all this mess, sometimes one needs to switch off and embrace this city.

Several years ago, when I'd just arrived in Kyiv to try my luck, I had no money at all. So I walked and watched, with the Wikipedia app in my hand. That's a beautiful thing about Kyiv—one can have a ton of fun without spending a single coin.

The Kyiv government quarter is an area we call "Lypky" ("The Little Lindens"). That's because Lypska Street is pretty close to the Presidential Office. Once a street of linden trees dating back to the eighteenth century, it's now a welcoming boulevard of green.

This place has always been our Beverly Hills, with its own flavor. And it's absolutely packed with big and little landmarks, especially if you pay attention to details.

Here one finds the centuries-old legacies of the rich and powerful, the movers and shakers of their time. The richest merchants flocked to the area, establishing exuberant villas and mansions in the nineteenth and the early twentieth centuries that are still around.

The street's very name says it all, Bank Street. The place still preserves its past—the street ends at today's National Bank of Ukraine central office.

Celebrated architects designed expensive revenue houses that with time became urban legends. Right in front of the Presidential Office, there's the weird gray House of Chimaeras.

The former owner, the Polish architect Vladyslav Gorodetsky, was really into hunting, so he bequeathed the city a house crowned with concrete sculptures of lions, eagles, rhinos, mermaids, and even toads.

The heads of elephants with their long trunks were used as rainwater pipes, as if the building was a wild African hillside set against a backyard garden of green. According to popular legend, Gorodetsky created this behemoth in loving memory of his daughter who'd drowned herself in the Dnipro River after an unhappy romance. Well, that's a lie—the architect's daughter lived a long life in a stable marriage.

The Lypky is still a reminder of how green Kyiv used to be.

Many years ago, Honoré de Balzac roamed these streets, always catching an unforgiving cold. Those mansions and palaces changed hands with the times, from millionaires of the old empire to warlords, then Soviet and Nazi generals during the periods of occupation, then to generations of Soviet bureaucrats.

I cross the Instytutska and Mykhailo Grushevsky streets that are so painfully familiar to all veterans of the EuroMaidan Revolution. The protests turned violent, though all is quiet now. And here we are right between the Verkhovna Rada, the Ukrainian parliament, and Mariinsky Park just in front of it.

It's winter now but memory surfaces. Few things are better in this world than ending a hot summer's day with an evening on a bench in the Mariinsky Park chomping an ice cream in the shade of century-old trees. The park somehow manages to stay quiet and calm even though the traffic in the government quarter can be wild.

The 250-year-old Mariinsky Palace, the colonial residence of tsars next to the parliament, was an ugly tatter when I first came to see Kyiv as a student for a couple of days in 2012. It took more than a decade of restoration work. And finally, voilà—today it's the ceremonial palace of Ukrainian presidents rising above an elegant square on which exuberant teen skateboarders bruise themselves daily.

There's a special spot at the palace's eastern corner—a viewing point from which a good half of the city can be seen. The Dnipro, the isles, the skyline of the east bank.

When the sun goes down, it's a shimmering city of lights as far as the eye can see.

What's great about the old Khreschaty Park are the small things. You can stroll the lanes past a series of wonderful fountains—and come across a top-level jazz band in the middle of an impromptu gig cheered by casual passersby. You walk on, and there's an open-air amphitheater where students declaim poems. And then suddenly there's the Museum of Water (yes!).

And those hills over the Dnipro . . . somewhere over there, on a day a thousand years ago, Prince Volodymyr and his guards of armor herded the people of Kyiv into the great river.

Rich and poor, they had to take baptism or die.

He had made a decision. He needed the powerful Byzantine Empire as an ally. So his kingdom was forced to accept a new faith, Christianity. The people of ancient Kyiv must have wept and cried as they mourned their old pagan idols. But the supreme god of sky and thunder was desecrated and exiled to the land of nomads.

That's what the old legend says.

Standing at the Dynamo Stadium on the hills rising from the river, I just couldn't help but take several pictures of Kyiv in the February sunset for Twitter.

This city is so worth fighting for.

SEVEN

C old and tired after so many days without much sleep, Ukrainian troops defy their mounting exhaustion and move on.

There was no end in sight for the battle of Pripyat.

The abandoned ghost of Chornobyl, after decades in radioactive desolation, was being tortured by yet another nightmare.

The front line of the war cut through what had been the city of Soviet atomic energy ecstasy.

Ukraine's National Guard troops control the city's south. The central square, with the sadly remembered remains of the Polissya Hotel and the Energetic Palace, is squeezed in the middle between the combatants' guns.

The house-to-house carnage is brutal.

Enemy forces, in yet another frantic push, manage to overrun the former Yubileiny Mall building on the northern side of Serzhanta Lazareva Street and establish a checkpoint.

A BTR-3E vehicle stops at the street's southern edge behind the rubble. Some dozen Ukrainian troops jump off the armor into the dirty snow and immediately seek cover among radioactive ruins.

The whistling clicks of sniper fire break through the buzz of drones floating overhead.

The assault force is ready for yet another attempt to break through.

But civilians first. Disheveled, trying to bundle up in whatever clothes they have grabbed, embattled men and women crawl out of the former Soviet supermarket's basement into the hands of the nearest emergency response group. They hastily cover the dazed civilians in blankets and take them to a safe place behind their vehicles, covering them with their bodies.

All is said and done.

At command, mortars launch their barrage on the enemy checkpoint. The building nearby collapses and fills the street with debris and acrid smoke.

The BTR roars up and begins slowly crawling along the street toward the enemy line. The thirty-millimeter turret cannon pours short bursts of fire.

Ukrainian guardsmen hide behind the vehicle's bulk and move on, rapidly scanning the charred windows of apartment blocks facing the street for marksmen. They crawl on through the snow mixed with ash and debris . . .

All right, yeah.

That was a simulated urban battle that Ukraine's National Guard and Special Police Service arranged in early February in Pripyat, the Exclusion Zone.

Of course, this was little more than a show aimed at a foreign audience.

But—foreign reporters got a chance to visit the legendary heart of Chornobyl, photographers got to take some juicy shots, and our Ministry of Internal Affairs got to show how sexy their troops look in full combat gear and how they are all ready for an all-out urban war with Russia.

Everyone was happy that day.

Especially when the Battle of Pripyat was over and organizers finally served us hot tea and sandwiches in tents next to the trashed "Russian checkpoint."

Sipping tea from plastic cups, we journalists swarmed the defense minister Oleksiy Reznikov and the interior minister Denis Monastyrsky and gnawed at them with endless questions.

"An offensive from the Belarusian direction is unlikely," Reznikov reassured the crowd of reporters. "We're paying close attention to the

Russian drills in Belarus via various intelligence sources and open data. I can confidently say that the concentration of Russian forces in Belarus is not sufficient for any sort of offensive operation."

As I was leaving the crowd interrogating the defense minister, I heard Reznikov telling someone: "It would be extremely hard for Russia to cross these woods and swamps. Can you even imagine those hordes moving through all this?"

I went on to see the guys. Soldiers were lined up next to vehicles behind their big bosses' backs, made available to the joy of TV reporters and photographers. The Rapid Response Brigade, the Omega anti-terror force troops.

All faces covered, but one could see they were young boys in their early twenties. Like ten years younger than me, and part of this country's most elite combat formations on the threshold of war.

And given the nature of their service, they'll be among the first to take up the fight if the unthinkable comes.

Reuters on February 6:

> If Russia were to invade the capital of Kyiv, it could fall within a couple of days, the United States officials said . . . Ukraine could suffer 5,000 to 25,000 troop casualties, while Russia's troop casualties could be between 3,000 and 10,000, and civilian casualties could range from 25,000 to 50,000, according to United States estimates.

In Western media, it was now only a question of when.

On February 2 and 3, the United States Chairman of the Joint Chiefs of Staff, General Mark Milley, told reporters during closed door meetings that in the case of a full-scale invasion, Kyiv could fall within seventy-two hours, with some fifteen thousand Ukrainian citizens and four thousand troops dead.

As people in Ukraine's Defense Ministry told us on many occasions, it was General Milley's initial assessment that led the West in general to have little faith regarding Ukrainian chances.

There began the infamous guessing game of how soon Russia would raise its flag over Kyiv.

Many at Ukraine's highest levels were not happy about all this. If you say the invasion is imminent and the Russians are determined, why are you sending us only Javelins and Stingers? Why not heavier stuff? Are you afraid of provoking Putin or do you expect from us nothing more than a guerrilla war?

Even in February, the contrast between the scare in Western media and regular life in Ukraine was mind-blowing.

Bild's Julian Ropke published a story describing an alleged Russian occupation plan for Ukraine acquired by German intelligence.

So, there were supposed to be three stages.

First—Russia inflicts a quick and devastating defeat to Ukraine's military and besieges key cities. Local collaborators seize power and make "agreements" with Russians to cede cities in a "peaceful way." Russians also seize key infrastructure facilities and install "new local authorities."

Second—Russia wants the takeover of Ukraine to be "legitimate and democratic." So it installs a new "parliament," the People's Council, that is to replace and outlaw the Verkhovna Rada and also form a new puppet government fully controlled by the Kremlin.

And of course, countless Kremlin-aligned foreign policy experts and politicians in the West and beyond, in a massive propaganda campaign, very carefully explain how justified and legit this all is.

Then things get really ugly.

Third—the "new Ukrainian authorities" declare the state of emergency. The occupation regime is to create a network of concentration camps incarcerating Ukrainian activists and suspected potential resisters. Detention lists were already in the making, according to *Bild*, and Putin had given an order to drum up Ukrainian politicians and eliminate the opposition.

The crackdown and terror would continue until the will to resist was broken.

In the end, according to the plan, the Kremlin wanted "the new Ukraine" to prepare a "referendum." There would be a trilateral state of Russia, Belarus, and Ukraine, the new Soviet Union under Moscow's full centralized control.

Meanwhile, in good old Ukraine, the year's biggest scandal so far: Alina Pash, the candidate chosen to represent the country at Eurovision 2022, was reported to have taken part in an illegal gig in Russian-occupied Crimea.

Good lord, that was a drama that shook the entire nation.

And those who replaced her, the Kalush Orchestra, ended up winning that annoying song contest later on in May—the most horrific month of insane hostilities in Donbas.

Now, from the distance of time, it is sadly ironic—or, frankly speaking, utterly infuriating—to see how voices in the West and beyond so audaciously called for "negotiations for peace."

Those who stood for "giving diplomacy a chance" would again be right on time when, after months of bloody battles, the Russian war in Ukraine stalled, went off the rails, and started sliding toward ultimate failure.

The more unexpectedly perilous the Kremlin's situation was, the more insistent the advocates of "compromises for saving lives" became. What a gross and deeply immoral stance—Ukraine and its Western supporters are determined to go on for as long as necessary until victory and are not even thinking about diplomacy, true?

But in the vocabulary of the freshly minted pacifists, the word "diplomacy" meant "let Putin keep what he's seized from Ukraine because the war's maximalist goals have completely failed and future prospects now look increasingly grim."

Let's recall how many opportunities of finding a peaceful solution were given to the Kremlin before February 24.

The United States and European leaders spent months trying to reason and smooth-talk Putin. Two rounds of talks with Biden, calls with Macron and Johnson. Germany, France, Italy, the United States publicly calling on Russia to return to the Normandy Four talks.

NATO was ready to cooperate on arms control and transparency, Blinken met Lavrov in Geneva. Germany publicly refused Ukraine's request for lethal weapons to avoid angering the Kremlin. Macron stayed glued to the telephone with Putin all the damn time.

On February 10, yet another useless nine-hour meeting of the Normandy Four advisers.

Two days later, again Biden called Putin with a warning against attacking Ukraine. Zelensky traveled to Donbas on February 17 and again invited Putin to have an in-person meeting—anywhere, anytime.

Not going to happen.

Dmitry Peskov on February 17:

> We have repeatedly received Kyiv's propositions on meetings, but on every occasion, Kyiv failed to give a response to a simple question: Why, what's the goal? We say: "Listen, when it comes to Donbas, you must talk to the people of Donbas. Do you have any other questions for us?" No answer.

Yes, several days before the biggest European war since 1945, Moscow was still putting on an act and insisting it had nothing to do with occupied Donbas.

Attempts to prevent the catastrophe continued until literally the last days.

Four days prior to the invasion, Putin promised Macron to try to broker a cease-fire in Donbas and initiate new Normandy Four meetings. Three days prior to the invasion, the White House confirmed it was ready to have yet another peace summit if Putin was to abstain from war.

But amid the West's most frantic diplomatic effort, the Kremlin and its mandarins were unfolding the most brazen clownery imaginary.

Victor Tatarintsev, the Russian ambassador to Sweden in an interview with *Aftonbladet* regarding potential Western sanctions in case of the Ukraine invasion:

> Excuse my language, but we don't give a shit about your sanctions.

Sergey Naryshkin, the director of Russia's Foreign Intelligence Service, in deadly earnest stated on February 10 that along with NATO advisers and instructors, Ukraine also deploys "multinational Jihadist forces" in Donbas.

Belarusian dictator Aleksandr Lukashenko was reaching his own lows.

His three-decades-long regime had barely survived the mass protests of 2020, and that was only thanks to Russian money and power. In a frantic attempt to keep his ass on the throne he had in fact almost completely ceded his own country to the Kremlin.

With Putin holding him by the balls, Lukashenko offered up Belarusian territory as a staging ground for a Russian attack on Ukraine—and went on buffooning as hard as he could in the media.

Lukashenko in an interview with Russia's top war propagandist Vladimir Solovyov on February 5:

> Ukraine will never have a war with us—such a war would last three or four days at best. After that, there would be no one left to fight. [The operation in Kazakhstan] demonstrated that we'd be standing at the English Channel even before they began to deploy their forces. Can't they see this? They understand that fighting us, primarily Russia, is pointless.

By early February, Russia already had some thirty thousand troops in Belarus, which was the Kremlin's largest military presence in the country since the end of the Cold War.

And Putin again demonstrated his excellent comprehension of how Article 5 works.

During a meeting with Macron, he stated that if Ukraine as a NATO member ever decided to launch a military operation in Crimea, other European allies would be automatically involved in a war with nuclear-armed Russia.

But the true performance happened while discussing Ukraine's grievances regarding the Minsk accords. Leaning back in his chair and holding his little chin, Putin chuckled his infamous line: "Like it or not, take the abuse, my beauty, it's your lot."

The soon-to-be resurrector of the Russian Empire and the big fan of dirty rape jokes was clearly having a great time!

Meanwhile, by the first weeks of February, all preparations were basically completed.

Russia had concentrated nearly 125 battalion tactical groups posed against Kyiv, Chernihiv, Sumy, Kharkiv, western Donbas, and southern Ukraine. That's a total of nearly 3,200 tanks, nearly 5,000 infantry fighting vehicles and personnel carriers, some 2,400 artillery pieces, 3,500 rocket systems, and a stockpile of thousands of ballistic and cruise missiles.

Russian aircraft were deployed at well over thirty air bases in Russian territory bordering Ukraine and in occupied Crimea, including all eight main airfields of Belarus.

Most of Russia's overall conventional military power was gathered within the seven thousand kilometers between Kaliningrad and Vladivostok.

The question was still: Were they really serious about invading? If so, how big would they go? And when? On that score, there was a narrow time window that would close with the coming of the spring mud season in March.

What could be a worse time for launching a new startup than an apocalyptic war crisis in your country?

What a great time to look for potential investors, advertisers, and business plans.

Anyway, the *KI* guys were still moving forward.

Ukraine of course was on everyone's lips worldwide. I think in January we received a grant from the Canadian embassy, and continued crowdfunding. We already had several hundred supporters on Patreon and considered ourselves incredibly privileged.

So, in early February, we finally said goodbye to our nomadic life in Kyiv coffee shops and rented our first office.

It was a very basic venue in Podil, right next to the Kontraktova subway station. Just two rooms with several desks in a very mediocre business center. Top floor, no windows except for tiny dormers, the noise and the vibration of trams arriving at their terminus below.

And for some reason, a huge potted tree rising to the ceiling smack in the middle.

"Well, if you think about this in a positive way, you might consider this a sort of penthouse," Oleksiy Sorokin, our political editor, said when we first saw the place.

He's a Ukrainian born here in Kyiv, he's twenty-four. He spent his teen years in Canada, graduated university in Toronto—and for some funny reason ended up back in Ukraine.

We inherited the place from some tiny IT company that left behind incredibly inspiring wall paintings such as JUST DON'T GIVE UP and SUCCESS IS OUR STRATEGY. Not sure about the strategy, but having to share the toilet with two other offices was definitely motivation to work hard so we might move to a better venue.

Anyway, the work was in full swing. Live updates from the Russian war crisis:

BORIS JOHNSON: WORST EUROPEAN SECURITY CRISIS IN DECADES,
NEXT FEW DAYS MOST DANGEROUS TO UKRAINE
RUSSIA'S MASSIVE MILITARY DRILL UNFOLDS IN BELARUS
BIDEN WARNS ALL AMERICANS IN UKRAINE TO LEAVE NOW

We were sitting behind desks in the small, dimly lit room, snapping at our keyboards and occasionally exchanging sad jokes.

"So you guys think we're all fucked?"

"Yes, we are. Now get the story filed already and let's go order some Chinese food, I'm starving."

My iPhone flicks.

It's a message from Denys Krasnikov, a friend of mine who's an editor at *Forbes Ukraine*. He used to work with us at the *Kyiv Post* and quit not long before the publication was killed.

Denys is twenty-seven, he's really tall and normally very cheerful and talkative. We became great friends during those years—the kind of office buddies who can call each other at two A.M. and crash on each other's couches when needed.

"Hi. I really need to talk to someone. Now. Can we meet up?"

I meet the guy somewhere outside our office building in Podil.

"Let's have a sit somewhere and get a beer," I suggest.

"No, I just wanted to take a bit of a walk, if that's all right with you."

Okay . . .

What happened? Troubles at work? You don't often see Denys so stressed out. He's literally ashen-faced. He feverishly walks down the sidewalk by my side, with his hands deep in his pockets.

We walk on and Denys says nothing. Then he finally ekes out: "I had this interview with . . . ehm, Michael Kofman. You know, the top guy on Russian military issues."

Oh, I see where this is going.

"He told me . . . well. He says . . . he's really pessimistic. He believes the Russians will actually start a war in the coming weeks."

Denys stares straight ahead.

"Kofman says we're greatly underestimating their recklessness. We're not taking this seriously enough. And our defense ministry seems . . . overconfident to him. And Zelensky is going too far trying to calm us down. We don't have enough power to prevent them from taking at least a huge part of the country."

Well, it's true we don't have seven fleets and twelve carrier strike groups worldwide.

But still, we have a considerable military and lots of civilians with military experience.

I'm giving it my best shot, for Denys's sake, and frankly, probably for both our sakes.

You know, those experts love to compare sheer numbers of tanks and artillery pieces on both sides and make simple judgments.

I think our military is large enough to inflict unacceptable losses and therefore render the whole invasion futile. And they know it. They can't expect to simply roll into Kyiv, without our military putting up a fight.

Denys doesn't seem to be buying that at all.

"Kofman says the Russians just don't care. Historically they've never cared about their dead. And we're overestimating their need for more troops against us. A swift war will reduce their risks and costs."

Well, that rings some bells for me but feels oversimplified. Blitzkrieg plans may look nice and well-thought-out on paper, but what if a million things go wrong?

Snatch a piece of Ukraine at a huge cost and then what? End up being a global aggressor, revitalize NATO, then spend enormous resources trying to maintain the unrecognized occupation—how long would this last?

And why opt for war when there are lots of much safer tools? Economic suffocation, internal destabilization, cyberattacks, insurgencies, extorting a deal with the West.

Why shoot yourself in the leg in such a dumb way?

"Besides, after all, we're not seeing them switch to attack formations. I don't see how one can be so dumb as to continue this very dramatic buildup for a year, brag about it in the media, and give us time to prepare," I say.

"I don't know, man . . . ," Denys sighs. "I am really, really worried."

"I know," I say. "Your buddy Kofman is right when he says we all should take the threat seriously. And we do. Zelensky might be a wind blower, but I'm confident Zaluzhny knows what he's doing. Everything is going to be all right."

"Yeah . . . Thanks for talking to me about all this. It's hard stuff to sort. I'm glad Daryna is in Riga now, away from this mess. And she's freaking out, too. Everybody in Latvia asks her about the coming of war all the time."

Daryna is his girlfriend, she's a tech journalist. And yes, it's good that she's abroad. For now and for the coming weeks.

"You know what?" I say. "I know what would cheer you up. We're having a housewarming party tonight at the new office. Why don't you drop by and see old friends? That's exactly what you need."

"Nah," Denys sighs again. "I'd better go home. There's too much tension in the air. I'll try to go offline and stop thinking about what's in the news. See you, man."

My unusually sad friend disappears into the deep of the Kontraktova subway station entrance.

Good night . . . and good luck.

That was a dark and, at the same time, very inspiring time.

Feelings got really acute. You thought more of people around you and of things we all believe in.

You get out in the neon nights of Kyiv. You see people smiling and minding their own business at tram stops, crowds of young people having fun in beer halls.

Supermarkets and gift shops running merry jingles—Valentine's Day is coming, make sure to check our special offers! The observation wheel at Kontraktova Square, long lines of cars making their way home through rush hour.

It's a great blessedness just to come into the office every morning, saying hi to friends in the room, thinking about summertime vacations or that nice IKEA coffee table you've had your eye on.

Knowing that there will always be another day, and that the never-ending circle of life for millions of people around you will go on. We're taking this all for granted, as we normally would.

But what if at some point you begin to see that a new tomorrow may never come?

It was unspeakably weird to see the abyss of the most hateful and bloodthirsty war hysteria the Kremlin was vomiting up every day. "You Nazis, you swine, you're not a real country, we'll finish you in three days, you American bootlickers."

And there's a giant death army standing 150 kilometers away from your city gates and rattling its battering rams.

You see how fragile and precious the little things in your life are.

All across Kyiv, many buildings and government offices, along with the yellow-and-blue national colors, also fly a European Union flag. It's a constant reminder of the nation's drive to become part of the United Europe some sunny day.

It's become something like the ultimate benchmark of success—similar, in a funny way, to the poor man's dream of starting from zero, overcoming all hardship, and finally succeeding in life.

My generation grew up and established itself knowing that we belong to a place better than a frowsy and poverty-stricken police regime obsessed with its violent imperial past and never-ending territorial grabs.

And now this tiny newsroom somewhere in Kyiv must write articles about a dark force that decries and denies all that is dear to us. It challenges the very legacy of the West here in Kyiv. It proclaims the end of our naive dream and threatens to clasp us in its arms forever.

And Europe seems to be ready to sacrifice its principles and roll over.

But—nothing is predestined yet. The unimaginable is still not happening. And if we put emotions aside, it's still very unlikely to happen—or I still believed then.

Anyway, it's Friday night—so it's party time, right?

At the *Kyiv Independent* office, there is loud music and spirits scooped up from the nearest supermarket.

We drag a desk out and load it up with cheese, hummus, fruits, and potato chips.

Some of us appear to have already had a decent jag of wine. Girls dance around with sandwiches in their hands.

"Guys, guys, guys!"

That's our chief editor, Olga Rudenko, taking to the floor and, as always, trying to scramble this noisy crew together for a minute.

She's thirty-two, a delicate brunette. She's the kind of boss who would never yell at you. But at the same time, you will always regret not living up to her expectations.

Shortly before the fall of the *Kyiv Post*, she unofficially resigned as a deputy chief editor and went to Chicago for three months. She never intended to return to the newspaper.

It was obvious she was the one to lead the *Kyiv Independent*.

"I just wanted to say thank you to all of you guys," she says, raising a paper cup full of semisweet red wine. "It's been a tough three months. We started a new media outlet from nothing, and heaven knows that was difficult. Especially considering the times we live in. But here we are—we have a website, a newsletter, and now an office! Yay!"

"Hooray!" we all shout.

"I wanted to say that I really admire and appreciate that everybody here worked hard without any clear prospects of things like . . . um . . . monthly salaries and all. We deserve a little bit of fun tonight. So let's drink to us all and to those who thought we weren't going to make it."

"Yeah!" we shout again and laugh.

The party continues in full swing.

During our office parties, I normally prefer to sit behind my laptop, sip beer, and make fun of my boozy colleagues dancing around. Maybe it's me getting old and increasingly boring. On that night, at some point, I noticed that all the editors had suddenly put their wine aside and started doing things behind laptops.

What's going on?

The news update.

The Guardian: BIDEN WARNS ALLIES PUTIN HAS MADE A DECISION TO GO AHEAD WITH UKRAINE INVASION, POSSIBILITY VERY DISTINCT IN THE NEXT FEW DAYS

The party is over now, apparently.

Several reporters and editors are going to have a lot of work.

We seem to have made yet another step toward the brink tonight, and the situation is serious enough for the president of the United States to speak confidently about it.

EIGHT

The Saturday morning of February 12 is cold and sleety.

The place is an abandoned asphalt refinery lost in the forest on the eastern outskirts of Kyiv, close to Brovary. The remains of a huge Soviet industrial belt.

An impromptu parking lot is full of civilian cars that somehow managed to make it through the mud. Incomers at their trunks hastily change into military fatigues, put on the gear they have, grab firearms with no magazines attached, and head for the processing line.

Winter camo, forest camo, those wearing ballistic helmets of every variety and model and those who have knit woolen caps, those dressed like Universal Soldier supporting cast members and those who have nothing but winter sports suits.

Young neat boys and round-bellied men in their forties, several women, clean cut lawyers wearing glasses, rappers with dreadlocks. All stand in the line, as diverse as the very streets of Kyiv.

Welcome to the 130th Territorial Defense Battalion, part of the just-formed civilian home guard of Kyiv.

In early February, Ukraine became obsessed with the novelty: becoming a weekend warrior.

The Territorial Defense Forces were inaugurated as late as January 2022, when new national security legislation finally went into effect.

A total of twenty-five brigades in twenty-five Ukrainian regions, over 150 battalions scattered across the county.

The idea was hardly new—you could join ranks to defend your own neighborhood and stay home.

Anyone between the ages of eighteen and sixty, males and females, with no criminal record or severe health issues, was welcome. That included foreigners who had legally resided in Ukraine for at least five years. The home guard network became a totally new branch of military service organized by career regulars.

One could keep his or her civilian job and go out in the field every once in a while to get combat training. Volunteers were to sign a contract with the armed forces and take an oath.

But as many officers told us back then, the whole thing was supposed to be very informal. As a volunteer, you were expected to be motivated enough to take your commitment seriously. No one was going to punish anyone if a Territorial Defense member couldn't show up for a training day because of admissible family issues.

That's peacetime. In wartime, the reservists were to become full-fledged service members under military command. But they were still expected to serve in their home areas as light infantry executing auxiliary missions behind the regular military. That might mean patrolling their own communities, manning checkpoints, safeguarding key infrastructure.

The movement was expected to enlist some 130,000 volunteers and form a nationwide network of men and women with basic combat skills ready to respond if and when the time came.

General Zaluzhny publicly suggested that Ukraine would eventually have up to two million in the popular militia—that's roughly 5 percent of the country's population.

Enthusiasm was massive.

Retired combat veterans of Donbas became activists and organized new formations in their communities. Many among them said they hoped to provide motivated civilians with basic fighting skills in as little as two or three months of intense training on weekends.

Regular people across the country were inspired by what they saw on Facebook about the Territorial Defense Forces. In Ukraine, boxing champions, pop stars, comedians, TV anchors all publicly announced their intention to enlist.

And many people were joining. In late January, there was an independent poll saying that 56 percent of Ukrainians were interested in joining home guard formations in their communities.

That's despite the fact that the newly created units had almost nothing provided by the military. Back then, the battalion could offer little more than standard summertime fatigues.

Volunteers rustled up their own clothes and personally registered firearms. They bought tactical gear with their own money.

I don't really know how many of those guys took the commitment seriously. Or how many came just because a volunteer automatically became a highly respected citizen in the public eye.

Nonetheless, on this morning several dozen regular Kyivans sacrificed their weekend to come to those factory ruins and crawl through the dirt. And beginners without airsoft guns of their own didn't seem to have a problem when the famous wooden Kalashnikov replicas were handed to them.

A very young guy, the basic training instructor, walks among reservists lying in the snow with their dummy rifles pointed forward.

"In combat, nobody fights all alone," he says. "You're going to practice in pairs now. Here's what you must do. First—you take cover and suppress the enemy. Your mate, meanwhile, moves forward and finds cover. Then you move as your mate gives you covering fire. Repeat until I say stop. Go!"

The minutemen, swearing and breathing hard, rise up and run to a nearest concrete ruin and then fall down again into the snow.

The basics tactic of fire and movement for small squads.

"Hey, how are you doing?"

That's Anton Goloborodko, one of the battalion's non-commissioned officers, putting a hand on my shoulder. A blond guy in his early thirties, he used to serve in Donbas as a mobilized draftee with the 80th Airborne.

Goloborodko—yes, just like Zelensky's character from the Netflix show—was actually a well-known TV anchor with Ukraine's Channel 24. We first met each other during yet another press tour to NATO headquarters in Brussels.

Once upon a time in 2019, Zelensky decided to hold the world's longest press conference to mark his first one hundred days in office. The administration rented a newly established food court at the Arsenalna. Journalists, in groups of ten, were to sit down with Zelensky and have thirty minutes for questions before the next group came in.

The whole thing lasted for fourteen hours.

There, among burgers and slices of pizza, my friend Goloborodko got into a *massive* altercation with Zelensky over his entourage's illicit influence on the courts. The president fought back and started questioning the journalist's own integrity. To which Anton, for want of a better response, fired off: "I am the one asking questions here!"

Ugh, that was a hell of a scandal.

And now, Goloborodko, as a Donbas veteran, is among the founding fathers of Kyiv's Territorial Defense brigade. He walks around in full combat gear organizing crowds of civilian newbies.

We're going to see each other again many months later, during the worst days of the epic Battle of Donbas.

The famous pictures of civilians executing tactical moves with plywood Kalashnikovs were from those days. Many laughed at that, especially the Russians. Now, from the distance of time, I wonder how many were still laughing when the Territorial Defense militias in Kyiv, Sumy, Chernihiv, and Kharkiv were fighting like hell and destroying Russian columns.

A slim guy with dreadlocks looking like a long-time Bob Marley fan splashes into the snow. His dummy shotgun pointed against an imaginary enemy in the distance.

The battalion's senior sergeant comes by and lightly kicks his feet.

"Get your legs together," he says. "Leave not a single extra centimeter of your body exposed to enemy fire. We don't need you killed, you understand? And if you get injured, you're distracting two or three of your brothers from the mission. Get a grip, soldier."

The Bob Marley fan obeys and keeps breathing hard.

When the field day is done, sandwiches appear and friendly conversations begin. And then it's back to their families for the rest of the weekend.

Among the hundreds of the battalion's newly hatched, there were IT specialists, people originally from Donbas, even a doctoral candidate in history.

Like I said, enthusiasm was immense. And just like so many others, as I was headed back to Kyiv with the battalion, I decided that I wanted to enlist, too.

What a nice plan for the upcoming year—to do something about my blood issues, maybe have surgery or something like that, and join the Kyiv home guard.

The *Kyiv Independent* culture reporter Artur Korniienko was thinking about this as well.

He filed his application to the 112th Territorial Defense Brigade Kyiv in late February.

Several days later, when the worst happened, this guy who wrote lifestyle and fashion stories for the paper answered a phone call and became a soldier of war.

Things were growing darker by the day. If not the hour.

Der Spiegel published an article: United States special operations forces warned the allies that a Russian invasion was expected to begin on February 16.

For the first time, amid all the fuss and countless, uncertain warnings, there appeared a specific date.

What followed was a massive Western exodus from Ukraine.

The United States embassy in Kyiv evacuates all nonessential staff and terminates all consular services. British and American military training missions leave immediately as well. European nations, along with Australia, New Zealand, and India, all call on their nationals to leave as soon as possible.

OSCE curtails its monitoring mission in Ukraine that has been around since 2014. Israel evacuates its embassy. Canada relocates diplomats to Lviv. All done within a few days.

This is bad. This is all really bad.

Every new headline shook Ukrainian markets. The national currency saw its biggest drop since 2015, when the economy was in tatters following the EuroMaidan and the war in Donbas.

Many businesses, foreign and Ukrainian, hastily developed contingency plans and relocated their staff abroad. Due to unprecedented tensions in the media, insurance and leasing companies declined to continue covering flights to Ukraine.

In fact, air traffic began collapsing within days, even though the airspace was open. Airlines withdrew one after another. First KLM, then SkyUp. Then Lufthansa and Swiss International Air Lines. The Ukrainian government was in disarray and trying to provide additional assurances to stop the avalanche.

As many in Ukraine were saying in those days, "It's Russia that threatens war. Why is it us who get punished for that, why not Moscow?"

But at the same time, there was always more than one explanation for what was happening.

One day, Biden is reported to have told the allies the invasion was imminent. Hours later, the media quoted Jake Sullivan as saying "we haven't seen anything that says the go order has been given."

For weeks, United States officials had said the invasion could happen any moment. It could be a massive cyberattack, a chemical weapons incident, a staged act of terror in Russian-held territory. Any sort of a false flag operation could give Russia a casus belli against Ukraine.

And this continued on and on.

The uncertainty was giving us whiplash.

Even the *Der Spiegel* story claimed that officials in Berlin did not know why the United States believed Russia would attack precisely on February 16. Although it was known that a lot of intelligence data was attached to the warning.

There was no absolute certainty about anything.

And then the announcement that the United States embassy was to be evacuated.

The impression was that Americans were being a bit over dramatic and emotional. Possibly, on purpose.

The angle kind of made sense. It was obvious that the Russians were up to something. Maybe not a full-scale war, but very possibly a bloody provocation.

So, this aggressive American drumbeat could purposefully be trying to anticipate the Kremlin's next step. Doing so, it kept Ukraine in the global spotlight and what was going on in the open. With all the focused attention it would be difficult for Russia to get away with a false flag in Donbas or elsewhere.

From that point of view, it seemed to make sense.

It was a big relief to see a CNN story saying that the Biden administration was deliberately feeding alarming headlines and releasing sensitive intelligence to disrupt Russia's planning.

We know that many American journalists were angry about the revelation. The administration was in many cases not willing to disclose evidence backing up its claims regarding the Russian invasion. Many in Ukraine were pissed off beyond compare.

The tactic was rather cruel and risky. But it really gave us some hope that Russia would eventually have to scrap its plans. You just can't reasonably expect a successful false flag operation when the other side sees your every step and exposes you in front of the world.

Nonetheless, the great exodus continued.

And in mid-February, it looked more like a panicked stampede.

I remember a lot of our friends, foreign nationals, telling us their embassies repeatedly called trying to persuade them to take the first available flight west. And many were feeling bitter.

"I feel ashamed to be leaving Kyiv, my home now," our German good friend Mattia Nelles wrote on Facebook at the time. "But our company has issued an order that we leave immediately . . ."

Yep, mate. See you soon back in town, hopefully.

But Russian drills in Belarus are in full swing. And they've also deployed over 140 warships and auxiliary vessels for "maneuvers" near

Crimea. Most maritime traffic in the Black and Azov seas along the Ukrainian coastline is in fact blocked until February 19.

Is this the beginning?

If Russians have planned a full-scale attack, we should expect a coastal landing operation. Possibly somewhere between Odesa and Kherson.

Or is this still a game of pressure? Russians are raising the stakes and threaten to jeopardize our southern seaports. A vital part of the Ukrainian economy.

But of course, Russia was still in absolute denial mode.

Russian deputy foreign minister Yury Ushakov, following yet another call with Biden on February 12:

> The facts are that Americans are deliberately escalating the hysteria over the so-called upcoming Russian invasion. They even set invasion dates and, in the meanwhile, along with their allies, are beefing up Ukrainian war muscles . . . The hysteria has reached a new peak.

The "unprecedented pumping of Ukraine with modern weapons" was still limited to a certain number of Javelins, NLAWs, and Stingers. That's it. The air bridge would still be active until the final hour. Western birds of metal were touching down in Boryspil every other day, bringing new supplies. Baltic nations were sending us everything they had.

Not many in the West paid attention to a joint statement by Ukrainian defense minister Reznikov and top general Zaluzhny.

This was on February 12.

The two posted a smiling selfie in the ruins of a textile factory in Avdiivka's Promzona. The legendary Position Skeleton. This happened to be my "favorite" front-line spot where once upon a time in 2017 I experienced a brutal mortar attack.

> This will not be the year 2014 all over again. The aggressor will never get Kyiv, Odesa, or Kharkiv, or any other city. Have no doubts. The Armed Forces of Ukraine are totally ready to fight

back. We're constantly improving our defenses, our cohesion, and our combat skills.

We have deployed battle formations and managed to swiftly unfold Territorial Defense units and armed them with tank killers and anti-aircraft weapons. We've reinforced the defense of Kyiv. We have seen war and undergone rigorous training. So we're ready to meet the enemy with not flowers but Stingers, Javelins, and NLAWs.

Welcome to hell!

"Guys, we need to decide what we're going to do now."

That's our boss Olga Rudenko taking the floor again. This is an emergency editorial meeting. Everyone present in Kyiv was very kindly asked to show up in the office if convenient. If not convenient, one was kindly asked to come anyway.

"This is not the kind of conversation I ever wanted to have," she continues. "But these are strange times. We need a contingency plan for wartime."

In the tiny newsroom, no one else says anything.

"We all need to know what to do if the invasion happens. Especially if Russian forces reach Kyiv. Illia, do you have anything to say?"

I winced.

"Yeah, it would be good to have a plan. But I want you guys to keep in mind that we're not doomed and we're talking about hypothetical things just to be safe."

Not everyone in the room endorses my optimism. That's for sure.

"Anyway, we need a plan," Olga exhales. "First of all, we need to stay operational. Our website is hosted abroad. So it should stay up even if we in Ukraine lose internet access. We have our guys Max Hunder in Georgia, Olena Goncharova in Canada, Lili Bivings in the United States. And we also have Jakub Parusinski in the United Kingdom. If there's no contact with us, they will take over and go on publishing everything they can on Ukraine, 24/7."

Yes. Russia would try to cut Ukraine off from the rest of the world. And do their carnage and chaos in the dark.

"We will also provide you all with info on how to run our website and how to get access to the stock image services we use. That's in case you have internet connection when the rest of us aren't responding," Olga said.

Frankly, I'm personally not sure if we will be mentally capable of working in the hell of Russian missile strikes.

"Another issue," Olga continues, "is your own safety. Please prioritize your survival and that of your close ones. If you feel like leaving Kyiv, consider your options. And please, everyone, as soon as possible, let me know your plan. And your emergency contacts."

Daryna Shevchenko, Olga's long-time friend and now our CEO, steps up.

"We're looking into possibilities for helping you relocate to West Ukraine if you can't do so on your own. But we assume many of you already have plans to move out with your family and partners."

That's a sensitive issue. A huge portion of us are foreign nationals. And some of them have partners here in Ukraine.

I remember looking at our foreigners in the office. Americans, Brits, the French. They talk about Ukraine as if it's their country, too. All of them can—and quite frankly should—leave now. Yet, they stay here with us. Talking about how they can go on serving journalism in wartime.

"Does it make sense to move now?" Asami Terajima, our Japanese colleague asks me. "We don't want to. How pressing is that, seriously?"

"Well," I said. "If you want my opinion, you should always have a good plan and watch the situation 24/7. Even if war breaks out, you will still have time to leave Kyiv. I don't think you need to jump this very second. That's my opinion. But it's your decision."

"Oh, and another thing," Olga said. "Please also let me know if any of you have an active driver's license. We might consider renting vehicles and moving out in groups. If the Russians reach Kyiv, we expect that most of us will leave the city and continue working from safe places."

"Hah," somebody chuckled. "I wonder if traffic rules are going to be a thing. There's a war, missiles, tanks, everyone's fleeing, and a Ukrainian military police guy gives you a ticket for a parking violation."

Everybody giggles.

Is that us being cheerful and optimistic? Or is that everyone being nervous and trying to hide it?

"All right, let's get back to work," Olga says. "Don't forget about your emergency contacts and wartime plans."

Wartime plans . . . the uncertainty was driving us insane.

We all need to decide.

We all have our loved ones. We need to choose a rendezvous point if we lose one another in the confusion. What about our work, our humble possessions, money? Do we have anywhere else to go? Should we?

We need to try to do the right thing. Something we won't be ashamed of years later.

So, I am sitting at a Lviv Croissants near the Arsenalna subway station, waiting for my girlfriend, Natalia, to show up. I take out my phone and send a message to Olga.

I've made a decision.

"Hi. My roommate, Ivan, is going to take my girlfriend to West Ukraine. I'm going to stay. I'll be working or joining the 130th battalion. I have friends there."

That's the plan.

February 13 was probably the last beautiful sunny day of the month. Life in the streets was continuing as usual. Lviv Croissants was as lively and busy as always. The buzz of idle talk, light music, and waitresses running around serving sandwich-style croissants with ham and cheese.

Life is good if you don't scroll through headlines.

UKRAINIAN OLIGARCHS LEAVING UKRAINE, AT LEAST 20 PRIVATE JETS SEEN TAKING OFF

ZELENSKY CALLS FOR BIDEN'S IMMINENT VISIT TO KYIV

POPE LEADS CROWDS IN PRAYER FOR PEACE IN UKRAINE

A waitress puts an order number on my table: "13."

Ah, fuck. You all must be kidding me.

Finally, Natalia comes in and gives me a peck on the cheek. She's always cheerful and a bit curly haired.

Appropriately enough, that's exactly what her family name means—Kucheriava ("the curly one").

We had been seeing each other for just three months. She's a Ukrainian-speaking girl from West Ukraine, I'm a native Russian speaker from Donbas . . . Zelensky should award us a medal for popularizing national unity in the country.

We're far from being unique in this regard though.

"Phew, what a beautiful day, and I'm just starving," she says, taking off her stylish black coat.

She works at a PR firm in charge of communications for various international companies with a presence in Ukraine. Natalia herself is responsible for corporations such as IKEA, Wizz Air, Shell, and Westinghouse. Oh yeah, she's a catch!

She just got back from some PR event in Lviv.

"On the intercity train, everybody was talking about nothing but war," Natalia says as she faces a difficult choice between a chocolate croissant and a roast beef sandwich.

"A dude was sitting next to me and listening to the news, no headphones. All those things on how to prepare a bugout bag. Another woman got so nervous she called her husband and told him to go buy as much medicine as he could.

"I was really looking forward to a coffee and switched to watching a movie. Can't stand it when people watch videos with Putin."

How was Lviv, anyway?

"A bit weird, really. Our American office is worried about us. There's a lot of anxiety. They're even developing a sort of mobile app so we can track one another's whereabouts in an emergency. And we are like, 'People, relax, it's okay, we've been going through this for years.'"

Yep . . . for years now.

"Sweetie, what's up, is everything all right?" she says, looking at me. "You seem a bit worried."

"No, honey, I'm fine," I respond.

"Everything's going to be all right."

NINE

The morning of February 16 brought nothing but the noise of a jackhammer outside our windows.

Workers were digging a new foundation at a nearby kindergarten.

No bombs, no tank tracks rattling, no helicopter engines roaring. Just construction noise early in the morning. The sweetest sound one could hope for. The day predicted to be the beginning of the end was just another day.

Doomsday hasn't come.

So, it's as always. A mug of coffee, the torturous ritual of shaving, the usual traffic jams of Kyiv.

Another working day is waiting.

Back then, my roommate, Ivan, had a workshop on Khoryva Street in Podil, right next to a seventeenth-century baroque church. He worked at a tiny company repairing iPhones, vacuum cleaners, laptops—all kinds of electronic stuff.

So, we drive through the morning sun of Kyiv, watching endless lines of cars crawling toward downtown.

Big city life.

"This is just depressing, people," Ivan grumbles.

He's bald, skinny, and stubbled. Your own personal Jason Statham behind a Daewoo Lanos wheel.

"If the Russians really want to attack us, I have bad fucking news for them. By the time they finally make it through our traffic to downtown Kyiv, we'll already have an army of super advanced space marines."

For six years, we'd shared a cheap two-bedroom apartment in Kyiv's far northwest. Just where the road takes a right turn and heads toward Irpin. Basically, the city's godforsaken fringe next to the woods where long-ago Neanderthals warmed themselves at the fire.

Ivan and I met each other in Mariupol as university classmates. As our beloved Quentin Tarantino described it, he is "a buddy who is more than a brother and a little less than a wife."

Once upon a time in February 2016, while still living in Donbas, we came to Kyiv for a short vacation. We ended up in a pub on Khreschatyk Street, partying all night with Nazareth, the rock band.

Still a bit drunk and absolutely blissed out, we came back to our hostel room at sunrise.

"Man, I'm gonna move to this city," I said, flopping down on my bed.

That's how it happened. I moved first and rented a god-awful room in a poor single-family house. Ivan came a couple of months later.

A new start from nothing.

And here we are, six years later. We're about to hit our thirties and we're still roommates. I've cobbled together a sort of a mediocre career in journalism and Ivan is a proud Daewoo Lanos owner.

". . . amid dire Western warnings of a full-scale Russian invasion, president Volodymyr Zelensky declared February 16 Ukrainian Unity Day," the car radio says.

". . . across the country, local authorities were ordered to host patriotic events in their communities. All large TV networks are currently running a live national telethon. In his morning address, the president called on Ukrainians to stand together against the war threat . . ."

Yep, for the want of a better move, Zelensky has signed a decree telling everyone to be cheerful and proud. The more Ukrainian flags and pep talks from officials on TV, the better. Of course, they were trying to tamp down the fear and apprehension running amok.

Not sure if playing the national anthem on all TV channels at ten A.M. was helpful. But Kyiv and the rest of the country were still carrying on life as usual.

Behind this veil of normalcy, there was a giant emotional seesaw. And the same chilling lack of clarity.

Secretary Blinken glided over the February 16 date and claimed the invasion could happen within the current week. NATO, as well as British and Ukrainian intelligence, said there was no de-escalation, and that Russia continued its buildup.

Increasingly, we were glued to the flight radar and the United States Air Force RQ-4 Global Hawk surveillance missions over Ukraine. The FORTE 11 call sign, now a legend of those days, repeatedly cruised the entire length of the Ukrainian border between Kyiv and Donbas.

Call sign HOMER31, a United States Air Force RC-135V/W Rivet Joint, did the same over Crimea.

Tens of thousands of people from every corner of the world all scrutinized these vigilance flights in real time.

Two things came out of this.

First—the United States was not kidding around. There is something. They seriously believe the threat is so real that they're sending out several reconnaissance missions every day.

Second—we're seeing everything Russia does. And we will be warned.

A lot of little things were getting under our skin.

On February 16, OSINT (open-source intelligence) researchers analyzing fresh satellite pictures noticed a newly installed military pontoon bridge cross the Pripyat River. It was located in the Belarusian part of the Chornobyl Exclusion Zone, just six kilometers from the Ukrainian border. It hadn't been seen on images from the same location just the day before.

It was pointed out that those areas were not listed among territories hosting Russian-Belarusian drills.

Any ideas on what this was supposed to mean? Is this part of their drills or is this preparation for invading Ukraine?

The mysterious bridge disappeared the next day.

And secretary of defense Lloyd Austin noted that the United States saw Russian troops stock up on their blood supplies:

I was a soldier myself not that long ago. I know firsthand that you
don't do these sorts of things for no reason.

February 17 was when it all began.

For weeks, the front line of Donbas had been mostly quiet and stable.
Nothing bigger than a few isolated shooting incidents a day. Pretty
typical.

But on that date, in the blink of an eye, all hell broke loose.

Beginning in the morning, dozens of attacks were reported. Again
and again.

At ten twenty-five A.M. local time, a school in the town of Vrubivka
in the Ukrainian-controlled part of Luhansk Oblast was shelled
with artillery. Some thirty students and fourteen staff members took
cover in a basement. 122-millimeter shells destroyed the town's gas
supply line.

In Stanytsia Luhasnka, also under Ukrainian control, a kindergarten
was targeted.

Ukrainian media published a picture of an impact hole in the facility.
Three teachers were reported to have suffered contusion traumas. The
kids were fortunately not hurt, because their classroom was elsewhere
in the building.

Russian media outlets claimed the pictures show a kindergarten in
occupied Donbas that was shelled by the Ukrainian military. After this
was definitively proved false, they claimed the kindergarten attack had
been staged by Ukraine.

Dmitry Peskov, of course, didn't miss a chance to accuse Ukraine of
escalating tensions in Donbas.

By the end of the day, nearly fifty cease-fire violations had been
reported along the front. Mostly artillery strikes and gunfighting.

But still not even close to a large-scale escalation. More like the
sporadic flare-ups we had seen dozens of times over the previous years.

But—on February 18, the day after, leading Russian collaborationists crawled out of the woods.

DNR's Denis Pushilin (a former Ponzi scheme organizer, as you might remember) and LNR's Leonid Pasechnik both issued video statements.

Both said the same thing.

Against common sense and international agreements, the Ukrainian aggressor has concentrated a large military force against Donbas. Ukrainian forces are already at their attack positions. Soon, Zelensky will give the go order. Ukrainian guns are pointed at "our families and our children."

So, starting from "today, February 18," the mass evacuation of women, children, and the elderly to Russia will begin. Russia, in its turn, was already prepared to host "refugees" in camps.

Once again, I was becoming fond of all these spectacular coincidences.

Zelensky planned a genocidal war exactly as Russia surrounds Ukraine with two thirds of its overall military power. And just exactly when Russia has completed all preparations for a full-scale invasion.

In a heartbeat, Russian-controlled media space plunged into hysteria.

In Donetsk, militants turned the air raid siren on, even though this city hadn't seen a single Ukrainian military aircraft since 2014.

Around six P.M. Kyiv time, Russian media launched an avalanche of reports saying a "very powerful explosion was heard" in Donetsk, and that the blast shock swept through the city. Of course, that was a "Ukrainian terror attack" against "the republican authorities and the civilian population."

In truth, what happened was that Russian collaborators blew up an old Soviet UAZ-469 military SUV in a parking lot next to the city council building. The task had been formally assigned to a high-ranking collaborationist warlord, "major general" Denis Sinenkov. Pictures from the scene showed a destroyed car with the license plate "ДК0101." That would have been Sinenkov's.

But the blackened, torn-up SUV was obviously an old beater. Sinenkov normally drove his much more comfortable and expensive UAZ Patriot off-roader.

My theory is that the militants were ordered to stage an "assassination attempt." But they felt bitter about destroying a nice, expensive

SUV. So they just put the license plate on an old car from someone's backyard and blew it up.

No one was hurt, of course.

Videos on social media showed long lines at ATMs and gas stations in Donetsk and Luhansk. Shops in Donbas were forcibly closed until further notice.

Militants in Donetsk said they were prepared to "evacuate" seven hundred thousand people. That's nearly half of the region's population under Russian occupation. For the sake of comparison, during the Chornobyl disaster, the Soviet Union executed a costly and complicated operation to evacuate and resettle some 115,000 from Pripyat and all nearby villages.

Putin, in his infinite generosity, immediately allocated 10,000 rubles ($130) to everyone coming to the "refugee camps" in Russia's Rostov Oblast.

We were all following every minute of that online.

Many in the occupied territories were openly asking questions on social media. Why, what's rush, what's even happening? Many were saying this all looked like a ridiculous panic show and they were not going anywhere.

In front of TV cameras, militants gathered confused women and children at buses in crowded parking lots. Bring nothing but papers, immediately needed clothes, and food supplies for twenty-four hours.

At the same time, Russian media aggressively pushed a story about "Ukrainian sabotage groups" that had tried to blow up chlorine and ammonia reservoirs near occupied Horlivka.

According to the reporting, the assailants lost two killed and three injured and were forced to retreat.

The Russian-backed militants allegedly recovered "foreign-made" combat gear and a body camera, and even managed to intercept "communications among Polish-speaking mercenaries."

Of course, no evidence was ever brought forward.

And the United States intelligence warned Ukraine that Russians might stage something headline-making, like a chemical attack, to justify an invasion.

Meanwhile, Bellingcat's Aric Toler checked the metadata of the evacuation video statements.

The date both videos were created: February 16.

That's two full days before they were published. A day before a "major escalation in Donbas" even unfolded, when the front was as generally quiet as ever.

Unbelievable.

Two shit faces serving a foreign occupying power stood up in front of cameras, one of them even wearing nice suit. And they read it all from a note. And they lied in cold blood about how "today, on February 18," everyone in Donetsk and Luhansk must run for their lives from "the Ukrainian offensive."

And they were theatrically wringing their hands and imploring "all men who can hold weapons to stand up and fight for their homeland."

All prepared in advance.

OSCE later in the day requested the Minsk group negotiations. Moscow declined.

And starting from eight P.M. Moscow time, the first "evacuation convoys" were supposed to start moving to Russia.

"Oh god, this may be a provocation," somebody in the newsroom said.

This might be it.

We need to get as much global attention as possible. Right now.

In a great rush, Ukrainian voices on social media started posting on multiple platforms in English. I jump onto Twitter, typing with my fingers shaking:

WARNING!
ANY SORT OF DEADLY INCIDENTS INVOLVING CIVILIANS IN OCCUPIED DONBAS IS A RUSSIAN PROVOCATION TO JUSTIFY AN ATTACK ON UKRAINE.
DO NOT LET THE AGGRESSOR POWER DECEIVE YOU.

General Zaluzhny in a statement late on February 18:

I address people who live in temporarily occupied territories. Do not believe lies from occupational authorities! You are being used to escalate the situation and unleash yet another bloodbath.

That was one hell of a night.

Fortunately, none of the evacuation buses were "attacked by Ukrainian subversives."

And in the morning, international news agencies and anti-Kremlin Russian journalists revealed what was happening at the "refugee camps."

Militants had transported several hundred people at best. And a huge portion of those ended up out in the open. The "shelters" quickly ran out of capacity. The unfortunate ones were chaotically sent to health camps. People ended up without money or food, and no way to communicate with their loved ones.

The Russians told those who wanted to return home a simple no.

And the "Ukrainian offensive" was still nowhere to be seen.

Within days, this "mass evacuation" was completely forgotten. It disappeared from the Kremlin agenda as if it never happened.

And oh, yes, this tidbit: According to metadata, Pasechnik's "LNR" video had been uploaded from a folder titled . . . "The Mongoose Jump."

Please remind me who's a big fan of references and quotes from Rudyard Kipling's tales?

Oh yeah, thank you, Vladimir V. Putin.

When the war didn't start on February 16, many here in Ukraine angrily questioned the reliability of Western intelligence. How many "invasion dates" will there be in the future? Yet another nervous prediction that goes nowhere and doesn't come true.

But I guess the February 16 date was correct from the very start.

On that day, Russia initiated the final stage of its preparation for war: what was supposed to be a high-toned casus belli against "the genocidal Nazi junta in Ukraine."

But it ended up being an unbelievably absurd farce and a giant tragedy.

★　★　★

"Mom, you have to leave. Just take a short break from work and come to Kyiv. Today."

I was nervously walking up and down our office corridor with my phone to my ear.

"What on earth for?" my mom, Iryna, replied.

Her reluctance was quite understandable. She was living in a quiet little town in one of the wealthiest areas of the Ukrainian-controlled part of Donbas. A place where nothing really bad happens.

Sounds of war hadn't come to our Volnovakha for years. Police and military checkpoints at the town's exits were removed as unnecessary a long time ago. The community was visibly developing thanks to the country's new decentralized home rule program.

As a mid-ranking local social security board clerk, she was relatively well-paid. In her early fifties, her life was slow-paced and pleasant enough. It rarely went beyond her daily routine: the morning coffee, the office, the supermarket, the TV shows.

And here I was breaking into this dullness and saying funny things about war and all.

"Because I'm asking you," I insisted. "Just take the night train. It would be better if you were by my side, here in Kyiv. Just come and stay for several days at my place. Ivan and I will meet you."

"Is this about what's in the news?"

"Yes."

"And? Do you know anything particular?"

"No, I don't. But things look kind of worrisome. It wouldn't hurt to take precautions. Just to be on the safe side. Please do it tonight, I'm gonna buy you a ticket online."

My mom gets annoyed.

"I'm going to come later this month, as planned. On your birthday. What do you think I will tell my supervisors? I'm a public employee, I can't just drop everything and leave."

"No, you actually can. I don't have time to argue with you. Take an unpaid leave. Just a few days. I'm not sure your beloved Russian liberators aren't going to do something stupid in Donbas."

She was openly pro-Russian. Before February 24, it was so pleasant to watch Russian TV all the time and dream of Russian oil money raining from the sky and reinstating a new Soviet paradise instead of that impoverished Ukraine.

But then February 24 came and the world turned upside down, bringing a torment of bitter regrets.

"Stop fooling around. You're panicking. I'm going to come as planned. Period."

You can't argue with her. But our hometown is located some twenty kilometers from the front line.

One thing made a lot of us call their loved ones late on February 18.

"President Biden: 'I'm convinced' Putin has made the decision to invade Ukraine."

The morning of February 19 brought more bad news in Donbas.

Pushilin and Pasechnik, the Russian puppets, stood in front of cameras again. They again obediently read what had been put on paper and shoved into their faces.

They had signed "decrees" announcing a general mobilization in Donbas.

Immediately, throughout the occupied zone, a giant manhunt was launched. All males aged eighteen to fifty-five were barred from leaving the region. Then it was catch as catch can for all they could round up.

In the streets, militant patrols began openly kidnapping people and then trundling them off to mobilization centers. Many regular folks in the occupied territories sent terrified messages to their relatives in Ukraine: "They are taking all the men. Literally sweeping entire city blocks off."

Business enterprises, public utilities services, transportation systems in Donetsk and Luhansk, all ground to a halt due to the lack of workers. Tens of thousands were forcefully "mobilized" regardless of health status.

Students, the Donetsk concert hall musicians, technical school-teachers. Soon they would join ranks: against their will, untrained, equipped with antique Soviet rifles and fatigues dating back to the mid-twentieth century. I remember a woman from a town deep in occupied Donetsk telling me shortly after the mobilization order: "There are no men living on our street anymore. All taken. Only women, children and the elderly are still around."

Those who had money could leave for Russia or pay a smaller bribe to be sent to noncombat units.

And, again, this nightmare was unfolding right in front of everyone's eyes, totally online, in masses of videos and texts on Telegram.

I wondered how many of those dragooned into ranks had voted in favor of breaking away from Ukraine on May 11, 2014, when Russian henchmen staged a bogus "referendum" in Donbas? Or how many relatives of those now held by Russian provocateurs had gone to "polling stations" throughout the region?

Back then, the demon was talking sweet and promising so much.

In the years since, the people of Donbas saw nothing but poverty and endless stagnation. It turned them into hostages in a place where time stands still.

And in February 2022, the demon started to devour them all.

It turned them into sadly remembered mobiks (conscripts). The countless cannon fodder sent to die by the thousands before Ukrainian machine guns to clear the way for Russian regulars.

Meanwhile, Russia continued hitting the gas on "the Ukrainian offensive" narrative.

Early on February 19, Kremlin media said the Ukrainian military shelled an old waste lot a kilometer inside Russian territory. No evidence presented. Then there was reportedly a BM-21 Grad rocket found at the same location inside Russia.

Then Russia's state-run Channel One issued an interview with "Ukrainian intelligence officer Anton Matsaniuk," claiming he was the one who blew up that cheap Soviet UAZ in Donetsk.

Russians even published an alleged map of Ukraine's grand Market Garden–style offensive in Donbas.

On February 21, Ukraine, in this fantasy universe of propaganda to justify a war, got even more impudent.

In the morning, the Ukrainian military for some reason again shelled a long-abandoned cabin in the middle of nowhere in Russia's Rostov Oblast.

Believe it or not, and later in the same day, Ukraine even sent small squads to invade Russian territory.

First, Russia's FSB service reported the elimination of two Ukrainian BMP-2s that had crossed the border. All five Ukrainians troops were allegedly killed, and the FSB press service was right at the scene to film the BMPs still burning in woods.

The FSB did not show any bodies.

Then, there appeared video footage of two Ukrainian BTR-70Ms, also at the Russian border, also stopped and destroyed by brave Russian military and border guards.

Oryx, the famous warfare research group, split its sides with laughter.

Ukraine's military had ceased operating BTR-70Ms years before. And the vehicles shown in videos had been lazily repainted in a lame attempt to imitate the Ukrainian camouflage pattern.

The Russians weren't even trying that hard to make their false flag look at least somewhat believable.

Later on February 21, as Ukraine "attacked" Russia with two BMPs, the Kremlin stooges, Pushilin and Pasechnik, were told to come forward again.

They both issued two totally identical statements asking Putin to officially recognize the puppet enclaves.

To "save the people of Donbas from massive loss of life," they said. Russia should also formalize "defense agreements" with them.

Meanwhile, Russian forces were seen moving into positions just kilometers away from the Ukrainian territory.

Russian soldiers, both conscripts and the contracted, were seen sleeping on a bare floor inside unprepared premises, clinging to one another in the cold. One couldn't expect to hold troops in such conditions for long.

Their command would need to send them back to field bases in the rear—or give them all a go order within the next few days.

An avalanche of photos and videos on social media showed tanks, artillery, and TOS-1 thermobaric rocket systems forming battle arrays. Field hospitals were ready. It was happening everywhere—Belarus, Russia's Bryansk, Belgorod, Crimea.

And we started seeing endless scores of Russian vehicles marked with a white-painted tactical symbol, "Z."

TEN

That was a weird time.

Imagine a Michael Bay–style disaster movie in which a one-hundred-meter-high tsunami rises on the horizon.

The main character stands on the beach crowned with palms and watches the wall of death coming from the sunset. He knows the wave is going to sweep this place clean.

It's coming, and there's not much time left.

There will be death and destruction. But there also will be many of the brave and daring in the beautiful city behind his back to clear up the rubble, tend to the suffering, and point the way toward a new dawn.

So instead of panicking and dashing for high ground, the character lights up what may be his last cigarette.

The tsunami is not forever. It will come, reap its harvest of sorrow, and then flow back into the sea again. And life will continue.

It's not true that Ukrainians were defiant in the last days of February. I remember seeing a lot of videos on Twitter showing Ukrainian shopping malls full of customers.

"Why aren't they freaking out?" many were asking in the comments section. "Can't they see what's happening? You just can't go shopping like it's just another day."

"Leave these people alone," many replied. "This might be their last weekend in peace."

We were being . . . fatalistic. And very confident in our military.

If you ask me, I'd choose that over hysteria and societal collapse.

And hey—life still had its lighter moments.

After all, it's Ukraine, the country where hilariously wild history occurs like clockwork.

In January and February, Kyiv authorities started to prepare the city for a Russian attack. In a shocking revelation, it appeared that most, if not all the old Soviet air raid shelters in the city were either long condemned or leased out as storage facilities.

On Velyka Vasylkivska Street, in downtown Kyiv, a large shelter in the basement of a spacious home turned out to be . . . a very posh strip club. Yeah, babe, that's the place where you want to outlast doomsday!

However, prices there were wild. Something like $5 for an espresso. I'm not even talking about cocktails and all. But one must pay for some extra fun during wartime, right?

It was suggested that we rename the place "Sex Bomb Shelter." Sometimes Twitter can be so much fun.

Another fun story.

As you might remember, around February 16, when the world was expecting a Russian invasion, Reuters installed a web camera at the Maidan. Its video feed showed the entire square from the height of the Hotel Ukraine.

Many here in Ukraine were genuinely pissed off.

"So you Westerners want to enjoy the fun of a live missile attack on YouTube?"

The stream was running 24/7 for several days. On the sixteenth, someone, probably a Putin sympathizer, turned the Soviet anthem on so it could be heard on the video.

The Ukrainian response was swift and merciless.

Later in the day, a drone appeared hovering in the air before the camera. It carried a sign that read: GARAGE FOR SALE IN THE SOLOMY-ANSKY DISTRICT. And shared the phone number of the Russian embassy.

Sadly, the performance's then-anonymous mastermind, Felix Kurtanich, was later killed in action in Donbas in April 2022. He had served brilliantly as a military drone operator. We learned of his death months later.

He was twenty-six.

February 21, afternoon, we at the *KI* have gathered in the newsroom to witness the latest episode of Moscow's extravaganza.

Pushilin and Pasechnik, the Donbas collaborators, had already "requested" the Russian recognition of the occupied region.

Now, Russia's security council, Putin's inner politburo, was expected to discuss this new and totally unexpected move.

According to official Russian statements, the meeting was to be broadcast live.

This was obviously to show the moment's solemnity on the brink of the almost inevitable Ukrainian genocide of Donbas that the Kremlin elders were generously trying to thwart, despite the West's vicious intrigues.

The meeting begins: six thirty P.M. Moscow time.

My iPhone buzzes.

"Hey."

An unexpected message from Anastasia. A girl from Mariupol who had been my university classmate. We were rather close in our student years, and our dorm rooms were near to each other.

Unlike me, she never left Mariupol. After trying out several professions, she eventually ended up becoming a policewoman. At the time, she was a lieutenant.

"Our superiors are asking us about the evacuation," she wrote. "Who wants to go and where to . . . if the shit really hits the fan."

I respond.

"What do you mean?"

"I think they're going to take us away. To Dnipro, Kyiv, Kryvy Rih . . . wherever one can go," Anastasia said. "Just like Donetsk in 2014."

"How is the city?"

"What can I tell . . . nothing. On Saturday at five A.M. there was a lot of loud rumbling. It's all quiet now though. But folks say there are heavy attacks in Luhansk Oblast."

"What does your department tell you? Any rumors?"

"Not much. It's all in a rush. Everyone's running around and arranging transportation. And making lists of their relatives in the city who may need to be evacuated."

Not a good sign if the National Police are already jumping.

"It's one giant fucking nightmare," Anastasia continues. "It just makes no sense."

"And what about you?" I ask.

"What about me . . . I don't know. I've packed up, just to be safe. 29 years of my life crammed into one small duffel bag. But . . . I have nowhere to go. I want to go to Kyiv. From there, I'd have options. And I could get a job."

"Don't you have relatives in Kharkiv Oblast? I'd suggest you go to them if things get bad and you need to leave Mariupol. And your plan B would be to come to Kyiv. Make it to the city any way possible. And we'll see what we can do for you."

"I don't want to go to Kharkiv Oblast . . . it's a very small town, no jobs. And it's pretty close to the Russian border, you know."

"I'm afraid job opportunities aren't our top priority now. But I still think it's too early for panic . . . It's not 2014 anymore. I'm 100 percent sure we'll show them some fucking hell if they dare to come in."

"Yeah . . . Our guys have been standing strong for so many years. And get this, I've been listening to intercepted communications from the Russian side. They're all freaking out too, they're short of food and water, and they have no idea what's really happening. But Mariupol . . . we're going to be so sad about Mariupol. Just like we were about Donetsk. But I'm not afraid anymore."

Just three weeks after this conversation, in mid–March . . . I'll finally see her on Facebook again. And learn that she managed to survive the Russian holocaust of Mariupol.

She will have spent weeks with barely any food or water in the basement of her police department headquarters. And then she fled what was left of the city.

Meanwhile, Putin's politburo is speaking.

Live from the Kremlin.

Defense minister Sergei Shoigu, the army general who never served a day in the military. The Federal Council chairwoman, Valentina Matvienko, born and raised in Ukraine. The security council chairman, Nikolai Patrushev, the gray cardinal behind the Kremlin's wars and assassinations across the world.

Dmitry Medvedev, the pathetic man who once sold out his dignity and agreed to serve as a dummy president to keep the chair warm for Putin. Dmitry Kozak, also born and raised in Ukraine, the Mouth of Sauron issuing threats of total elimination to his own former homeland.

Viktor Zolotov, the Rosgvardiya head and Putin's former bodyguard living the life of a Saudi prince. Vyacheslav Volodin, the State Duma chairman threatening to annihilate Ukraine and Europe with nuclear weapons. Sergey Lavrov, the foreign minister enjoying a lavish lifestyle with his mistress amid villas and yachts fully covered by the Russian oligarch Sergey Deripaska, whom he serves.

The Russian foreign intelligence service's Sergey Naryshkin—stumbling, obviously frightened, embarrassed and ill at ease, clearly realizing the very depth of hell things are going to.

And Putin—slouching on his throne at a distance from his Nazgûls, enjoying himself and relishing the inevitable heyday of his reign.

All the key war criminals gathered in the same room.

Of course, everyone says what he or she is supposed to, giving an absolute yes to the salvation of Donbas from the clutches of "the Nazi regime in Ukraine."

Valentina Matvienko during the meeting:

> For seven years, a real genocide, a blockade, no welfare payments, the shelling. Donetsk and Luhansk became victims of an anti-Russian project. What has Russia done wrong to Ukraine over these thirty years?

And Putin theatrically leaves the council, promising to make an uneasy decision after hearing from his peers' honest, individual, and absolutely not predetermined recommendations.

A small detail pops up in the media a bit later.

The stream at several moments shows traces of editing.

And again, the live broadcast from the Kremlin was launched at five thirty P.M. Moscow time.

But Shoigu's wristwatch clearly shows twelve fifty P.M. and then one thirty P.M. during his second speech. And the Moscow mayor Sergey Sobyanin's watch at another moment shows twelve ten P.M.

This wasn't live.

It was filmed midday, edited, and then published at the comfortable beginning of the workday in Washington, D.C.

Another small detail: The Kremlin had this "emergency council" *before* the "republics of Donbas" even issued their "official requests" of recognition at three forty P.M.

From the very beginning, this all was a complete shit show. A very poorly executed performance.

However, was it a surprise to anyone?

No. But it was simply sickening to see.

In front of the whole world's eyes, this bunch of filthy, ridiculously rich kleptocrats in their sixties and seventies were playing out their cheesy shenanigans, just like that.

Like a cheap fool's bargain, but at the level of nations, giant armies, with millions of lives at stake.

But they had no other choice. This was genocide and America was fanning the flames.

Their propaganda absolutely went bonkers with the prospect of devouring Ukraine "within three days."

In all seriousness, Russian media was painting a world in which Ukraine was waging a full-scale punitive war in the east. River-crossing operations, sudden rushes, maneuvers, armed clashes, sorties into Russia—things that never happened in the real world.

It was more than obvious to any honest-minded human being watching the situation that this was about just one thing: concocting an excuse for annihilating Ukraine.

But as sworn Soviet formalists, they continued with their lame show: councils, papers, addresses, decrees, "mutual friendship and defense agreements."

They wept crocodile tears over "the people of Donbas" oppressed by "Nazi Ukraine," and then turned the whole region into a desolation of cities razed to the ground.

Dmitry Peskov on February 20:

> Throughout its history, Russia was never the one to attack first. And Russia, which survived so many wars, is the last European country to ever want to even pronounce the word war.

I want to say that these people have no shame. But no words can really describe how far into the darkness humans can tumble.

"So . . . any thoughts, guys?" Our political editor, Oleksiy Sorokin, decides to engage us in a debate over the Kremlin clownery.

"Well," I said, taking a sip of the day's fifth cup of coffee. "They are going to do that. And that's going to be the end of the Minsk agreements. They may potentially want to 'recognize' the occupied zone as independent nations, formalize their military presence there, and freeze the whole thing forever. Something like Transnistria."

Yes, hope always wants another chance. No matter what.

"Here's the thing: They do not mention the borders. Do Russians recognize the 'DNR' and the 'LNR' as what they are now? Or do they want the whole of Donetsk and Luhansk oblasts?" said Toma Istomina, our deputy chief editor, from behind her desk in front of me.

The Russian puppet enclaves in their "constitution" claimed the full of the two Ukrainian oblasts. Even though they controlled no more than one third of the region.

The newsroom was growing darker.

As if on cue, the office's main light went off. There we were sitting in the gloom of desk lamps, in the agonizing wait for the inevitable.

People were really changing in those days.

Some fell into a quiet despair and idly or obsessively planned escape routes abroad. Others filled up long queues at the shooting ranges of Kyiv, despite ridiculously high prices.

It was almost impossible to sign up for first aid and tactical medical courses. All the decent organizations offering training were booked solid for the next several weeks.

Even Zelensky began to change.

These were the days when he finally started showing some temper.

After the February 16 attack date prediction, scores of the country's top tycoons and pro-Russian lawmakers fled Ukraine.

During a joint press conference with Germany's chancellor, Olaf Scholz, Zelensky told them all to get back to the country within the next twenty-four hours—"otherwise, the government and the leadership will have to come to some serious conclusions, and believe me, we will."

Whoa, not a bad move. Not something we expected from our comedian.

And yes, on February 17, the country's top oligarch, Rinat Akhmetov, returned to Mariupol, walking on the cold Azov seaside with his entourage.

There was a mixture of bitterness and high resolve in the air.

Zelensky in his speech at the Munich Security Conference on February 19:

> We're going to defend our homeland. With or without the support from partners. Regardless if they give us hundreds of modern weapons or five thousand helmets.
>
> These are not noble gestures for which Ukraine should bow low. This is your contribution to the security of Europe and the world. Where Ukraine has been a reliable shield for eight years. And for eight years it has rebuffed one of the world's biggest armies. Which stands along our borders, not the borders of the EU.
>
> And Grad rockets hit Mariupol, not European cities. And after almost six months of fighting, the airport in Donetsk was destroyed, not in Frankfurt. And it's always hot in the Avdiivka industrial zone—it was hot there in the last few days, not in Montmartre. And no European country knows the toll military burials every day in all regions take. And no European leader

knows the heartbreak of regular meetings with the families of the deceased bring.

Finally, in the evening, Putin speaks.

Guys in the newsroom turn up the volume on someone's laptop as high as it goes.

Huddled around the computer, we're listening to the most imperialistic speech since Adolf Hitler.

> . . . the contemporary Ukraine was fully and completely created by Russia. Or to be precise, by the Bolshevik Communist Russia. This process was initiated almost immediately following the 1917 revolution. And Lenin and his peers were doing that in a way rather brutal to Russia, tearing away parts of its historic territories . . .

The dictator's face is twisted with barely veiled, morbid hatred.

> . . . Ukraine never formed a sustainable statehood. Corruption has gained a sort of a special nature. It has literally infiltrated and corroded the Ukrainian statehood, the whole system, all branches of power . . .

"Oh, fuck your face!" the newsroom guys burst out. "How are things with your own billion-dollar palace at the Black Sea?"

> . . . so you want de-communization? Well, we're quite fine with that. We're ready to show what a real de-communization means to Ukraine.

Our chief, Olga Rudenko, sits on a floor pillow and wipes tears from her face.

> . . . with Ukraine acquiring weapons of mass destruction, the situation in the world and Europe, especially when it comes to Russia,

will see the most radical change. We can't help but react to this real danger. Especially considering the fact that Western masters can facilitate Ukraine in acquiring such a weapon to pose yet another threat to our country . . .

I shut my MacBook down.

All is said and done.

It's time to take care of our loved ones.

Putin was still reading out his endless list of grievances and complaints to the world when I took the subway from Kontraktova station.

Of course, he did that. He officially recognized his fake republics in Donbas. Claiming the Ukrainian-controlled part as well. On that night, endless columns of hundreds of Russian military vehicles rushed toward the front line near Donetsk and Luhansk.

Almost everyone in the subway car in Kyiv was staring into their phones.

Do they know? Do they realize what's coming? Are they all checking the news right now? Or are they all scrolling through Instagram and playing puzzle games as hell cracks the gate open?

Anyway, my girlfriend Natalia's bus departs in an hour and a half.

"It's better that you just go to your parents' place now." I've been texting her all day. "Not for too long, maybe for a week. Just to be safe. It's just a precaution. No, please don't be worried about me, I'll be fine here in Kyiv. I've got a whole lot of work to do! We'll be in touch all the time, I promise. You'll see your mom and dad, your sis."

Thank the Lord, she can listen.

The farewell kiss at the Demiivska central bus station. It's getting close to midnight.

"Please promise we'll be together on your birthday this Friday," Natalia whispers and stifles a tear.

Chernivtsi is a nice place. A city in the country's west facing Moldova and Romania four hundred kilometers away from Kyiv.

A good place to outlast the day of all days.

As Natalia's bus finally departs, I take out my phone and type a message before getting a cab home: "Mom, I'm sending you a train ticket to Kyiv. Just fucking take it and leave NOW!"

You know who wasn't freaking out amid all this doom and gloom?

My roommate, Ivan.

The guy did himself a favor and decided not to check the news every second of the day.

"You're into this thing," he told me once. "Let me know if the shit hits the fan."

And Ivan was the happiest man in this country. In the final days of February, he was drinking beer, messing around with his car, and binge-watching our favorite shows on HBO.

Lucky bastard.

I came back home from work to find him slouched in his chair, mixing his Johnnie Walker with Pepsi and watching *The Lord of the Rings*.

On the screen, the shadow of Mordor was rising from Mount Doom in the east and the Elves, feeling the touch of evil, reluctantly begin to leave Middle-Earth.

"Whoa," he grunted. "That's just what our Westerners are doing now!"

I went to my room to get some rest in the dark.

Yes, those were moments of truth.

The NATO liaison office evacuates its staff from Kyiv. United States embassy staff evacuated to Lviv are told to spend their nights in Poland and then return to Ukraine every morning.

They are waiting for the night it all begins.

When Putin "recognized" his monkeys in occupied Donbas, the West, despite its infinite desire to prevent the worst, gave up.

Blinken canceled yet another meeting with Lavrov. The White House abandoned plans for yet another peace summit with Putin. Even Germany terminated the certification of Nord Stream 2.

They're giving up trying to persuade Putin. He wasn't listening. He never listened. Diplomacy has failed.

Even here in Ukraine, the most optimistic (or, shall we say, denialist) voices have ceased trying.

And I cease trying to put myself at ease.

It's coming.

Rationality has failed. Along with human sanity and propensity for goodness.

Now is the time to face the ugly side of truth.

The countdown is ticking.

On February 22, as a reaction to Putin's "official" deployment of the Russian military in Donbas, Reznikov issued his own address to Ukrainian soldiers.

It popped up on Facebook late at night, just as I was trying to get some sleep. My whiskey-inspired roommate reasonably compared the Shire to Ukraine.

> The choice is very simple—defending our country, our homes, and our loved ones. Nothing has changed for us. Now we see our real friends, and there are more of them. Now the "friends" who have spent years trying to persuade us into surrendering can't hide anymore.
>
> Dark ordeals are coming our way. There will be losses. We will have to endure pain and defeat fear and frustration. But there will be our inevitable victory. Because we are home and ours is the truth. Our people support the Ukrainian military. The truth shows we are doing everything right.

In the morning, on February 23, all private chats for Ukrainian journalists were saying one thing: Zelensky had finally signed a decree calling up thirty-six thousand reserve troops. And the National Security and Defense Council was considering declaring a state of emergency.

No curfew yet, but everyone is advised to have passports at the ready. The SBU and the National Guard introduce maximum security regimes at the country's vital infrastructure facilities.

I shoot Ivan a message he was told to expect: We're stocking up on food, right now.

Ivan is ready.

We head to the nearest supermarket at Kontraktova Square. We need everything nonperishable, nutritious, and simple. Water, chocolate bars, coffee, tinned meat. Everything that will keep us going. Also, fuel from the nearest gas station. A lot of fuel and a full trunk of canisters.

The state of emergency was declared starting at midnight, February 24.

But, in the final hours of that evening, there was absolutely no binge-buying or panicking. Just two dudes running around with their cart and scooping up the whole stock of instant noodles.

The catastrophe is getting close.

In Mariupol, anti-war rallies in front of the Drama Theater under Ukrainian flags.

In Berlin, the Brandenburg Gate is illuminated with Ukrainian colors. The Ukrainian parliament approves an emergency bill on simplified civilian firearms regulation.

Come Back Alive, Ukraine's biggest charity assisting the military, is far surpassing its record of civilian donations.

In Lviv, the last Canadian aircraft takes off after having delivered its cache of weapons.

In Odesa and Kyiv, Russian diplomats burn papers in their backyards before being evacuated from Ukraine.

Late on February 23, the guys at the *Kyiv Independent* office didn't want the workday to end.

This was unspoken. But we all stayed together in the newsroom until late at night. Meanwhile, Zelensky was meeting with the country's top businesspeople at the Bankova. We knew they were discussing the situation, but Zelensky did not give them a definitive answer about the likelihood of war.

At nine P.M. I receive a message from my mom: "I took the train, everything's all right."

All that needs to be done is done.

"So . . . I think I'm gonna get going," I say to the crew, and get up reluctantly. "See you. See you all tomorrow."

For crying out loud, I can't express how much I want tomorrow to start with just another annoyingly boring editorial meeting.

"See you, man. Good night and good luck."

And I walked into the darkness of night.

Some of the *KI* guys stayed in the newsroom until the very last hours of the night. Still working.

In our crappy apartment, Ivan again said "Fuck this shit, I'm going to bed."

But I couldn't.

In private chats for Ukrainian defense journalists, a message: "Guys, it's due at five A.M. Not 100% confirmed yet."

Ukraine's journalists stay up. All linked with one another via a zillion chats.

This is going to be a long night.

Scrolling through news headlines again.

The Kremlin stooges, Pasechnik and Pushilin, issue yet another identical "statement." They request Russia's military help in "repelling Ukraine's military aggression."

Reuters: BLINKEN BELIEVES RUSSIA WILL INVADE UKRAINE BEFORE NIGHT IS OUT

Wouldn't hurt to have a good late dinner and pour some whiskey.

It's probably the last night of quiet.

Two thirty-five A.M.

This has been happening for so long. For nearly a decade.

If you think about it, a Ukrainian thirty years of age has spent one third of his or her life amid Russia's war on their homeland.

We in Ukraine neglected our armed forces. As if a war in the hinterland of Europe was unimaginable. Then Russia seized Crimea and unleashed a bloodbath in Donbas.

We attempted to build a brand-new military for our nation's survival. And yet we proceeded as if we had all time in the world. We did not.

Time is over now.

The Kremlin had been preparing all this time.

For years, they poisoned their citizenry with insane propaganda of hatred and revenge. And we laughed at their idiotic grimacing on TV, not believing they could be serious.

Moscow got half of Europe hooked on its natural gas and appointed corrupt European politicians to the juiciest positions in its state monopolies. It made and spent countless billions to rearm its giant military and prepare for a major war.

So many in the West turned a blind eye on Georgia, Crimea, and Donbas. They've fed this beast all these years, calling on "both sides to de-escalate."

The movers and shakers of Russia's state machine enjoyed their unspeakable wealth in the West. Their kids grew up and lived in the West. And, meanwhile, state propagandists in Moscow with villas at Lake Como and condos in Miami year after year nurtured an all-encompassing, absolute appetite for territorial grabs.

Year after year, the Kremlin made new encroachments with little resistance or pushback. They perceived this as an open invitation for more.

The world's greatest nuclear power has concentrated the largest military force in the region since the peak of the Cold War. And it was shamelessly bitching about a batch of Stingers sent by Lithuania to help Ukraine at the last moment.

NATO has been present two hundred kilometers away from Saint Petersburg since 2004. Yet, even after 2014, all along the eastern frontier, the alliance nations never had anything that might possibly be construed as a conventional invasion threat to Russia.

I remember how in 2018 the RAND Corporation issued a report comparing NATO's available forces in Poland and the Baltic nations with what Russia had in the region. Russia had 2.5 times the size of NATO manpower, 6 times the number of NATO tanks, 4.6 times the number of infantry fighting vehicles, 10 times the number of self-propelled artillery pieces, 270 times the number of rocket systems.

And that's Russia's Western Military District alone.

In early February 2022, we could only give a sad smile to the American deployment of one thousand additional troops to Romania and two thousand to Germany and Poland as a response to the crisis in Ukraine.

And now, in the age of intercontinental ballistic missiles and nuclear-carrying submarines, Putin threatened to wipe out Ukraine because "NATO ballistic missiles near Kharkiv could reach Moscow within seven minutes."

Putin never explained why it wasn't a problem that "NATO ballistic missiles" fired from Estonia, Latvia, and Lithuania could potentially target Moscow and Saint Petersburg from the very same distance and within the very same impact time.

And the Baltic nations had been alliance members for almost twenty years and had never hosted any missile systems or nuclear weapons. Russia's elite 76th Airborne Division in Pskov, just thirty kilometers from Estonia, was alone considerably stronger than anything NATO had in the region.

And Russia didn't see as a problem their own ballistic missile systems in Kaliningrad, just 270 kilometers away from Warsaw and 530 kilometers away from Berlin.

And it was fine deploying nuclear-carrying submarines around the world that could target the West pretty much anywhere and from the shortest distances. Same as the United States and NATO.

The stable nuclear balance of power had worked all these years.

And now, on this night, Russia had concentrated 75 percent of its armed forces at Ukraine's borders. Deployed from across their country, from central Europe to the Far East.

They never really cared about NATO.

They knew the West was weak, spineless, and actively demilitarizing. Russia, with its immense conventional and nuclear power, had always been totally safe.

They only cared about NATO when small nations joined the alliance and automatically became no-go zones for their tanks. And then, worse, turned into successful societies whose happy, prosperous people might incite cross-border envy and thus destabilize things back home.

High-minded, useful idiots in the West spent decades warning of the "existential threat of NATO's expansion to Russia."

In truth, it was thanks to this "expansion" that not a single bomb fell on Tallinn, Riga, and Vilnius.

We in Ukraine fucked up our main chance. We leaned into our fake neutrality in the 1990s, as the West tried to be nice and appease the Kremlin for far too long.

NATO feared nuclear holocaust, Russia used that fear as a weapon.

So here we are now, after all these years of permissiveness, blatant lies, and omission.

Sipping whiskey in front of a laptop and waiting for the H-hour.

But nothing's over yet.

They keep talking about Kyiv falling within days. They keep painting maps with scary red arrows pointed again at Kyiv, Dnipro, and Kharkiv.

Russians will burn this country to ashes, that's for sure. There will be a lot of blood, fire, and grief.

But the Russians will face a nightmare of their own making. A million things can go wrong. All those splendid little wars never ended well.

We have our elite 95th Airborne from Zhytomyr. South of Kyiv, we have the 72nd Mechanized Infantry I spent so much time with in Donbas. We have our 93rd Mechanized, the glorious one.

In Mykolaiv, we have our 79th Airborne, the defenders of Donetsk Airport. We have the Azov and the 36th Marines in Mariupol. We have tens, if not hundreds, of thousands in civilian life who have combat experience.

I strongly advise anyone against underestimating the frantic anger of the doomed fighting for their own homes and families.

There will always be a way to resist. Even if our military is broken and scattered, we'll switch to relentless guerillas. Try to tame the fighting nation the size of France that hates you to the very core.

The resistance will switch to small unit tactics. It will be harder for Russians to spot them. We have NLAWs and Javelins. We have dense woods, swamps, and mountains. Time will be on our side.

Nothing is predestined.

We'll see how they like a conveyor belt of scorched dead bodies and eviscerated tanks coming back to Russia.

Two forty-five A.M.

A United States Air Force Global Hawk makes its last surveillance mission over Ukraine. The aircraft closely scans the Donbas front line.

I look up at a book on my shelf. It's the young Winston Churchill. Still fit and slim, about my age. Our deputy chief editor, Toma Istomina, once upon a time gave me the book as a Secret Santa present.

"We shall fight on the beaches, we shall fight on the landing grounds . . ."

Yes, Grandpa Winston.

I know you would have been by our side with all your heart now.

Three fifteen A.M.

In New York City, the United Nations Security Council is holding an emergency meeting. In Ukraine, meanwhile, airports in Kharkiv, Kherson, Zaporizhia, and Dnipro block runways with utility vehicles turned over and set aflame.

CNN: RUSSIA ISSUES NOTAM NOTIFICATION CLOSING CIVILIAN AIR TRAFFIC NEAR NORTHEASTERN BORDER OF UKRAINE

On Twitter, OSINT researchers post security camera shots from Kalanchak, a Ukrainian border control point at the entrance into Crimea.

Armed men in military uniforms break into the facility, and the Ukrainian staff runs for their lives.

Four forty-five A.M.

In journalistic chats, a message: "Guys, Putin is going live again."

The dictator's face on my laptop is twisted with sick rage.

> . . . they have simply left us with no other option to protect Russia
> and our people but the one we will have to adhere to today. The
> people's republics of Donbas have requested Russia's assistance.
> I have made a decision to execute a special military operation . . .

I shut the laptop down.

No emotions. Nothing but a deliberate rehearsal of practical plans to get me through the day of all days that's coming.

I knock on my roommate's door.

Ivan's sleepy face peeps out from the dark.

"Wake the fuck up. It's a war."

"Okay . . ."

ELEVEN

Ivan jumps to the floor and struggles into his jeans.

"Call everyone," I say. "Wake your parents up."

His mom and dad live in a distant town on the Azov Sea coast. His little sister is in Mariupol with her husband.

I grab my iPhone, too.

Natalia isn't answering. Long beeps. Moving on through the contacts list. Denys from *Forbes Ukraine* is still sleeping, too. Maksym, our friend living in Lviv, murmurs ". . . mmmkay . . ." And then he suddenly realizes what we're trying to tell him through his sleep.

"What, what?!"

"I'm gonna go get some fuel," Ivan says, putting his jacket on as he rushes to the front door. "I think I'm still half-empty."

"I fucking told you to keep your car gassed up. Why?"

"Because reasons!"

"Okay. Don't waste a minute, people will begin fighting at gas stations any minute now. I'll try to go buy some more food. We'll meet up here at home if the phone connection is out."

We split up at the parking lot.

Our neighborhood is silent. Almost no window lights. Kyiv is still sleeping.

Our 24/7 supermarket, Silpo, appears to be open. I grab a cart and sweep up all Snickers and Bounty bars the place has.

There's only me in the aisles. And there's still mild generic music playing from speakers.

"Dear customers! Don't forget to check our discounts! Sausages, special beer brands brewed just for you, baby food! New special deals this week only!"

Just one cashier is working. The half-asleep lady lazily beeps a new batch of our wartime food stock.

"Excuse me," I say for some reason. "Have you checked the news lately?

She lifts her dazed eyes on me.

"No, I haven't."

"I highly recommend that you do so now," I say and leave quickly. "Especially if you happen to have relatives in Donbas."

I'm getting nervous. Not good.

5:09 A.M.

I carry my bags back home across our neighborhood of shitty nine-story brezhnevkas, typical specimens of Soviet low-cost panel construction.

And then the night brings the sound of distant thunder.

A heavy bang. Then another. And again. They're coming from the northwest. As if a kettlebell fell onto an empty steel barrel.

One more blast. Now rolling down from the west.

This sound is so familiar.

Missiles.

Russians are striking the city.

Guys in the *KI* work chat are all awake, too.

"A real fucking heavy bang just a minute ago here," Toma Istomina writes in our work chat.

Media report dozens of heavy impacts across the country. This is way bigger than Donbas.

Zhytomyr, Odesa, Zaporizhia, Kherson. Massive conflagrations in Mykolaiv. In Kharkiv, the glowing light from heavy blasts fire up the night sky. People on Facebook tell of shock waves shattering their windows.

All along the northeastern border, Russian artillery and rockets devastate Ukrainian border control points.

So it begins.

As expected, Russia opens the invasion with a massive shock-and-awe bombing campaign.

No air raid sirens roar in the city still.

Back to the apartment—Now.

Check all documents. The passport, the press card, all copies. All devices and power banks charged. Take a shower while it's still possible.

Missile hits roar almost every minute. I recount all the cash I have on me and time after time flinch from the shock waves shaking the building.

Windows across the neighborhood light up with every blast. Kyiv is waking to the last day of Pompeii. Facebook shows the first hits in the city's residential areas.

This better be just a bad dream.

Finally, Natalia picks up the phone.

"Listen to me very carefully now," I say.

One more blast, a really loud one. The sound of car tires begin squealing.

Natalia is currently in Chernivtsi, a major city two hours' drive away from her parents' place.

"Wake your parents up and go to their town as soon as you can. It's better that you stay away from big cities."

"I know, I know, I know, I've just seen it all in the news . . ." Natalia's voice is trembling. "Please tell me how you are. What's that sound on your end? Is Kyiv all right?"

"It's not, sweetie, we're being bombed right now," I say. "Please don't waste any time."

Her parents live in Sokyryany. That's a little town just hundreds of meters from the border with Moldova. A distant, quiet place on the banks of the Dniester River. A perfect place to weather the storm.

"And please . . . ask them if my mom can come to your place. Ivan can take her to your town. I have some money."

"What are you even talking about?" Natalia shouts. "Of course, we want all of you to come as soon as possible. My dad told me they'd welcome everyone in need. And you come, too, please! And bring anyone you want with you. Please, come."

"Listen . . . ," I say, rubbing my forehead. "Phone and internet connections are getting worse. If we lose contact . . . please just expect Ivan and her. She'll move farther to Moldova to my sister."

Easier said than done. My mother is stubborn as hell.

Seven A.M.

There seems to be a lull in the airstrikes across the city.

Russia has completed the first massive wave of missile attacks on Ukraine's military infrastructure, command and control centers, and airfields. Nearly 160 cruise and ballistic missiles launched from strategic bombers and the sea.

Estimated total damage: unknown.

In the first post-attack hours, we don't know if our military has survived as a functional force. We do not know how much of our air defense is still operational. Footage on social media shows dozens of civilian and military airfields burning across the country, from Kramatorsk to Lviv.

The General Staff, the Border Guard Service, the national police department all report active status in the coming hours.

Civilian authorities are still functional as well. At eight A.M. the Verkhovna Rada overwhelmingly endorses a bill to introduce martial law in all regions. The parliament's speaker, Ruslan Stefanchuk, declares the bill passed and tells all lawmakers: "Whoever among you leaves Kyiv now is a traitor!"

Zelensky has a brief conversation with Biden and goes live on Facebook saying that Russia has launched "a special military operation in Donbas."

> We need you to remain calm. If you can stay, stay indoors. We're working, the military is working, the whole of Ukraine's defense and security sector is working. I'll be with you live again soon.

Don't panic, we are strong, we are ready for anything, because we
are Ukraine. Glory to Ukraine.

Security cameras at Ukrainian border control stations show giant
military convoys breaking in from Belarus and Russia. They all funnel
into roads running to Kyiv, Chernihiv, Sumy, and Kharkiv.

Way, way beyond just Donbas.

It's a full-scale invasion.

The phone rings.

"Illia, it's me." My colleague Anna Myroniuk is on the line. "There
was a huge impact not far away from me . . . I think the military base
was hit, smoke is billowing high. Can I come to you guys now? You
live closer than anyone I know."

There's no other option.

"Yes, sure . . . but we can't give you a ride right now. You'll have to
come by yourself, you know the address."

"That's the problem now. The streets are absolute chaos. One giant
traffic jam, nothing is moving. Everyone's fleeing. I've been trying to
get a cab, but nothing and no one can get to me."

"I see . . . grab some basic stuff and walk your way to us. Talk later."

Ivan is back.

"The tank full," he snaps. "And I also got a couple of gas canisters.
We're good."

"How are your parents in Mariupol?" I ask.

"They're fine. I told my sis to leave the city, but she doesn't want to.
The twat never listens to me."

We take his car and drive out into the streets. My mom's train should
arrive in Kyiv at ten.

The first wartime morning breaks colorless and cold. Light drizzle
smears onto the windshield. We live in the city's very outskirts, so the
roads are still okay. But there are already long lines at ATMs and
pharmacies.

People gather in small groups and talk. Some even manage to buy
their morning coffee at their usual kiosks. No panicking, no pillaging,
even though there's no police or military presence as of yet.

"Okay, I see no point driving to the central train station," Ivan says. "The traffic across the entire city is an absolute mess. Peremohy Avenue is packed full, with no movement whatsoever. The cars are all going in one direction. We can drive toward the downtown, but we'll never make it back home."

The Google Maps traffic monitor shows most of Kyiv's streets in red. Millions are already fleeing.

"We're better off leaving the car at the Akademmistechko and hitting the subway. I'm gonna go to my workshop and secure all the money we got. You take care of your mom and we'll meet up somewhere."

Fortunately, the Kyiv subway is still working as always.

The city authorities immediately canceled the passenger fare and flung open all pay-gates. Our subway has finally lived to see the day when it will switch to its main secondary function—an all-city network of wartime bomb shelters, some of which may be able to sustain nuclear strikes.

Sorry, dear Soviet engineers of the 1960s, evil capitalist warmongers in the West never forced that function on the fruit of your labor. Vladimir V. Putin of Moscow did that—today.

Subway trains weren't busy at all.

However, people were already sitting on platform stairs, with laptops on their knees, learning the rules of their new life.

. . . The Kyiv Central Train Station is gray and inhospitable.

People rush in and out. Many are dressed in military fatigues and throw their giant canvas duffels onto benches. Police patrols in full gear walk here and there and help ladies with heavy suitcases and perform other small miracles.

Dozens of passenger trains are hours late.

Denys of *Forbes Ukraine* meets me at the station, too. Dazed and confused, he has nothing but a small backpack and a gray pet carrier. That's his precious cat, Cocos.

"It's better that you stay with us now," I told him over the phone. "We have enough room at our place. I really don't think it's a good idea for you to stay alone at home now."

Eleven thirty A.M.

My mom's train was supposed to arrive more than an hour ago, but it's not even on the station's display. And over the phone, my mom is truly freaking out. She knows what has happened.

Denys looks really depressed.

"What's going to happen to us all now, Illia?"

I wish I knew. But we must do the right thing. As of now, that includes taking care of our loved ones.

Also, the work.

Guys in the *KI* chat exchange messages about who can update the news on the website and who will get a couple of hours sleep. I'll be back to work as soon as I make it home.

Our boss, Olga, decided to spend this morning at the office for some reason.

Beginning at seven twenty A.M., Kyiv city authorities started pushing online notifications of air alerts. But still, no sirens.

This all looks more like a scene from an old Soviet book about World War II. The day when Nazis invaded their former ally. The death army is marching somewhere far away, cannons roaring far beyond the horizon.

But here, deep in the rear, there's this turmoil of facing an unspeakable dread.

Natalia sends a message: It's a complete mess in Chernivtsi. But she somehow managed to take a shuttle van to her parents' town.

"You know what, I'm gonna get going," Denys sighs. "I'd better be at home."

"You sure?"

"Yeah . . . I'll maybe team up with *Forbes* guys in the city. They're moving west. *Forbes* has rented a vacation camp in the Carpathians to relocate us all. I don't know."

"I see . . . it's up to you. Let's stay in touch."

We hug each other. And Denys walks away with his cat.

Finally, the train arrives. Just an hour and a half late, which is lucky, considering the circumstances.

★   ★   ★

One fifty P.M.

"I'm not going anywhere. I'm staying here in Kyiv with you. You may drive me out of this apartment right now but I'm staying close to you in the city."

As I've said, my mother is stubborn as hell.

And now this trait is multiplied threefold.

She arrived in Kyiv with nothing but her purse. And it took a lot of screaming into the phone to make her admit the un-admittable and take her real estate property documents. A small apartment in a village near Volnovakha in Donbas. She might never see it again. Ivan is running around our apartment with his phone.

"Katya, I'm telling you, get your hubby up and go to mom and dad's. What are you waiting for? There's nothing to be gained in the city, you're under attack."

The Russians are advancing fast.

By early afternoon, invading forces had reached the outskirts of Kharkiv. Russian tanks were seen moving through downtown Sumy.

In the south, they'd reached Nova Kakhovka and seized the local hydroelectric power plant. That's sixty kilometers inside the Kherson Oblast. Another strike force had entered Melitopol with little to no resistance.

Since early morning, media have also reported Russian coastal landings near Odesa and Berdyansk. But this turns out to be false. In the east, the city of Shastya (which means "happiness") was 80 percent occupied, but Ukrainian forces were still holding on.

North of Kyiv, Russian forces move from Belarus through the Exclusion Zone. Ukrainian National Guard units take up the fight at the Chornobyl Exclusion Zone, but they are doomed.

It's the blitzkrieg.

Dmitry Peskov, when asked if the objective of the "special military operation" was to topple Ukraine's leadership:

> It is necessary to liberate Ukraine, clean it out of Nazis, pro-Nazi individuals, and ideologies.

And then the worst begins.

Videos on social media show Russian helicopters roaring over the northeastern suburbs of Kyiv. Dozens coming from the north, flying low over the Dnipro River. KAmov Ka-52s and Mil Mi-8s.

Hostomel.

The Antonov Airport.

A classic textbook move—securing key airfields near the target and then landing reinforcements.

Ukrainian air defenses are largely suppressed.

Ukrainian military units manage to down only two Ka-52s. From their own balconies, the people of Hostomel see one crash in a nearby field. Another is critically hit and abandoned by Russian pilots.

I instruct Ivan and my mom to rush to the bathroom if anything big happens. In case you didn't know, bathrooms can be the safest place (or let's say, the least dangerous) to be during a shelling. They're normally situated within the walls of other rooms and usually have no windows.

We live on the top floor of a shitty Soviet panel apartment block that could crumble in a wind gust, but the bathroom is where you want to be. And avoid windows. Always the golden rule.

One eleven P.M.

A sharp roar swells overhead. It's getting louder. The windows rattle.

"All take cover now," I say and walk out of my room.

My mom is bewildered. Hearing the terrible noise coming closer, she sways from side to side in the kitchen.

"Into the fucking bathroom, now!!" I yell.

She comes around and jumps into the loo.

The whistling roar dies down quickly.

"I think it was a fighter jet . . . ," Ivan says from his corner.

Yes. The air battle unfolds right over the Kyiv metropolitan area. Hopefully, that was our guy engaging Russians. Or providing support to our troops. Hopefully, we still have some aircraft able to fight.

"Let's keep the bathroom door open," I say. "Remember, stay away from windows and take cover in places where there are two walls between you and the outside."

From the northwest of our place come sounds of fighting.

Natalia sends a message on Telegram.

"How are you?"

"Still hoping to wake up in cold sweat," I reply. "There's fighting in Hostomel."

"Honey, I'm so scared. Even though I'm totally safe."

"God willing, we'll endure this. Tell me about what's happening there."

"I'm not sure I can tell you anything comforting . . . We're glued to the news. People are emptying the groceries, stocking up on everything. Everybody's asking about you, even my friends. Please take the car and come here, please."

"I can't. I'm a war reporter. I need to be with my military now . . . but mother's driving me nuts. She's not going anywhere without me. And there's no way she can stay here with me. I guess I'll need to get her to a safe place before anything else."

"Take her and come here. At least for a time . . . Sorry, I don't want to pressure you."

Three twelve P.M.

From the street behind our house a loud rumble. But it's not like the others. It's coming from somewhere on the ground and isn't fading away.

I walk into the stairwell.

Our tanks are rolling down the street. A full-fledged T-64BM company makes a turn onto the Irpin Highway, fencing off civilian cars.

The military is probably reinforcing Hostomel.

The work chat buzzes.

"Everyone, there are credible reports Kyiv will be bombed within one hour. TAKE SHELTER OR BE NEAR ONE."

"EVERYONE: YOUR SAFETY IS THE NUMBER ONE PRIORITY, OUR WORK COMES SECOND. TAKE SHELTER."

The *KI* guys are keeping the news feed updated. Some of them, just like so many across the city, are already working from inside subway stations underground.

Miraculously, we have good internet connection. And mobile networks are still working, even though they're clearly overloaded by zillions of people calling their close ones. We expected a total communications blackout by now.

Okay, let's go and check out the nearest shelter.

An online map from Kyiv city authorities says it's a five-minute walk from our place.

Turns out it's even closer, a dark and damp basement underneath a nine-story panel house. It's been closed for like forty years, and locals have only just now cracked open the lock. The same was happening in apartment blocks across the country.

This hole can reasonably shelter no more than thirty people at best.

Some women have brought small stools for themselves. No cell coverage inside, of course. My mom finds a place to sit. Ivan and I find a bench just outside the entrance.

Nothing happens.

People walk in and out. Some look into the sky, no doubt trying to see the predicted Russian bomber breaking through the clouds.

Still, nothing happens. Not even an air raid siren.

4:06 P.M.

CNN's Matthew Chance goes live from Hostomel.

Just behind him, his cameraman shows troops marked with white sleeve patches in a parking lot at the airbase perimeter. Russians. They unload their supplies and move in. They pay no attention to the reporter.

Motherfucker . . .

"The Russians have secured the Antonov," I tell Ivan.

CNN: "The VDV airborne. They will now proceed with their main landing forces."

Ivan flinches. He says something he has clearly kept to himself for quite a while. "We need to get out of the city. While we still can."

Oh god, please don't.

"What are we waiting for? The moment when they storm the city and all hell breaks loose?"

Ivan is freaking out. I am freaking out.

"You wanna stay—you stay." Ivan goes a bit bonkers. "I'm leaving. You decide."

I rub my face.

"Man, I just can't . . ."

"May I ask you a small question? What are you going to do here? Alone? With your mother among the ruins? Go and join the military with your fucking weak legs. You can barely run for more than a hundred meters."

Ivan plunges on.

"And please allow me to remind you that according to your own media outlet, the Russians have hit lists of journalists. You're more than welcome to tell your own personal FSB interrogator that you felt some responsibility to stay."

CNN: "Four ballistic missiles fired from Belarus."

I close my eyes.

"I'm going to Lviv," Ivan says. "I can go via Natalia's parents' town. You decide. Now."

My temples are pulsing.

If this is a bad dream, now is the time to wake up in a warm bed and say phew.

"Okay," I finally force myself into murmuring. "We're going to Sokyryany. Now."

"Oh Jesus, finally!"

Back to the apartment.

No bombing still. Nothing but police establishing a checkpoint at the nearest intersection next to our house.

Five forty P.M.

Ivan is hastily packing up. He unplugs his PC, his most valuable possession. My mother clutches her purse and looks lost.

Russian tanks already in downtown Melitopol. That's over one hundred kilometers away from Crimea. They are crawling deeper into the country with every passing hour.

Well, at least I'll make sure my mom is safe.

Temptation.

It comes.

What if the game is up? What if it's all over?

Another jet whistles over the neighborhood. A hollow boom rolls down from the Hostomel area.

What if it's time to think about ourselves now? What if our days are not necessarily over? There could be something other than death and destruction. Somewhere far away from this doomed place. A new start. We have only one life to live.

Temptation.

And I'm slowly succumbing to it, with an army of death standing fifteen kilometers away from this apartment.

I pack up my PlayStation 4 and my robot vacuum cleaner. Some of the little things that I've acquired over these several years of my stubborn pursuit of happiness in Kyiv. Also—some papers. Documents that prove my future ownership of an unfinished one-bedroom apartment in Bucha.

But that little dream is probably never going to come true.

Well, at least my mom will be safely transported abroad. And then we'll see. Get a grip.

We pack all the food and water we have into the car. As I close the front door, I'm also leaving behind my favorite black tactical jacket and my Ukrainian press pass. We'll have to move via Irpin. There's no other route we can depart from Kyiv now. If the enemy troops from the CNN video stop our car, that is the last thing I should have on me.

We're moving out.

We'll make a huge detour via Stoyanka and then hopefully pour onto the E40 Highway running straight west to Zhytomyr.

Six P.M.

CNN: "Bellingcat's Christo Grozev: 18 Russian Ilyushin Il-76 airlifts bound for Hostomel, estimated arrival within 1 hour."

Now we are just a very small particle in a giant storm sweeping across the highway. It's getting dark, and there's nothing but an endless line of red brake lights. Cars inch forward, stop and start. The immense traffic jam drags on for at least a hundred kilometers.

Ivan clenches the wheel and spits swear words from time to time.

Hostomel . . . the Russian-captured Antonov Airport somewhere in the dark of night to the north.

The testing facility of the grand old Antonov engineering bureau, the masters of large freight aviation based in Kyiv since the 1950s. Also, the truly giant cargo airport, with its endless expanse of extra thick concrete runways.

The company had struggled through hard times for many years, but it always remembered what it was.

In October 2019, a bunch of journalists were invited to the Antonov Airport near Hostomel to celebrate the sixtieth and the fiftieth anniversaries of two legendary aircraft types, the An-24 and the An-26, respectively.

Emblazoned with THE ARMED FORCES OF UKRAINE in yellow, the blue An-26 was shining in the bright morning sun and roaring with its turboprops. She went up into the sky and released a handful of tiny specks into the deep blue over our heads: members of a local skydiving club, one of them a very beautiful young girl I was too shy to interview upon her landing.

And there was an old man wearing a Columbo-style raincoat walking around the airfield. With undisguised pleasure, he dished out enthusiastic commentaries to TV reporters on camera.

I can't really describe the shining love and pride in his eyes as he watched an An-24 takeoff from Antonov that morning. Sixty years before that day, in the late 1950s, he had co-engineered that aircraft as a flight test specialist.

His name was Yakiv Ryzhyk, and he was among the legends of the Antonov bureau. He was a very lively man. While talking to reporters, he would pull out his smartphone from his Columbo raincoat to answer calls from fellow aviation engineers congratulating him on the anniversary.

Afterward, he sent me an email asking that we send pictures of him at the airfield. The guy was ninety-two years old! A couple of weeks later, I learned on Facebook that the famed engineer had passed away peacefully at home.

And Hostomel is the home to the Mriya . . . the iconic Antonov An-225, the world's largest cargo aircraft.

In April 2020, we were honored to see her take off for her first COVID-19 mission. After much modernization and repair work, it was off to transport some four hundred tons of medical equipment from China to Poland.

All hail to the king of the skies as he returns to his kingdom, roaring loudly like a dragon at the start of the runway. Yep, those who've once heard the Mriya roar will never forget.

As if we reporters were not impressed enough, pilots made the Mriya waggle a bit in the air, bidding us all farewell with its giant wings.

And now, we're leaving this all behind.

A Ukrainian Buk-M1 air defense system moves toward Kyiv on the highway's opposite lane. Then there's a convoy of Humvees with DShK turrets. The military is preparing to give a warm welcome to the Russian landing operation in Hostomel.

"What's in the news? Read it all aloud," Ivan says.

"Snake Island is probably lost. There's no communication with our garrison there. Curfew has been declared throughout the country starting at ten P.M. tonight. The Russians are trying to bypass Kherson from the east and attack Mykolaiv. Then they will block Odesa and enter Transnistria."

I take a full swig from a whiskey bottle. I still can't force myself to send a message to Natalia that we're leaving.

"Can I have one, too?" my mother calls from the back seat. She's been unusually silent.

The traffic is not moving at all. We've been on the road for several hours, but we're not yet even close to Zhytomyr.

Fierce fighting is reported at the Antonov Airport. People on social media say they're taking cover in basements, and towns nearby see gleams of fire over Hostomel. Journalistic chats say Ukraine's special operations team Omega is attacking the Russian airborne on the airport premises.

"Oh, fuck this crap!" Ivan suddenly cranks the steering wheel and breaks out onto the highway's opposite lane, against traffic. He hits the gas. Hundreds of other cars are already doing the same, keeping the right lane free for the military and ambulances.

Police patrols do nothing or angrily blast their horns in an effort to shame the offenders. In Ivan's defense, unlike so many others, we return to our side of the highway once we've passed the blockade's most impassable kilometers.

The doomsday night rolls on. Of course, no one out here gives a damn about the curfew. Including the police.

In the outside world, there's a heated diplomatic battle between the United States and Europe over disconnecting Russia from SWIFT. It seems that witnessing a forty-million-person nation steamrolled with missiles and tanks is still not serious enough for some.

Ten ten P.M.

Damn, I haven't slept for like fifty-five hours.

Checking Facebook again.

Zelensky begs NATO to declare a no-fly zone over Ukraine. Totally hopeless.

And then this: Ukraine's National Guard Rapid Response Brigade has just posted a picture. Three Ukrainian soldiers holding up a national flag riddled with bullets. And they beam from ear to ear.

"Defense Ministry: Ukrainian troops reinstate control over Hostomel, Russian landing force destroyed."

"Yeah, babe!" Ivan and I shout together. "Get some! Woo-hoo!"

Among all that chaos of misinformation, desperation, and confusion, that little message was gold.

Not many really comprehended the real significance of that picture. But that, as we know now, was really the first and one of the greatest, long-lasting Ukrainian victories in this horrific war.

I memorialized it as the moment light sparked in the darkness.

The first real breath of true hope. As if a predator's bleeding prey, in an immense spiritual upwelling, discovered a newfound power to carry on and fight back.

The Russian landing operation at the Antonov Airport, an essential part of Russia's blitzkrieg, just . . . failed.

Starting before dawn on February 24, Russian Z-milbloggers on Telegram went absolutely nuts in their exalted euphoria.

In their world, the "special military operation" was running "flawlessly." In the invasion's earliest hours, following the waves of missile strikes, they declared the whole of the Ukrainian Air Force and air defenses nonexistent. Russia's aviation destroyed everything not wiped out by missiles just like that, in a single sortie.

At seven A.M., two hours into the war, the whole of Ukrainian armed forces were fully demoralized and defeated, and civilian leadership paralyzed.

By nine A.M., they had already pronounced Kharkiv occupied. The people of Mariupol, in their world, were meanwhile putting out Russian flags. They declared Ukraine partitioned and ready to be absorbed within Russia's Union State, just like Belarus.

"Hooray, hooray, hooray! Russia has changed the world. Pride is overwhelming," they shouted online.

Here's what really happened.

On February 24, the Kremlin opted for a full-scale invasion—the most adventurist and risky option of all. This plan was developed by a very limited group of officials and outlined by Putin himself. Most of top Russian civilian and military officials, ironically enough, were not aware that their scripted war hysteria had actually been for real.

This absolute secrecy, however, did not save the plan from being totally exposed by Western intelligence, in great detail.

As is widely known, the whole plan and the decision-making was based on the totally false, chauvinistic perception of Ukraine as not being "a real nation"—that is, not overwhelmingly loyal to its own statehood and, except for a handful of grotesque Nazis and armed nationalists, without the resolve to resist.

Such delusion happens when a system traffics in nothing but good news and rewards subordinates who tell their superiors only what they want to hear. One lie entangles another lie, at every level, up to the highest echelons of the Kremlin.

As a result, here you go with a dangerously overconfident plan of defeating Ukraine within three days amid weak resistance and a governmental collapse.

This was supposed to be a luminous, flawless shock-and-awe campaign that would make history and herald Russia's triumphal return as a military superpower of the twenty-first century. The Kremlin never envisioned the years-long giant meat grinder war it would come to be.

This was planned as a combination of the 1968 Czechoslovakia invasion and the 1979 Operation-333 in Kabul. Groups of elite airborne and special forces would seize key airfields, secure the ground for more landing forces, paralyze key governance functions, and eliminate the political leadership, all clearing the way for the main occupation forces.

Thus, "the special military operation." Not a war.

The Antonov Airport was the linchpin. It's located just northwest of Kyiv, less than one hundred kilometers away from the Belarusian border. The vast expanses of the Dnipro river and the woods of the Chornobyl Exclusion Zone spread out all the way north to Russia's lodgment area in occupied Belarus.

The Ukrainian airfield is located just kilometers away from the E373 Warsaw Highway running straight into Hostomel and is surrounded by dense woodlands. And it's perfect for landing Il-76s, aircraft that can carry hundreds of troops and vehicles.

Securing Hostomel, with Ukrainian air defenses wiped out and its ground forces disoriented and demoralized, shouldn't have been a major problem. It was to be shockingly rapid and bold.

Major ground forces were to follow at a great speed and, with total Russian air supremacy, overwhelm the paralyzed Ukrainian military, in Kyiv, the south, Donbas, and elsewhere.

But.

Approximately several days before the H-hour, in a great rush and acting on extensive intelligence from the West and of its own, the Ukrainian military did everything it could to dodge the blow. It dispersed its forces and munitions from bases and arsenals. Just hours before the invasion, the Ukrainian Air Force also moved its aircraft and air defense systems.

As a result, the initial massive missile attack failed to totally disrupt the Ukrainian defense. The country's command and control systems and military stockpiles largely survived the first crushing blow.

In many instances, Russian strikes were inaccurate or totally futile. In one of Ukraine's military bases in Kyiv Oblast, a Russian Kalibr missile destroyed nothing but the facility's summer dining hall.

Moreover, during the missile bombardment and air assaults, Russia made a critical mistake in its battle damage assessment. It failed to double-check whether a target was actually destroyed.

As a result, a lot of clever deception came into play. Ukrainian air units took aerial pictures of their damaged aircraft hangars, then printed those images on enormous sheets of paper and covered their hangars to imitate damage. They then could go on using those facilities the Russians believed were confirmed as destroyed.

To Russia's great surprise, the Ukrainian Air Force survived and took up the fight.

A lot of things went terribly wrong on the Ukrainian side, too.

Despite multiple Western warnings, the Ukrainian military quite rationally expected the main attack line to be in Donbas, where Russia had the largest force. What Russia had amassed near Kyiv was considered insufficient and therefore seen as a secondary threat meant to divert Ukrainian forces from the east and the south.

And there was always the major issue of full mobilization. As the attacking side, Russia had the benefit of determining timing. In the event of aggressive Ukrainian mobilization prior to the invasion, the Kremlin could comfortably reschedule. And wait for as long as necessary as Ukraine's economy effectively crumbled before the war even began.

The Ukrainian command had to choose.

And they had to distinguish between Russia's actual intensions and possible deception. As a result, they opted for what seemed to be the most logical and rational plan of invasion. More than ten Ukrainian regular brigades were deployed to hold on to the Donbas front and buy time for the country's mobilization.

Up to 50 percent of the Ukrainian military power was committed to the east.

The bulk of Ukraine's 4th Rapid Response Brigade guarding the Antonov Airport was deployed to Donbas in February. That's despite direct warnings from CIA chief William Burns about a possible

Russian landing in Hostomel that he personally brought to Kyiv in January.

And, in the final moments, it turned out that the Russians nonetheless went for the riskiest assault possible.

What we had against the main Russian strike in Kyiv Oblast: the 72nd Mechanized, the 44th Artillery, the Territorial Defense Forces, the 40th Tactical Aviation Brigade, as well as elements of special operations forces, the National Guard units, and a handful of volunteer paramilitaries.

The skeleton staff of Ukraine's Rapid Response Brigade had to lead conscripts into a battle with Russia's elite 45th Airborne and down advancing helicopters with MANPADs.

But by the end of the day, a fierce Ukrainian counterattack spearheaded by the National Guard and special forces, with air and artillery support, effectively pushed the Russians out of the Antonov.

Survivors retreated and disappeared into the forests of Kyiv Oblast.

The Russian Il-76s expected to bring more reinforcements never came. Later, Ukrainian forces rendered the Antonov runway unusable for large transport aircraft.

This was a very sudden—and definitive—failure of one of the first key steps to seize Kyiv in an audacious and overwhelming rush. It was supposed to be a brilliant triumph of Russia's elite VDV force upon which the Russian command relied so heavily.

Instead, there was a smoking moonscape heaped with dead bodies and destroyed assault helicopters on the Antonov takeoff strip.

But that was just the beginning.

Gargantuan Russian columns were moving toward the city on the ground, blazing through everything standing in their way.

The Battle of Kyiv was about to kick the gates of hell wide open.

Two fifty-two A.M.

Ivan stirs me awake as I slowly succumb to sleep in the passenger seat. "Look! Look!"

Swarms of Ukrainian attack helicopters roar near Vinnytsya. Probably bound north for Kyiv. Time and again, white armored SUVs marked "OSCE" outpace the slowly moving traffic on the road to Moldova.

So much for the international monitoring mission . . .

5:06 A.M.

We finally make it to Sokyryany.

Twelve hours on the road.

A small and very quiet town close to the border with Moldova. A tiny shelter in the dying world.

Those window lights have expected us all night long.

Natalia and her parents welcome us at the front door and immediately set out the table.

I'm not seeing straight. I haven't slept for like sixty hours.

"Thank you for your hospitality" is all I'm able to murmur to our hosts. "Sorry, I need to get some sleep."

If you ever need tips on how to have the world's worst meet-and-greet with your partner's mom and dad, feel free to contact me.

Natalia takes my hand and leads me to the nearest double bed.

Without getting undressed, I pull the pillow over my head and crash on a dime.

Happy thirtieth birthday to me.

Vladimir V. Putin of Moscow is more than welcome to give me the greatest birthday present ever by shooting himself in the fucking throat.

TWELVE

I wake up mad as a hornet.

The warm bed, the sweet silence, the mild midday light seeping through the window. There's no one else in the room. Somebody in this house thoughtfully covered my senseless body after I passed out several hours before.

Checking the work chat and the news.

Zelensky has declared full mobilization. Russian tanks stopped at a crossroad near Ivankiv. That's nearly halfway between the Chornobyl Exclusion Zone and the outskirts of Kyiv. Guys from the *Kyiv Independent* are leaving the city, too.

Railroad communications are still working in Kyiv. But tens of thousands of people are trying to make it onto any train out of the city. Rumors have it that the train cars are for evacuating women and children only. And for foreigners.

An ambushed Russian armored advance group is burning on a highway near Hostomel.

That's the news so far.

It's a single-floor, one-family cottage with a garage and a fruit garden in the backyard. A village guy like myself can't help but appreciate the mild crackling of firewood in the heating stove.

I quietly push open the door into the house's main area.

Everyone is already sitting at the dining table in the kitchen. Including Ivan and, surprisingly, Denys of *Forbes Ukraine*. Last night, at the last moment, he suddenly changed his mind and decided to stick with us.

But it was too late. The Kyiv subway wasn't running. There was no thought of even attempting to get a taxi. Kyiv was paralyzed from east to west. Its streets a solid parking lot.

A friend of mine trying to flee the city got to his car with his wife early in the morning. They lived downtown and decided to take the worst way possible—Peremohy Avenue, Kyiv's main thoroughfare. And they ended up stuck in the monstrous jam, barely moving over the next twenty-four hours of war.

But Denys and his cat got lucky. Natalia's friends were also fleeing Kyiv toward Chernivtsi, so we arranged for them to scoop up the guy and his beloved cat and bring him to our new refuge.

"Look who's up now, our big-time sleeper." Natalia smiles as she sees my rumpled face.

Her mom bustles about at the stove with her oven mitts on.

"You're just in time!" She puts a bunch of hot pancakes on a plate and pours some condensed milk over the stack. "Have a seat now, come on."

Hot coffee, pancakes, chocolate, cheese, a vegetable salad. My friends still feel somewhat shy, but they eagerly shovel everything in.

Natalia's mom, Galyna, is the model Ukrainian homemaker. Extremely lively, restless, and always going to extremes to give her guests the warmest possible welcome.

"Guys, guys, guys, are you up for sausages? Oh, I also have varenyky in the fridge. Let's boil some for you all now."

"Mom, that's okay, we have more than enough. We're stuffed," Natalia says.

Her mom is not even listening.

"The boys are all tired from the road, they need to have a decent dinner now. Illia, why don't you eat? Come on, have a bite."

"Thank you, thank you, thank you." My friends cherish her.

Natalia's father, Oleksandr, is just the opposite of his wife's beaming energy. In his late fifties, he's gray and rather silent. He walks into the kitchen to see his guests now and then and to ask: "You doing all right now, boys?"

And again and again, he retreats to his computer corner in the living room to see what's in the news. All the country's largest TV networks are broadcasting the same news telethon, their anchors going live from various sheltered compounds.

> . . . The Ukrainian military continue fighting at Antonivsky Bridge over the Dnipro near Kherson . . . we have reports saying that Ukrainian defenders had to withdraw from the city of Henichesk . . . Marine Vitaliy Skakun of the 137th Naval Infantry Battalion sacrificed his life blowing up an automobile bridge to stop advancing Russian tanks . . .

Natalia's dad walks out of the house to have another cigarette alone.

His right arm is almost dysfunctional and secured across his chest. A pinched nerve or something of the kind. He's been suffering from the condition for quite a while.

Natalia's parents are both teachers at the local school. Galyna teaches history. Oleksandr offers classes in computer science. And to survive beyond a Ukrainian teacher's poor wages, they also maintain their orchard and sell fruit to juice manufacturers.

"How are you, guys?" I ask Ivan and Denys.

"Fine," Ivan answers dryly.

As Natalia told me, last night, after I conked out, they couldn't calm Ivan down. He sat at the dining table, gulping whiskey from my backpack, and he didn't stop talking. On, and on, and on.

People tend to react to shock and trauma in different ways.

Denys can't stop cracking his favorite dad jokes. His cat is frightened in this new uncharted territory so far from home, and he's huddling underneath a bathtub. Denys later tries to talk to his pet (literally) and coax him out from his hiding place.

My mom is silently freaking out. She's bitterly upset that I forced her to leave her sweet little home in Donbas and brought her to this place. Of course, her emotional distress is to be expected. Her world has just collapsed. That very day, Volnovakha would see the first brutal shelling across many of its residential areas.

The Russian military was quickly approaching Volnovakha from the south and the east.

And I'm mad as hell inside, even as I try to stay calm and look complacent. Everything we love and care for in our lives is literally dying, and I'm sitting here and enjoying coffee with pancakes.

Time is moving slowly.

But weirdly enough, in all this warmth and coziness, we relax and come to our senses, step by step. In times like these, people can get along very easily. A short coffee breakfast—and everyone's worst nightmare, meeting one's partner's parents, goes rather smoothly.

"Mom and Dad really like you," Natalia whispers in my ear. "They really appreciate you taking care of your family and friends. And they're also really thankful you made me leave Kyiv when I did."

I sigh.

I wish my mom had listened to me and come to Kyiv before the invasion got underway . . . But yeah, she would have never left Kyiv without me. She's madly stubborn.

"Yeah . . . ," I say. "I hope we're not too much of a burden on your family. My sister will soon take Mom to her place in Moldova. Denys is going to go to Ivano-Frankivsk, where *Forbes Ukraine* has rented a sort of camp in the Carpathians to relocate its writers. And Ivan . . . I think he's off to our friend Maksym's in Lviv. I'll pay your parents for our stay."

"I don't want to listen to this. You stay here."

Natalia's family is also hosting another family from Kyiv. They will couch surf their way to West Ukraine over the coming days.

"You want to hear something funny?" Ivan suddenly perks up.

Before this, he'd spent hours just sitting by himself in a chair, his gaze fixed.

"The other family staying here . . . they're nice people. It seems I once hooked up with the dad on some business in Kyiv. The world really is a small place."

"Let's maybe invite them for a drink in the kitchen?"

"Yeah."

Natalia's mother is already bustling about for a large dinner.

There will be roasted chicken and parsley potatoes with mushroom sauce. It feels like we're having a hearty family weekend in the countryside, with the hosts' neighbors also invited.

Back in Kyiv, city authorities warn residents of the Obolon district to stay away from windows: missiles are approaching the city from the north. Russian subversives have reportedly infiltrated Kyiv with Ukrainian vehicles and uniforms. Here and there in the city, locals record the sound of heavy gunfighting in the streets.

Videos on social media show the police unloading trucks full of ammo boxes. They're giving out hundreds of Kalashnikov rifles in the streets of Obolon to whoever wants to fight.

The last resort of the desperate.

Russians are drawing nearer.

Oh god.

Why I am here, three hundred kilometers away from home.

I need a ride.

Now.

"Listen, buddy . . ." I pull Ivan aside to a quiet room.

"I think I'm going back to Kyiv."

"What?" a flustered Ivan whispers. "Are you nuts? Don't even say that in front of your mother and your girlfriend."

I rub my face and exhale.

"I have to . . . I'll never forgive myself if I don't do it now. Let's go home in the morning. You've got a car, we've got a lot of food, we have a lot of friends still in Kyiv."

Ivan stares into the corner of the room and shakes his head no.

I try to make one more push.

"Man, I need a driver by my side . . . let's give it a try. At least for a couple of days during the battle. The military is taking up the fight. We'll see what the situation is like and what we can do to help. And if shit really gets hot, we'll slip away again."

"I'm not going back to that place . . . I can't."

Ivan has got nothing to get back to in Kyiv, essentially.

He's jobless now. His little iPhone-repair service has closed up shop.

The two other guys working at the company are enlisting in the military. Ivan keeps making phone calls to one of them, named Vetal, only to learn that the guy has waited for more than twenty-four hours in a long line to sign up for the Territorial Defense Forces and get a rifle.

"See?" I'm still trying to persuade Ivan. "All our friends are in Kyiv."

Ivan sighs.

Having faced unexpectedly fierce Ukrainian resistance, Putin issued yet another weird statement on day two of the war. He overtly called on the Ukrainian military to execute a coup d'état. With the failure of the Hostomel gamble, the Kremlin has decided to undermine Ukraine from within.

> Do not let Neo-Nazis and Banderites use your children, your wives, and your elderly as living shields. Take power into your own hands. It looks like it will be easier for us to come to an agreement with you than with that gang of drug addicts and Neo-Nazis that remain in Kyiv and have taken the whole of the Ukrainian people hostage.

Russians were still not getting it.

The Kremlin was still blindly following its own Ukraine delusion. And Kyiv, as evening drew nearer, was bracing for the first major Russian assault.

Tonight . . .

Of course, there was quite a lot of fuss and shock as I announced I'd be going back to Kyiv. But I wasn't listening. The decision has been made. Do not try to talk me out of this.

It's better to do what's right for once than to end up feeling sorry for the rest of one's life.

But that's easier said than done.

In this chaos, there are no buses going anywhere. I neither drive nor have a car. Maybe there will be someone going to Kyiv? Maybe someone wanting to volunteer to fight for the capital city?

I need to make it to at least Vinnytsya, some one hundred kilometers to the northeast. People on Facebook say it's still possible to catch an evacuation train to Kyiv.

As the night progresses, the boys, including Natalia's dad, again gather at the table to talk about boyish things.

We all sound expert-like and move battalions and divisions around on Google Maps, trying to second-guess Russia's plans against Kyiv.

By late February 25, the main Russian forces are nearly one hundred kilometers deep in Kyiv Oblast and have reached the city's northwestern outskirts. The main mechanized force again entered the Antonov Airport near Hostomel, but the runways had already been destroyed.

They also reached the banks of Irpin River, all the way from Demydiv, where the tributary flows into the Dnipro, and down to Hostomel. This thin blue line was shielding Kyiv from the northwest.

The Ukrainian military blew up a bridge connecting the cities of Irpin and Kyiv. This spot was next to the neighborhood Ivan and I lived in. And Russians were moving fast from the northern occupied towns and cities of Kyiv Oblast.

They were already close to the M-07 Warsaw Highway, the northwestern passage to Kyiv coming through Borodyanka, Vorzel, and Bucha. My god, we're talking about places where we used to have awesome bike rides on weekends.

"Chernihiv and Sumy keep holding on," I say. "But the Russians are trying not to get bogged down in fighting. They are bypassing large cities and their defenses and moving deeper along our major highways. Toward the eastern part of Kyiv, I suppose."

In the south, it was an absolute nightmare.

Russians had entered Berdyansk on the Azov coastline. Without a fight. Mariupol was just sixty kilometers farther along the road to the northeast.

Day two. It's a collapse.

"I'm really worried about Belarus," Ivan says. "What if Lukashenko sends his own army against Kyiv? Hasn't he already?"

"I'm actually surprised, but this doesn't seem to be the case yet," I say. "I was sure from the beginning that Putin's mustachioed ass-slave would attack us, too. But I don't think that would make a huge difference now. Lukashenko's army is pretty small and it has no real combat experience."

Natalia's dad rubs his weak arm and sits up, alert.

"In the Soviet army, as a sergeant, I had Belarusian guys in my fire section. And let me tell you one thing, young men: Belarusians stand up for one another. They will fight like hell if they see one of them killed."

We still sit together talking in the kitchen.

There are reports of heavy fighting in Vasylkiv, south of Kyiv, at the 40th Tactical Aviation Brigade base. Russians are supposedly trying to seize another airfield. How come? That's twenty-five kilometers south of the city, over forty kilometers away from Russia's nearest positions at Hostomel.

Are our defenses so loose that the Russians have managed to send a force large enough to try to capture one so deep in our rear?

The Ukrainian Air Force says at least one Russian Il-76 airlift has been downed at twelve thirty A.M. local time . . . then, after three twenty, another Russian aircraft reportedly downed near Bila Tserkva.

Are they trying to airdrop more troops to seize Vasylkiv? How is that possible?

My heart is beating hard. This will be another endless night.

Keep holding on, my sweet little home.

Everyone except me is in bed.

At some point, Natalia's dad goes back outside to have another cigarette. The pain from his arm makes sleep difficult. Full of his thoughts, he quietly paces about his house.

Eventually, he finds me alone in the kitchen in front of my laptop.

"I am coming to Kyiv, too."

I look up at him. Not a bad start, given the fact that I've been seeing his daughter for less than three months. During dinner, he even gave me one of his hunting knives as a birthday present. But dang, a year later, I learned that he had purchased it on AliExpress.

"Sure . . . sure."

Of course, he wants to. This is how the world works. It has always been this way since the dawn of time.

But his arm . . . it's bad. He can't drive for long, and Kyiv is at least a seven-hour drive away. And I don't drive at all.

Anyway, we'll figure out something in the morning. Good night . . .

I quietly slip into a bedroom and crouch by Natalia's side. But no, sleep must wait. The dramatic night rages on through my iPhone.

In Kyiv, insane fighting just outside the Beresteiska subway station. Pictures on Twitter show a large plume of fire. Russian subversive groups are already on the city's main avenue ten kilometers inside Kyiv's outer limits, media say . . .

They are attacking the 101st General Staff Protection Brigade base. The Dehtyrivska Street overpass running over Peremohy Avenue, a place so familiar . . . Streetlights illuminate the plumes of smoke from the fighting. People living in houses along the street witness a dramatic fight right outside their windows in the dead of night.

Breathing hard.

Natalia wakes up.

"Dad wants to come with you, doesn't he?"

"He does."

Natalia quietly sheds tears.

"I know you won't listen to me . . . but Dad . . . He can barely hold a spoon in his hand."

Yes, that's true. But there's also this sense of duty always beating in the chest. Everybody must do his or her part. That's going to be hard, counterintuitive, dangerous, maybe even futile.

But at least, when the moment comes, we'll know we did the right thing. Or, if we're lucky, many years after, we'll remember these days with pride and peace of mind.

Get some sleep now. We'll talk about it more in the morning.

Closer to sunrise, good news pops up in live feeds.

The attack on Vasylkiv is repelled. The Russian subversive group at the Beresteiska subway station is destroyed. An enemy tank, two trucks, and several lighter cars have been demolished.

Morning comes to Kyiv again.

That was indeed a dramatic night. Not only in the sense of a giant death army standing at the gate. But also in terms of the deadly mayhem within the city itself, especially after nightfall.

Kyiv had been overtaken with a contagion of spy fever. Rumors about Russian subversives dressed in Ukrainian fatigues spread rapidly, fueled by official statements. Heaven knows how many Ukrainian personnel were fired on and arrested, or even killed at checkpoints.

In that mess, reports of "Russian tanks breaking into Obolon" seemed credible, and they gave license to all sorts of hotheads. In numerous ill-fated episodes, the Ukrainian police, military, National Guard, and the local militia immediately opened fire on vehicles they couldn't identify as friendly in the city.

The same was happening to countless ambulances and civilian cars that seemed suspicious.

What happened that night at the Beresteiska wasn't a clash with a Russian combat group that had suddenly materialized out of nowhere deep in the city. As we now know, at least eight Ukrainian soldiers with the 101st Brigade were killed by friendly fire as they moved along the city avenue in the night.

We still do not have any clear evidence that Russians indeed managed to attack Vasylkiv. No evidence of any Russian airlifts downed were ever found. Just as there were no confirmed Russian fatalities.

The mayhem of the first days of the Battle of Kyiv caused a lot of grief.

But we're moving on.

The sun rises again.

The grand war's day three begins.

And it opens with the image of a twenty-six-story residential building on Lobanovskoho Avenue hit by a Russian missile. Russians were likely trying to hit the Zhulyany Airport, just a kilometer away.

Instead, a chunk of the building between the seventeenth and eighteenth floors is ripped off. The tattered remains of individual apartments yawn in the dust.

The mayor of Chernihiv posts a video address calling on fellow townspeople to get ready for urban combat. All are invited to come to Territorial Defense stations in the city to help prepare Molotovs.

Natalia's mother serves us a very rich breakfast again.

Ivan silently blows on his mug of hot coffee. And then, out of the blue, he goes: "I've been thinking here . . . we're going home."

For the love of god, for crying out loud . . .

Finally.

Of course, we are.

We came to Kyiv six years ago, and the city gave us a new life. We started by renting a crappy hovel in the distant suburbs, got low-paid jobs, and teased ourselves with inexpensive cheesecakes from the nearest grocery on Fridays.

This city had given us so much. It gave us opportunities, new friends, a chance to work hard and move forward in life. And we knew and loved every single corner of Kyiv. We had nowhere else to go, realistically.

If the story is coming to an end, we want to be with our city in its finest hour.

Thank you, Grandpa Winston, for this lesson in wisdom.

We're going home because it's the right thing to do. We'll see how we can help in the battle for our capital. We'll probably have a couple of days. And then it doesn't matter.

Natalia's dad is more taciturn and gloomier than ever. Again and again, he walks out to have a cigarette and comes back to look at us laughing behind the breakfast table. And he keeps binding up his weak arm with an elastic bandage, as if that relieves him of pain.

Of course, he can't go. On the edge of the great unknown, with the nation going into an enormous battle, his daughter's tears stop him.

Well, he's not going to lie back idly. In the coming weeks, he'll collect clothes and food for war refugees, and along with two other male teachers from his school, he'll take on night watch duties and deliver humanitarian aid.

Finally, the last hugs goodbye.

"You take care over there, boys," Natalia's father says as he puts fuel canisters into Ivan's trunk. "And come back as guests early and safe."

Natalia's mom makes the sign of the cross over us and puts more canned food into the car.

"Please go to Moldova," I tell my mom. "Your daughter is ready to welcome you."

"I will not," she replies and puts something into my jacket's pocket. It's a small Christian icon. And a piece of paper with a handwritten prayer on it.

Goodbye, all.

We're going home.

We feel like eagles flying free.

The world is falling apart, but let's listen to heavy metal and keep the stupid jokes coming. At a National Guard checkpoint at the Dniester hydroelectric power plant, there's an enormous, kilometers-long queue of cars moving toward Moldova.

People wait for so long that they get out of cars and helplessly stare at the wide river in front of them. We are the only ones moving the opposite direction, with no obstacles whatsoever.

I poke my head out of the car.

"What's up, dudes, why so many of y'all over here?" I yell against the wind. "Is there a war or something?"

Ivan chuckles.

We're going home!

I shoot a message to Natalia.

"How are you?"

"I'm devastated . . . but I'll get through this. Don't worry."

"Just remember that we're not going to take risks . . . I'm not going to blow it when I have such a great girlfriend."

"I'm glad you understand this. And I'm glad the meet-and-greet parents thing went so smoothly. And please don't worry about your mom. She's in shock, but we'll take care of her. We're going to take a walk in the town tonight."

"Thank you . . . our village near Volnovakha has been occupied. I've been told our house is damaged from the fighting."

"Yes, your mom knows that. Your neighbors told her by phone."

We're moving on up north along deserted highways.

Here and there, utility workers remove road signs indicating names of cities and towns and distances.

Local townsfolk near villages, mostly men carrying their own hunting shotguns, bring down trees and hastily erect barricades and checkpoints. Their arms are marked with yellow tape tied over their everyday civilian clothes.

The Territorial Defense militia in action.

The whole country is diving into the gloom of war.

Judging from these preparations, the Russians must be expected to reach the very heartland of Ukraine. And soon.

At some point on the road, a new internet hit pops up.

Westerners are very quick to create fresh memes and have even begun selling T-shirts featuring Zelensky's face.

"I need ammo, not a ride."

Who could have thought that our guy from that dumb comedy show, whom many in Ukraine perceived of as a joke of a nothingburger, would be a globally admired wartime leader one day?

". . . we are all here." Zelensky says, making a selfie video with his colleagues outside on Bankova Street late on February 25. "The parliament faction leader is here, the chief of the presidential office is here, the prime minister is here, adviser Podolyak is here, the president is here. We are all here. Defending our independence and our nationhood. And that's how it's going to be . . ."

And meanwhile, Russian propaganda was running its mouth off trying to guess where Zelensky and his people had already fled to—was that America, Poland, or Turkey? All life is a mystery, indeed.

At entrances to major cities, like Vinnytsya, there are giant traffic jams. At every corner, police patrols stop cars and check the hell out of them, down to our pants and mobile phones.

A bridge on the Zhytomyr Highway has been blown up. So we try to enter Kyiv from the south—the Odesa road.

Bila Tserkva, Vasylkiv . . . and finally, in the dark of the last day of February, the southern outskirts of Kyiv.

On the E95 Highway, a giant queue at an entry checkpoint.

But Ivan still knows how to do some magic with opposite lanes. And we slip away from the crowded highway onto a tiny suburban road in Hatne.

A Territorial Defense guy waves his hand in the darkness to invite us into his checkpoint.

"Watch out," the guard says, peeping into our car window. "We've been told missiles are incoming."

Thanks, bud.

And here we are on the Kyiv Beltway.

We still have less than an hour to go until curfew.

"Look at this all," Ivan says mournfully. "The city is empty."

There's no one else on the multilane motorway close to the Zhulyany Airport. Streetlights illuminate nothing but the mist and road markings. High-rises and giant malls are all lost in the shadows.

Somewhere far away in the east, a bright orange arrow of fire soars up into the sky from beyond the skyline.

"Holy shit, S-300s working."

Another arrow bristling.

A heavy blast roars behind our backs. Russian missiles have reached their target.

"Go, go, go!"

No luck tonight.

We drive on toward our neighborhood.

There's absolute silence. No cars in the streets. Almost no window lights. Barely any cars in parking lots, where one normally must fight for every space.

It's a ghost city in the dark.

Just one more police checkpoint near our house: "Territorial Defense, the 6th company."

Finally, some thirty minutes to curfew, we enter our apartment and put our food stocks into plastic bags at the front door.

We are back.

It's only been several days, but it feels like we're unsealing a long-forgotten vault many years after the apocalypse. In our building's section of several dozen apartments, we are alone.

There's absolute, deathly quiet. As if we're trapped in the middle of a space void, surrounded by millions of kilometers of empty cold and dark.

The first thing we do is cut up the huge cardboard box my bicycle was shipped in and cover all our windows.

And we dim all lights.

The less visible we are in the night, the better.

Welcome to living in a city under siege.

THIRTEEN

The morning begins with the very fascinating procedure of unspooling Scotch tape in crisscross patterns over all our windows.

It's a useful thing in wartime. But holy cow, I may regret this if there ever comes a time when I'll want to rasp them clean.

The date is February 28, 2022.

The battle situation status: gruesome.

The defiant Russian jump at the Antonov Airport has failed. And now they're switching to plan B: an outright frontal assault on the ground.

Giant Russian forces move quickly along roads leading to the northwestern outskirts of Kyiv.

Swarms of vehicles marked "V" have broken through Ukrainian defenses in the forests of Ivankiv and entered Borodyanka, where the northern road running from the Chornobyl Exclusion Zone crosses the E373 Warsaw Highway. From there it runs straight east to Vorzel, Bucha, and Hostomel.

Also, they are moving south to sever the M-06 Zhytomyr Highway, the western entryway straight into Kyiv. Two other major roads—the M-05 Odesa Highway and the M-03 Poltava Highway—remain free.

And they gain a foothold on the banks of the Irpin River from Demydiv to Hostomel—basically, the capital city's northwestern boundary. All along the river, the Ukrainian military have blown up every bridge leading into the city—from Hostomel, Irpin, Stoyanka.

From the start, the Russians bet on speed and little resistance from Ukrainian units that were supposed to be demoralized and disorganized.

No luck so far. A Russian column ripped to pieces in Bucha's Vokzalna Street on its way into Irpin on February 28th. An even bigger column of lightly armed Rosgvardiya completely devastated on the bridge over the Irpin just east of Bucha.

Vorzel is occupied, but Bucha, Irpin City, and most of Hostomel are holding on. Heavy fighting concentrates in Kyiv's northeastern outer districts.

This is where the action is.

The head of the Kyiv defense is General Oleksandr Syrsky, the ground forces commander.

In the beginning, he has mainly the 72nd Mechanized and 43rd Artillery brigades, Special Operations units, the 112th Territorial Defense militia, National Guard units, the police, and self-organized paramilitaries.

Meanwhile, the Russians in Kyiv Oblast will end up with nearly thirty thousand troops, including the elite 76th Airborne Division, elements of the 29th, 35th, and 36th combined armies, as well as the Spetsnaz and the 155th Naval Infantry Brigade from as far away as the Pacific Ocean.

Also, numerous Rosgvardiya and special police units—ready to baton-charge civilian protesters in Kyiv, after it is occupied.

East of Kyiv, the Russians are trying to move with speed toward the Chernihiv and Sumy areas. Their communication lines stretch along large highways running through woodlands and turn out to be highly vulnerable to constant Ukrainian ambush. Entire Russian columns are obliterated near Nizhyn and Pryluky on the M-02 and H-07 highways, over one hundred kilometers from Kyiv.

In Chernihiv and Sumy, fierce battles rage that keep the enormous Russian forces from advancing on Kyiv. Kharkiv is still holding on, too. Even though Russian forces have made it to the city's outer circular road to the north. On February 27, a Russian Spetsnaz column of nearly ten Tirg vehicles and several trucks burst into the city only to be wiped out by the defending Ukrainians.

Speaking of Russian tactical signs.

In the invasion's early days, there was a lot of wild speculation about the menacing symbols painted white on the dark green of the enemy armor.

It's now more or less clear that "Z," the new swastika of yet another war of Lebensraum in Europe, denoted groups of Russian forces commanded by the Western ("Zapadny") Military District concentrated in Kursk, Voronezh, Belgorod, and occupied Donbas.

This group was to encircle and cut off a large Ukrainian military group stationed in Donbas.

Forces marked with "Z in a square" were commanded by Southern Military District headquarters and concentrated in Crimea. They were in charge of Ukraine's south from Odesa to Mariupol.

The group "V," commanded by the Eastern ("Vostochny") Military District, was to attack Kyiv's west flank from Belarus. The group "O" was commanded by the Central Military District and concentrated in Russia's Bryansk region. Their task was to surround Kyiv from the east.

Why did the crusaders of the "Russian World" opt for Latin letters? My own guess is that Latin tactical signs were simple, eye-catching, and easy to recognize from a distance. And the Cyrillic letter "В" (for "Восточный") instead of "V" could be easily misinterpreted as the number "8," and Russian letter "З" (for "Западный") instead of "Z" could resemble the number 3.

So, in the Battle of Kyiv, we had to deal with "V" and "O."

Three of us from the *Kyiv Independent* made it back to the city in the battle's first days to work: our Ukrainian-American journalist Igor Kossov, our investigative reporter Anna Myroniuk, and yours truly.

It was time to experience wartime Kyiv, firsthand.

My favorite tactical jacket, the PRESS shoulder patch, and the olive kaffiyeh are back in action.

The city grew dark and gloomy.

Same streets, same buildings, but it was hard to recognize the place we'd known. Kyiv was cluttered with endless stockades of rust-colored anti-tank hedgehogs.

Peremohy Avenue, the city's main thoroughfare, had been transformed into a twenty-kilometer barrier line. At every crossroad, a barricade or a strongpoint of concrete blocks. Old, nonfunctional BTRs scattered here and there on roads as obstacles.

Also—digital billboards show nothing but messages to uninvited guests in Russian: "Russian soldier! Don't be a murderer! Think about your families and get back home alive!" Or, in some places, a bit less diplomatic: "Russian warship, go fuck yourself!"

The city was very empty.

Civilian movement was generally pretty free, but hardly a fraction of Kyiv's usual traffic moved about. The four-million-person capital city had turned into a grieving ghost under the depressing sky.

Almost no venues were open. A handful of supermarkets and pharmacies opened as normal for several hours until around three P.M. And many people, especially in densely populated commuter belts, had to wait in endless lines to buy just enough food or fresh water to get by.

Ivan and I drive on, bound for the city center.

My suddenly jobless roommate is starting a brand-new career in media—he's our driver now. And believe me when I tell you, it wasn't an easy job. In the early weeks of the battle, there was an enormous shortage of fuel available to the civilian population.

Ivan had to apply every last ounce of his talent as a car enthusiast to finding bits of gas here and there in the city.

At the Akademmistechko subway station, a fifty-meter-long queue at the NOVUS supermarket stretched out into the parking lot in front of the mall.

"A guy I know from the neighborhood told me last night he had waited for several hours," says Ivan as we move down the road. "All in vain, he didn't make it. And the morning after, the shelves were almost empty."

Life in the city broke down in a heartbeat.

The shock detonated all supply chains. And hundreds of thousands of people were still living here with their everyday needs. Getting things like pet food became a quest, with many people sharing information online on pet shops still open and with available supplies.

Near the Beresteiska subway station, you could still see the charred frames of the "Russian trucks" that came under fire on February 26.

The Territorial Defense militia struck a white commercial van on the road and furnished it with a menacing caption: WELCOME TO HELL. Under all bridges, heaps of tank traps lay in the ready.

In the very heart of Kyiv, Kherschatyk Street, nothing is open. No restaurants, no coffee shops, no fashion boutiques.

Nothing but the rare pedestrian roaming amid fields of metal crosses on Maidan Square. And several Territorial Defense troops filling sandbags at an Instytutska Street intersection.

The Independence Monument still proudly rising high.

The Maidan, the place it all began.

Almost a decade ago, in 2013, we were very young and hot-tempered. Even young people from Ukraine's Russian-speaking east, like myself.

We grew up hearing phrases like "the Euro-Atlantic integration." In high schools and universities, we were engrossed in reading Montesquieu and soaked up tantalizing concepts like the rule of law, democracy, and human rights.

We grew up fully integrated into the Western worldview and values. We were a generation open to the world around us as never before, unlike so many of our parents, whose lifetime's greatest journey was the Soviet Army conscription service in Central Asia and maybe even the 1980 Olympics in Moscow.

We wanted clean streets, polite police, and government officials who resign when confronted with petty corruption scandals. We wanted to be able to start a business without passing money under the table and to trust that the courts of law would render justice.

We did not want irremovable, lifetime dictators who packed their governments at every level with corrupt cronies flush with ill-gotten cash. We did not want these creeps to tell us what to do. We wanted governments that serve the nation's will instead of releasing their goons to beat us up in our streets.

Moscow and the Kremlin were not the center of the universe to us anymore. It was New York City and Brussels.

We were idealistic and thrilled.

So, when in November 2013 Yanukovych boldly refused to sign the association agreement with the EU, there was just one thought in everyone's head—revolution.

There was almost a physical need to stand up and give free reign to our youthful ambition to make history here and now.

And, just like so many others across Ukraine, we joined pro-Europe rallies whose times and places could be found on an online map.

First, Mariupol, just a handful of students and a couple of university lecturers with handwritten picket signs.

Then—Maidan Square.

Our parents told us not to mess with the strong and the powerful. But hell no—we were not slipping back into Moscow's embrace just because Putin palmed Yanukovych a $3 billion bribe.

We were not of that kind anymore.

When my university buddy and I were on a night train bound for Kyiv, a piece of news came: Riot police had violently dispersed a student rally on the Maidan just as it was winding down. All hell broke loose across the country.

The following day, November 30, the Maidan was fully occupied by Berkut riot police. I remember a full-fledged company of "cosmonauts," as we called them, descending to Kherschatyk from Instytutska Street, with their black helmets and batons glistening.

The protest shifted to Mykhailivska Square up the hill, with huge crowds demanding justice for the crackdown. Cars passing the square leaned hard on their horns to express support.

"They think they can batter our children?" somebody yelled into a microphone. "No, they can't! And we will prove them wrong!"

And then, on December 1, an endless sea of people swarmed the heart of Kyiv. There were no less than one million in the streets that day. Everyday citizens, common people, no political symbols. Many came with their kids in strollers.

The revolution had begun.

And then, months later, in the early days of March 2014, a scorched battlefield on the Maidan—the place where month-long street battles with the riot police had culminated in the massacre of February.

The embattled square had been turned into a giant fortress of barricades and tents set up on a thick layer of ash and broken glass.

And flowers.

Literally endless armloads of flowers brought to the site of desolation to commemorate the dead of our tragic revolution.

Yanukovych fled the country that despised him and which had spiraled out of his control.

That was the beginning of a new Ukraine. And—the beginning of a decade-long war of independence. The Kremlin, full of wrath and thirst for revenge, was already sending its unmarked soldiers to seize Crimea. We lost the peninsula in March.

And in April, the war in Donbas erupted. Retired Russian FSB operative Igor Girkin and some fifty armed men under his command crossed the border and seized the Ukrainian city of Slovyansk.

But now, in late February 2022, eight years after, who says the anti-tank hedgehogs on the Maidan mark this long endeavor's bitter end?

We decide what's next for us in our city.

I couldn't resist a selfie next to the Independence Monument. Now Twitter will see the power of our resolve in this city: "Fuck you, Putin, your death army sucks ass."

After the first four or five days of the Battle of Kyiv, it was obvious that the initial Russian plan had gone off the rails.

There wouldn't be an easy and fast takeover. The grand offensive in the north was stalling.

If Russia wanted to seize Kyiv, it would have to fight a hard and extremely costly battle, including the carnage of urban warfare in the city.

Starting from approximately February 28, the Russian military began sending large reinforcements from Belarus to the Kyiv theater.

The very fact that Russia agreed to hold the first round of direct talks with Ukraine without any preconditions as early as February 27 was telling. That signaled quite a change since February 24, when the Kremlin boldly issued simple demands of surrender to Kyiv via deputy prime minister Dmitry Kozak and then via the Belarusian defense minister Viktor Khrenin.

The talks were of course totally pointless. The Russians had nothing to offer but ultimatums about Ukraine installing a pro-Kremlin government, dropping its rapprochement with the West, and giving up on Donbas and Crimea.

But there was another dark issue hanging over our heads: the Belarusian military.

Since the Russian blitz failed to bring a fast victory, it seemed just a matter of time before Putin would drag his puppet Lukashenko into the war.

Diplomatic cables indicated Lukashenko's army was preparing to join the invasion. Our sources close to Ukraine's Ministry of Defense told of the first Ilyushin Il–76 transport aircraft preparing to take off with a load of elite Belarusian paratroopers at five A.M. local time on February 28.

An extensive anti-war info campaign targetting Belarusian service members and anti-Lukashenko activists kicked into gear.

As part of this, for instance, the retired high-ranking Belarusian airborne commander Valeriy Sakhaschik (he's friends with our big guy Zaluzhny, by the way), on February 27 issued a tremendous video statement to all Belarusian paratroopers:

> The Russian military with its vast military experience has just had its three days in hell. The death toll runs into thousands, there are hundreds taken prisoner, rear hospitals are swamped with those wounded in action. No operational objectives have been achieved. Neither Kyiv nor any regional capitals have been captured.

The Russian military is already quite exhausted. And Ukrainians have endured the first and the hardest seventy-two hours, successfully launched the mobilization, got organized, adjusted their logistics, received global support, both moral and technical.

And most importantly, they've realized that their attackers are mortal men. They've stopped fearing and have tasted victory. This army will never retreat or surrender now.

Russians have become victims of their own propagandists who vowed the Ukrainians would welcome them as liberators. But you know everything now . . . This is not our war. You will not defend your fatherland, your home, and your family. You will not obtain glory but shame, humiliation, and blood, death, and the status of rogue nation for the Belarusian people for decades. Brothers, find a way to avoid this quagmire.

It remains to be seen why exactly Russia's would-be ally blinked. Whether it was an extensive diplomatic effort from Kyiv, or low Belarusian morale, or Lukahsenko's stubborn unwillingness to follow Putin into the abyss. Perhaps all of the above.

One thing was clear—Russians were suffering surprisingly heavy losses. Starting from day two or three, there began an unbelievable, staggering torrent of reports of destroyed Russian columns, especially near Chernihiv and Kharkiv. Not just official Ukrainian military communiqués— pictures and videos of scorched debris directly from the battlefields.

Dozens, if not hundreds of servicemen yielding themselves as prisoners of war—often poorly equipped, dirty, hungry, disoriented. Yesterday's conscripts frightened to death after relentless road ambushes.

At some point in late February, somebody sent me an email.

It read "Please keep my anonymity" in Russian. A media file was attached. A WhatsApp voice message recording.

A sad female voice spoke against the backdrop of music coming from a TV and baby chatter and laughter.

"Hello, girls . . . We're having a clusterfuck in Aleysk . . . our tank brigade was totally destroyed. Out of 150 guys, just 18 survived. The first batch of coffins is coming today."

The voice begins weeping.

"Forty-five KIAs in zinc coffins coming to us in Aleysk, parents are waiting. Our upstairs neighbor has been killed, a young boy, he had a year-old kid . . . A whole fucking lot of them. Three or four from our factory, the rest were from the city and villages. Young boys, contracted members.

"We learned that yesterday, and now we're all crying our eyes out. It's a madness . . . here they go with the fucking war."

Holy shit.

Googling . . . The city of Aleysk, Russia's Altai region, 3,500 kilometers away from Ukraine. Home to Russia's 35th Guards Motorized Rifle Brigade. The woman on the recording is probably talking about one of the brigade's companies.

The 35th has indeed been seen and battered near Chernihiv . . . for instance, the brigade's tank battalion leader, Major Leonid Shetkin, lost several tanks and was taken prisoner. Twisted into a pretzel with a lot of duct tape by Ukrainian troops.

The woman on the recording also mentioned a Russian serviceman named Yegneniy Zhilin. And yes, the Russian social media network VK used to have a profile under that name. City of residence: Aleysk, Russia. The profile had already been deleted.

And meanwhile, at that point, the Russian military publicly admitted no losses in Ukraine whatsoever.

I sent a brief reply to the anonymous Russian: "Thank you."

Heaps of twisted metal, concrete debris, and cars turned upside down litter the road out of Irpin. It is scarred but it is the road of life for many.

People come to the destroyed bridge over the river by the dozen. Some come on foot with nothing but a couple of handbags. Others are lucky owners of bicycles they carry in their arms as they dash through a pathway of broken wood planks and concrete slabs.

Those fleeing the war leave their cars forever on a highway at the bridge's frayed edge. They take all they can carry and hastily descend to the riverbed without a backward glance. People leave behind suitcases and baby strollers.

Somebody even dumped a dozen good turkey carcasses in the middle of the highway.

The lines of abandoned cars on the highway grows longer with every hour.

To the north, toward Irpin and Bucha, the constant, heavy rolls of artillery blasts.

A couple of Ukrainian soldiers and policemen stand among the bridge's rubble and help young mothers with their crying babies.

"Come on, no need to rush, careful, just like that." They take the elderly gingerly by their elbows.

Several men try to carry an old man in a wheelchair over the battered crossing. Waiting on the other side is a line of yellow buses and the road straight to Kyiv and relative safety.

The salvation.

A nearby parking lot at the Fora supermarket is a sort of a rendezvous point for a crowd of journalists, Ukrainians and foreigners.

The military has told us not to stick our necks out for the time being. So, we hang out behind the wall of what used to be a small grocery at a pedestrian crossing. The toffs of global media all wrapped up in heavy armor.

Everybody but me, yeah.

The road near the broken bridge bears scars of mortar impacts.

A Ukrainian guy with round glasses under his black helmet approaches ambulances at the parking lot.

"Can you do something for the poor thing?"

He holds a small dog, probably a Yorkshire terrier, its paws clotted with blood.

Time moves on.

Nothing really happens, bad or otherwise, and the civilian evacuation goes on.

I get up from my improvised seat, an empty Javelin container, and walk onto the broken highway past a Humvee with a DShK machine gun turret.

Giant plumes of black smoke rise from the horizon. That's somewhere between Bucha, Hostomel, and Moschun. Heavy thumping comes nearer to Irpin.

I walk along the messy highway toward the city's residential quarters two kilometers away from the destroyed bridge.

Beginning in early March, the Battle of Kyiv entered a new, and its most bloody, phase.

Due to frantic Ukrainian resistance and slow advances, the Russian grouping "V" threw in all its reserves from Belarus. Such an intense battle, for so long, was never anticipated.

Almost immediately, the grouping sustained heavy losses and its first troubles with fuel and ammo supplies. Logistics became a big issue.

That's when the legendary Russian sixty-four-kilometer column in Kyiv Oblast came to be.

The giant convoy of tanks, trucks, infantry fighting vehicles, and artillery pieces stretched along a few large roads running parallel through the forests of Polesia —from the Belarusian border across the Chornobyl Exclusion Zone, then to Ivankiv, then down south to Borodyanka area, and then east toward Hostomel.

Basically—a humongous traffic jam of nearly ten Russian battalion tactical groups, with up to nine thousand to ten thousand troops, one hundred tanks, four hundred armored fighting vehicles, and a myriad of support and maintenance vehicles.

And that's just the second half of what Moscow poured into the battle west of Kyiv since February 24. In March, they already had way too much military power for the traffic capacity in the occupied part of Kyiv Oblast, and more would only make matters worse.

Closer to the outskirts of Kyiv, Russia dispersed these forces to engage Ukrainian defenses in Bucha, Hostomel, and Irpin, and to move farther south toward the Zhytomyr Highway.

And while this leviathan inched its way slowly across the Kyiv Oblast, the Ukrainian Territorial Defense militia and special operations scout teams got busy disrupting Russian logistics and communications far behind the lines.

Hit and run, seek and destroy. Wreak havoc and eliminate Russian fuel, food, and ammo supplies as their forward forces try to break through Irpin, Bucha, and Hostomel.

Here's your Here's your manual from the Ukrainian military on how to deal with Russian columns.

As a guerrilla fighter in Russian-controlled territory, your mission is to undermine Russian logistical support. If you see a column of Russian armor moving through your town, just let it go. The regular military will take care of them.

Tanks and fighting vehicles will be followed by trucks transporting fuel, munitions, and food. They are the target. Rear support groups are normally poorly protected by personnel with little combat experience.

They can be interrupted or stopped with road obstacles. Or you can even attack the trucks with hunting weapons and/or Molotov cocktails. Anything can be put to good use.

At the end of the day, armor stripped of fuel and munitions very soon turns into useless pieces of metal. And hungry Russian crews and troops will have to abandon the safety of the column to forage for food.

Roughly speaking, the main Russian objective in this phase of the battle was to fight its way to the Irpin River and find a spot to cross. Then to secure a foothold on the other side and then break into Kyiv.

Ironically enough, in an age of advanced warfare, this not very wide local river became a serious obstacle, like a medieval castle moat.

And the Ukrainian military made good use of this natural ally.

In late February and early March, the Ukrainian military dynamited several key dams on the Irpin River to inundate the area and mire the Russians. A whole range of local towns, such as Demydiv, were tragically flooded.

Irpin, Bucha, and Hostomel still held tight, thanks to the demolition of their bridges. So the Russians found a spot where they had a chance of installing pontoon crossings—Moschun, a little town in the woods east of Hostomel.

Just a couple of kilometers away, across a forested zone, there's the recreational district of Puscha Vodytsya and the entry into the northern part of Kyiv.

The next two weeks would witness the frantic defense of Moschun by a small company of Ukrainian troops with the 72nd Mechanized supported by special operations teams.

The race to the river was brutal.

On the morning of March 4, the main street of Hostomel near the local glass factory was literally spangled with bodies of Russian VDV troops from a destroyed BMP-3 column.

I walk along the messy highway toward the thunder of war.

In the Irpin-Bucha-Hostomel triangle, the city of Irpin was the most attractive and most comfortable. A quiet suburb ideal for restful nights at home after a busy day in Kyiv.

Well-kept parks, green lawns, pine trees next to cottages and apartment blocks. Inviting coffee places and barbershops at street level. Along with Bucha, Irpin enjoyed a very popular housing market, with first-time buyers investing in planned developments to secure an apartment. Irpin is about modern, attractive, and rather expensive residences, the opposite of the ugly Soviet panel buildings we all knew too well. What's sad is that many people who fled the war in Donbas in 2014 and 2015 eventually settled down and started a new life in Irpin. In parking lots, one might notice that half of the local cars had license plates issued in Donetsk Oblast.

The war has come to haunt these people once again. And it's unbearable to see our little local Beverly Hills dying under the shrapnel of Russian artillery.

At the roundabout near the city entrance, Ukrainian soldiers construct barriers of sandbags. A row of NLAWs is carefully laid out on the ground.

At the stronghold, dark rumors spread among troops.

"I've been told all those towns along the Warsaw Highway don't exist anymore," one of them says. "All the way up to Borodyanka. Wiped out by Russians. I wonder what the Kyiv Oblast map will look like after the war."

The thunder of blasts to the north rumbles up again and again. And then dies down for a few minutes.

Reporters walk in and out of Irpin. I have absolutely zero idea who these people are or who they write for, but we journalists marked PRESS greet one another from across the streets. Kind of an international professional solidarity of those heading into that hell space to serve the cause.

Irpin is half-empty now, but still mostly intact.

On Soborna Street, there's chaos and rattling.

Civilian volunteers in cars marked with "Children" and "Evacuation" shuttle between the city and the destroyed bridge hoping to rescue as many as possible.

Farther down the street toward the road to Bucha, pickup trucks full of Territorial Defense fighters move out. They're a motley crowd equipped with store-bought tactical gear and yellow sleeve patches.

They all head toward the front line holding their Kalashnikovs ready—and all smiling.

In parking lots all over Irpin, locals pack their belongings into cars. Shockwaves from distant blasts rattle the display windows of closed flower shops.

They will rip this city to pieces soon.

Not everyone is fleeing though. There are long lines at a few pharmacies still open. And the people in the queues couldn't care less about the sharp whistle of projectiles over their heads.

A soldier with a heavily modified Kalashnikov, probably a military intelligence guy, stops me in one of the local backyards.

"Can I see your papers?"

Sure.

"You're going there?" The fighter hands my passport back to me and points down the roadway to Bucha. "Good luck, buddy."

Moving on.

At some point near Nezhaiko Park, the rumbling intensifies so much I begin to regret my recklessness and dive into the nearest ditch under a fence.

What am I even doing here?

Yes, I'd like to say my goodbyes to the pleasant city amid the pine-wood I've spent so many weekends in.

A middle-aged woman stumbles my way. She meanders from shock and fear—and cries.

"Easy, easy there," I call, running to her. "Easy. We're not being shot at, that's not for us. We're safe here. Easy. You'd better not go that way."

"Where to?! I live just over there," the woman weeps.

"So please go home and get sheltered."

The deafening roar of fighting seems to be coming closer.

It's time to think about the way back.

On Universytetska Street, a little miracle—an AromaKava coffee kiosk still open for business. Possibly, the last of its kind in the city. Territorial Defense, predominant troops gather at the booth and casually stir their coffee in paper cups with popsicle sticks.

One can't resist grasping this last breath of normal life under the sound of shelling.

Unfortunately, the kiosk doesn't serve cocoa for some reason, and I have a craving. A mediocre Americano will still be nice, given the circumstances. Cash only, no change. Thank you.

At some point, a teenage boy on a bicycle breaks into the backyard.

He literally jumps off his bike on the run and then is standing before us. He gasps with exertion, his eyes popping out.

"It's . . . it's a total nightmare," he says between gasps. "What's happening . . . Russians . . . Russians are coming. They're breaking through from the west and from Bucha."

"Fuck," the militia fighters murmur and go on blowing on their hot coffee.

Later in the day, when I get back home, Telegram channels pour out tons of footage of Russian "V" tanks and trucks churning up the streets in northwest Irpin.

FOURTEEN

Ivan drives along Lugova Street in Kyiv through the pouring rain.
He checks every single gas station in the district along the way.

"Empty . . . empty . . . empty . . . a long-ass queue standing still just as it was hours earlier . . . empty."

Price signs at most of the city's gas stations are turned off. If you're lucky and you know where to look, mostly in Kyiv's perimeter, you may get like thirty liters of A-95 gasoline at a time.

Since the beginning of the Russian invasion, prices have at least doubled. The country has been cut off from two thirds of its energy supplies. And that's during wartime, when the military and the police need all the fuel in the world and even more.

In the middle of the biggest European battle of the twenty-first century, we still have wheels.

Ivan is like the character Kat from Erich Maria Remarque's *All Quiet on the Western Front*. He's got a sort of a magic radar when it comes to racking up useful goodies, especially automobile things.

If there's some fresh fuel at a gas station nearby, he'll sniff it out. The night curfew ends at seven A.M., and be sure that by seven fifteen A.M., he's already been there to top off his old Daewoo Lanos.

And yes, all hail capitalism and the free market. In the middle of this giant battle, we regularly see fuel tanks from Poland entering Kyiv via the Odesa Highway. Gasoline may be expensive as hell, but it's still kind of available.

We have pulled into a half-empty parking lot near the Karavan. That's a giant shopping mall in the northern part of Kyiv.

Sometimes, journalists need to resort to certain tricks to get to places no one in their right mind would want to be.

Hostomel and Bucha are still generally under Ukrainian control, but entry for reporters is next to impossible. But rumors have it that civilian volunteers helping evacuate people and bringing in humanitarian aid sometimes manage to make it through military checkpoints.

Many Kyivans with access to cars and a bit of extra money have become aid providers.

As a journalist assisting humanitarian transfers to combat zones, it's an opportunity to do two good things at once—help your fellow people in need and possibly get a story.

I've made a deal with a married couple I found on Facebook—we're going to try to enter Bucha to bring food and basic necessities. They need another ride and helping hands.

And here we are with Ivan, watching the raindrops knock at his car's windshield at the shopping mall.

The volunteer guy's job is to buy stuff with his own money and suffer through the queue at the checkout. Then, with two cars (that's apparently the rule) we'll go to Bucha.

We're waiting for him and his wife.

". . . the Russian military are reported to have taken full control of Kherson," news updates on the radio say. "Russian forces are seen at the regional government's office, as well as the central railway station and the seaport. The Kherson mayor has issued a statement calling for a relief corridor to bring in food and medications. He noted that the city must recover multiple dead bodies, specifically Territorial Defense troops . . ."

Kherson is lost.

We did not know it then but on March 1 some thirty Ukrainian militiamen tragically tried to hold out against advancing Russian columns at Buzkovy Park. The regular Ukrainian military had already abandoned the city.

". . . in other news, the Ukrainian General Staff says at least 17 Russian battalion tactical groups are currently trying to advance at Horenychy, Hostomel, and Demydiv to envelop Kyiv from the north and the northwest . . ."

Finally, the volunteer guy comes around with his better half pushing two carts.

"Listen, erm . . . ," the guy says. "We can't go. I couldn't get any fuel anywhere in the city. I'm almost empty. No luck."

I mean . . .

"If you guys go to Bucha, please take what I got here. I'll send you all the addresses and contacts. Phone connection is rather poor now in those parts, but people on the list will be waiting on you guys."

He indeed sends me something on Telegram. It's not Bucha alone, it's also several delivery addresses in Kyiv.

"And also," he continues. "There's a restaurant near Minska station, it cooks free hot meals for elderly people who live alone. They will give you some. So, thanks a lot, guys! Good luck!"

And the dude disappears in his car.

Okaaaaay then.

Huggies, baby food, a lot of bottled water, crackers, essential medicines, bread, cereals, sunflower oil, chocolate, sugar, and many more things.

"Man, I must admit that was an awesome plan." Ivan enjoys his petty triumph. "What could possibly go wrong here?"

"Shut up and help with this stuff," I say.

We load the car up with huge white plastic bags full of goodies.

So, the list . . . we drive here and there across Kyiv through endless checkpoints and barricades. Near Minska, a small backstreet eatery indeed gives us a huge bag of hot food portions packed in plastic to-go boxes.

That goes to yet another aid provider in Obolon who will distribute the meals in her neighborhood, door to door.

That was one of many great things that happened in the city during the Battle of Kyiv. Indeed, a lot of fast-food chains and restaurants, including posh places, switched to cooking free meals for the military and those in need, mostly the elderly.

Even McDonald's and KFC, despite being closed from day one, donated their kitchen stuff to the effort. And many ad hoc volunteers helped ferry meals around the city. Many bakeries delivered bread at their own expense.

I remember a lot of elderly people coming to a restaurant on Velyka Vasylkivska Street. There were several such places feeding retirees for free.

Well, now we are also unexpectedly part of the movement. And we are cool—we have a car!

Follow the list.

Water packs and bread go out to a couple of old ladies living by themselves somewhere between the Akademmistechko and Zhytomyrska subway stations.

"I always knew your dubious career in journalism would sooner or later bring you into the food delivery business." Ivan can't stop having fun behind the wheel. "It's a pity that McDonald's is out, you could have had even broader opportunities."

We're done with the Kyiv addresses.

Now, Bucha.

Let's try to give it a shot.

Ivan turns onto Kyiv's northern beltway leading toward the Warsaw Highway—the straight passage into Hostomel and Bucha. The nearly empty road runs through dense forests that surround the city like a crown.

We move slowly, weaving between concrete blocks scattered over the roadway. The cold rain of early March keeps pouring.

A soldier steps onto the road and gestures for us to stop. He doesn't approach the car but indicates that we must not move until further notice. Another car also stops behind us.

All right then, waiting.

"Why isn't he even checking us?" Ivan asks.

And a minute later, the air and the ground around us shudder violently.

A deafening growl shakes the car's windshield and the highway begins trembling. We sink down in our seats and flinch with every discharge.

"Damn, that's something heavy!"

Ukrainian artillery shelling Russians from the forest close to the highway. The barrage rolls on for like two minutes.

On the opposite side of the highway, a car stops, apparently coming from the Bucha area. A woman and a little girl hastily clamor out.

Then a guy jumps out of the car behind us and helps the newcomers climb over the concrete barrier. The soldier who stopped us also runs to help the girl and lend a hand with the suitcases.

And the car from Bucha leaves quickly.

Another family seems to have managed to flee Bucha and reunite with someone close in Kyiv.

Finally, the artillery rampage calms down. We're good to go.

Next, a checkpoint on the road out of Kyiv.

Waiting again. If these guys let us through, we rock.

"Got two civilians here on wheels, one of them a reporter," the checkpoint guy on duty talks to a radio set on his shoulder. "They want to go to Bucha, got some humanitarian supplies on them, do you copy?"

"Asking our CO," the radio buzzes back. "Standby, over."

More heavy whoops rolling down across the forest from the Hostomel area.

Ivan taps the wheel.

Come on, the 72nd Mechanized, for the sake of everything we've been through together way back when in Donbas.

Waiting.

Finally, the radio buzz is back.

"Got a plus on the reporter's car."

In the language of those wearing pixel camouflage, that's a yes. We've just melted the invisible CO's heart of iron.

Rolling on.

Rare civilian cars still appear on the Warsaw Highway coming our way. So there should be a way through.

And it's in the news that yesterday and today, Kyiv city authorities managed to get humanitarian aid into Bucha, even though the bridge over the Irpin River has been destroyed—or just heavily damaged but still usable for light vehicles (which was the case, by the way).

It's been a week since the invasion's H-hour, but the strongest Russian axis still can't pass Bucha and Hostomel. According to their grand plan, day ten was to see the initiation of "stabilization efforts" throughout the overwhelmed Ukraine.

We pass the Hostomel stele at the town entrance.

But . . . another checkpoint down the road to Bucha.

We stop, the checkpoint's Territorial Defense guard remains at his station.

"Dudes seem to be a bit nervous," Ivan says. "We got a license plate registered in Donetsk Oblast."

All right, let's talk.

If the military has already let us through at the previous checkpoint a kilometer back, doesn't it kind of mean we're good to go?

I get out of the car.

"The bridge is destroyed. Entry banned," he says.

"Guys, it's okay, the army back there gave us a plus to Bucha," I say, trying to exercise my awesome military diplomacy skills gained in Donbas. "We've been asked to bring a humanitarian stash to the city. We have people waiting. Is there a way we can . . ."

"I said get the fuck out of here!" the guard yells suddenly.

And he points his rifle at me and racks the slide.

"Fuck off now!"

Wow, wow, dude, relax.

If you say the bridge is closed, the bridge is closed. I get it. We're fine, yeah? I get back into the car.

As we drive back home to Kyiv, Ivan has only one thing to say.

"We both have learned a lesson today," he says very thoughtfully. "And the lesson is: Your job sucks."

★   ★   ★

Life during the Battle of Kyiv was a bizarre mixture of inconceivable inspiration, unity, and pride—and at the same time, of dark grief and mourning.

Amid all the evil that people witnessed throughout March, there came the year's first warm days, just as was meant to be. The sun shone brightly and often and stray cats warmed themselves on benches in our neighborhood.

We had so many military weddings back then. A soldier guy would propose to a girl (often a military service member, too) right on the battle-field or at a checkpoint. And then a chaplain would officiate the blessings, and the newly married couple would climb back into the trenches and back to their duties.

Spontaneous picnics with guitars and singing and shared food were commonplace in the subway stations we now used as bomb shelters. Thousands of people in Kyiv spent their nights in tents and sleeping bags on the underground platforms they used to go to work from every morning.

At our nearest subway station, the Akademmistechko, all entrances but one were sealed tight with massive metal plates. The dead lock. Most essential if there's a confirmed nuclear strike threat, but those plates made us feel safe during missile strikes.

There was immense pride in the military.

Everybody loves stories of underdogs. But after all those Kyiv-will-fall-within-seventy-two-hours mantras coming from every corner, what the yellow-and-blue colors were doing in Mykolaiv, Irpin, Kharkiv, Mariupol was simply jaw-dropping.

It was a time of wild yarns and crazy legends.

Like the Roma people who allegedly snatched a tank from the Russians near Kherson. Or the woman who was rumored to have downed a Russian drone with a cucumber jar.

And the Ghost of Kyiv . . . this whole thing started with a rather lame attempt to boost the popular morale in the first days of the battle.

A mysterious MiG-29 fighter pilot that comes out of nowhere beyond the clouds and downs six superior Russian aircraft over Kyiv. Just like the army ripping Russian tanks into shreds on the ground, there's a guardian angel in the skies over the sacred city, the cradle of fifteen hundred years of our history.

Many in the media, and even some politicians like Petro Poroshenko, sniffed out this potentially viral story. There was a thrilling game of trying to identify the newfound mysterious ace, the successor of World War II heroes.

I swear to God, things were so ridiculous that a couple of large Ukrainian media outlets used a 2019 picture of yours truly (yes, me) at the Vasylkiv Airfield to illustrate their "The Ghost of Kyiv's Identity May Have Been Revealed" stories.

The media tale had a life of own as an internet meme. Of course, no sane person now seriously believes that was a true story. But it became a legend—a symbol of Ukrainian pride in their military.

Behind that meme, there were many untold stories of the valor of real Ukrainian Air Force pilots. With their long-obsolete aircraft and poor odds for survival let alone victory, they nonetheless took up the fight against a far superior power when the time came.

Many of them had returned to the Air Force from civilian life.

And only heaven knows how many of them were lost to the sky forever in the last days of February.

One of Ukraine's top guns, Colonel Oleksandr Oksanchenko of the 831st Tactical Aviation Brigade, was killed in air combat on February 25 while drawing off Russian jets.

Lieutenant Roman Pasulka of the 40th Tactical Aviation Brigade went down in combat on February 24 when his MiG-29 crashed into the Dnipro River. He was twenty-two.

Fifty-five-year-old Lieutenant Colonel Volodymyr Kokhansky of the 114th Tactical Aviation Brigade was among the first to take off in the earliest hours of the invasion. He never returned to home base after a combat mission over Kyiv.

We were what London was during the Blitz of 1940. It was our own finest hour.

Air strikes quickly became a new normal.

In the middle of the night, you sit at your desk and write a guest op-ed for the *Guardian* as windows rattle and shake from blast waves. Our air defense is again trying to intercept something over the city.

Night is the time of tense anticipation.

The darkness comes down, and we again cover our windows with cardboard. Not sure what that's really for—whether it's for hiding the light or protecting us from shards of glass or shielding away the world that descends with curfew at eight P.M.

You don't want to read any books, or watch a movie, or listen to music. You stay indoors and check online war maps, on and on. You don't even want to turn the light on.

That deathlike, unspeakably uncomfortable stillness was the worst.

Ivan was spending his nights sitting alone in this room staring into his phone in the darkness. Beginning around March 5, almost all communications with Mariupol were severed. We could only hunt for bits of information about the city from the military or from those who managed to go online.

Photos and videos from the streets. The Russians had isolated the city and were turning it into a giant cemetery among the ruins of our life as students. On March 16, the Drama Theater, whose grounds were marked with giant letters spelling out KIDS, in Russian, to indicate there were children sheltering inside—was devastated by a Russian gravity bomb.

A howl of despair deep inside.

For weeks, Ivan had no idea if his sister in Mariupol was still alive. And we could only guess what was happening to dozens of our friends, former colleagues, ex-girlfriends, university mates, acquaintances, all trapped in the absolute holocaust.

And my hometown, Volnovakha, was wiped out within days.

Those who managed to survive the devastation later told us that many in the town had been trapped in shelters and basements for days, without any heating, food, or water.

Furious fighting continued nonstop.

Many in my hometown, driven by desperation and thirst, tried to leave their basements and find a way out. Later in March, the Ukrainian military was policing a civilian evacuation corridor out of the city. And those who were lucky to leave later told us that the ruined streets were swamped with dead bodies.

My mother's best friend, Oksana, one night took a bicycle during a short lull in hostilities and went through the pitch dark trying to escape that hell. She was lucky to randomly come across a Ukrainian checkpoint.

On March 12, Ukrainian authorities declared that Volnovakha ceased to exist as a habitable human settlement.

At night, you suddenly wake up to the roar of artillery every other hour. Or to the distant rattle of machine guns.

Ukrainian artillery was deployed across the forests near the western boundary of Kyiv, not far from our neighborhood, so we could hear guns blazing day and night. The artillery duels were insane.

Sometimes the rounds were so heavy that their echoes quaked the fragile walls of our poor Soviet-era panel building. And you get used to that very quickly.

You might also wake up in the middle of the night and hear nothing but dead silence. Why, what's happening, why aren't our guns working? Is everything okay? And then the roar would resume in the early hours of the new day.

At still other times, you would wake up to something really loud and heavy. Is that an incoming strike? Are we being shelled? Nah, it's okay, that's probably our air defense working. You can turn over and go on sleeping.

Days were going by in our fragile apartment at the very edge of Kyiv. And we continued to slowly deplete our wartime food stocks and to foray out to try to get decent war stories.

By the middle of March, the battle had reached its peak moment.

The Russians completely occupied Bucha, Hostomel, and parts of Irpin. They began slowly moving south across (what was left of) the Zhytomyr Highway to envelop the city from the west.

By March 15, they were in full control of the highway from Makariv to Stoyanka, just on the outskirts of Kyiv. And they tried to move even farther south to threaten Fastiv. At that point, the nearest Russian lines in Stoyanka were something like seven kilometers from our house across the woods.

The battle was still mainly about the Irpin River.

The small river continued to heroically fulfill its historical role established ages ago. It was always predestined to be the first major defensive barrier for the city.

During World War II, an eighty-five-kilometer line of bunkers and engineered obstacles along the Irpin was used to impede the Nazi advance into Kyiv. Many of those old bunkers are still around today. Many were restored as war museums.

On weekends we would take bicycle rides to see those old concrete monsters in the forests northeast of the city. And in 2022, the same World War II–era bunkers were used again by the Ukrainian military in their fight against a new invasion.

The Russians, nonetheless, were all that time a hairsbreadth away from breaking through the Irpin defenses and pouring into the city. The Russians had spent weeks pounding Ukrainian positions particularly around Moschun. With not many more than eighty troops of the 72nd Mechanized and support from special operations units, Ukraine was holding out. If the Russians were able to ford the river they would have a straight shot to Kyiv.

East of Kyiv, brutal battles continued as well.

The Russians managed to come close to Brovary, although with heavy losses and less promising prospects. In a famous episode, Ukrainian artillery devastated a massive armored column with Russia's 90th Tank Division on a highway between Velyka Dymerka and Brovary.

But along the road to Chernihiv, the Russians stood only a few kilometers from Kyiv.

We had our contingency plans.

If the Russians eventually broke into our part of the city, we had a backup apartment closer to the center of town. If things went really bad in our neighborhood and we couldn't use the car, we'd take our bicycles and try to escape via the woods. Or we'd walk. We know those pathways.

Ivan decided to stay in the city for as long as the southern highway was passable. I decided to stay and work until the bitter end. I thought fighting would eventually pour into the city streets. And the slipknot would be pulled tighter and tighter around downtown Kyiv, the government's headquarters.

I wanted to stay online for as long as possible. Maybe I'd use military Starlinks to deliver a last word from besieged Kyiv to the wider world. And then it wouldn't matter.

After all the military and civilian valor we'd witnessed, it seemed impossible to leave Kyiv behind again.

There were dark rumors coming from the occupied northwest.

Starting from as early as March 8, Ukrainian authorities managed to organize fragile civilian evacuations from occupied towns. Women and children only. Long columns of yellow buses were parked just inside our neighborhood, and our community became sort of a transition hub where the evacuees could get medical aid and food.

It was very busy in front of our apartment block.

One day, the mother of one of our journalists, Anna Myroniuk, managed to escape Bucha via the yellow rescue buses.

The people arriving from Bucha had stories to tell.

Russian FSB officers were raiding houses and apartments looking for men. They had lists of local journalists, activists, Territorial Defense members, of those known to be loyal to and actively aiding the Ukrainian military.

Russian troops were often seen pillaging homesteads.

Many in Bucha and elsewhere tried to cross the front line with their own cars. And many disappeared without a trace. They never made it to their loved ones in Kyiv or other towns still under Ukrainian control.

Communication with the occupied zones was almost nonexistent. But some things leaked out online. Around March 10, video footage went live of a mass grave in Bucha near Andrew the Apostle Church.

Dozens of black body bags put into a pit next to the tall white church. A blossoming, quiet town with an awesome municipal park turned into a mass grave.

The Hostomel mayor was executed by Russians.

In Irpin, makeshift graves near cottage houses. I remember the infernal dread at seeing a picture of Maryna and Ivan Mets, a mother and her twelve-year-old son, buried at a parking lot in Irpin under funeral crosses made of raw wooden planks.

That was a dark time.

One day, Ivan disappeared with his car for the whole day.

He only said: "I'm out, will be back home later."

He got back home close to the curfew time and sent me a message: "Get out to parking lot, I need a hand."

Okay.

He cracked his trunk open to the day's beautiful spring sunset—and holy shit—the car was full of booze.

Back then, the sale of alcohol was prohibited in Kyiv and throughout the region. But Ivan somehow managed to travel nearly one hundred kilometers and get some spirits from some minor grocery somewhere near Bila Tserkva. Like I said, in wartime, Ivan discovered a very unexpected talent for getting his hands on essentials.

It was very cheap beer and vodka, though.

"Oh, good lord," I could only say.

"You should have seen the face of a military guy at a checkpoint on the Odesa Highway," Ivan said triumphantly. "The dude was so astonished by my boldness that he only said, 'Okaaaay then,' and let me go."

You must be kidding me.

"Don't get too excited though," Ivan continued. "Two thirds of that go to an investor next door who shared this intelligence with me. And you owe me a lot of money now."

I think that was the first time that we truly managed to switch off.

In the evening, Ivan served up pretty decent eats from our depleted wartime food stock. We selected a movie to watch, cracked our windows open to the fresh air of early spring—and declared the boozing session begun.

"Man, this is just awful," I said, tasting the cheap village vodka. "I can't drink that, ugh."

"Nobody's forcing you," Ivan noted as he murdered a hot varenik and poured another shot.

Finally, a quiet time. As if there's no war and no Russian front line just across the forest. Even the battlefield around the city had seemingly died down.

"To victory!" Ivan was still going strong and knocking them back.

"Whoa, I like things much more now," I said, already quite tipsy. "And those fucks seriously thought they could take this city within three days? Screw them, our 72nd guys will make mincemeat of those orcs."

Ivan was now inhaling tinned stew from our emergency survival kit.

Man, I was getting really drunk.

"When this shit is over, I swear I'm gonna have a long, lazy vacation," I continued. "I'm gonna switch the internet off and binge-rewatch war movies. First, *Generation Kill*. Then, *Band of Brothers*. Then, *The Pacific*. And by that time, HBO should have completed the third miniseries . . . what's that title? *Masters of the Air*."

"Bro, you're sick," Ivan says, taking another shot.

"No," I said. "I've got a better idea. I'm gonna buy a Harley-Davidson and hit the road. No news, calls, nothing. I'll be traveling the country like a nomad for three months. No, six months! We'll go to Mariupol again."

"We'll see about that," Ivan yucked. "With your job, you'll go bananas long before this is over. And I will go on fixing all those pesky iPhones."

And suddenly the world around us corkscrewed.

A very strong pulse hit hard from somewhere. Our apartment walls slipped out. As if in a second, the whole apartment block concussed like a piece of jelly and started falling flat on its side.

"Fuuuuuuuuuuck!" we both shouted and dropped onto the floor from our chairs.

A second passed.

Everything was okay. Nothing was crumbling anymore.

"What the hell was that?" Ivan shouted. He was suddenly sober.

That was an artillery shell fragment.

It came from across the woods in the direction of Irpin and hit our house's facade.

In the morning, we and other residents could see what it was all about. The shell fragment left a not very impressive wrinkle between the second and third floors. Within the next couple of hours, go-getters still living in our building got that fixed with some concrete in no time.

And even though that fragment nearly collapsed our panel house, we, those living a forest strip away from the battle zone, had every reason to be glad.

Throughout the entire Battle of Kyiv, that was the only hit our neighborhood had seen.

FIFTEEN

A dimly lit radio studio lost in a godforsaken industrial sector of Kyiv in between the Kontratkova and Tarasa Shevchenka subway stations.

A round table with a row of microphones.

Two sit at the desk behind their laptops both dressed in hoodies with armbands of yellow tape stuck to their sleeves.

Both plug in their ear monitors. A commercial break ends in several seconds.

I know these characters well.

The first is Yuriy Matsarsky. He's a brutal-looking black-bearded dude with an unexpectedly silky voice.

Matsarsky was born in Ukraine, but he has also spent a long time working in Moscow as a Middle East correspondent. And he has been to every single corner of the Arabic world that's been on fire in the last decade and a half. From the 2011 revolution in Egypt to the war on ISIS in Syria, or the rule of Hamas in Gaza.

We used to hang out together. As a radio host here in Kyiv, he invited me to be on maybe ten episodes of his own talk show. He's a single dad and asthmatic. As he says, his greatest interests are rock and roll and extreme Shia sects.

The second guy is Pavlo Kazarin. Unlike his mate, he's bald and lightly stubbled. He's originally from Crimea, and he's one of Ukraine's top political commentators and authors.

Now, they're also volunteer Territorial Defense fighters.

And they've gotten back to their studio for a brief moment for another episode of their long-running radio show.

Live straight out of wartime Kyiv.

On air now.

"All of a sudden, this is the 'Double Standards' talk show with you now," Kazarin opens the gig.

"Same people, same place, with you again," Matsarsky slips in. "It's been a week since we last were on air, and we skipped the previous episode."

"Yes, we have some big news," Kazarin says.

"Last Friday we went to a recruitment office and joined the Territorial Defense Forces. And now we have two hours off while it's all quiet."

"Let's tell our listeners how it went," Matsarsky says, climbing closer to the mic. "Apart from the usual service duties every Territorial Defense fighter or anyone in ranks has, we've been asked to take media matters upon ourselves."

Kazarin gives a short laugh.

"Yep, apart from manning checkpoints, Matsarsky lost his voice last night. How many interviews did you give? Eight? I'm telling you, dear listeners. When we win this war, don't be surprised if you read it on English Wikipedia that Matsarsky defeated Russia all by himself. He was live on CNN, CBS, Romanian television, also with the Finns, who illustrated his interview with two pictures from Facebook in which he looks like a cutthroat."

Matsarsky splits his sides with laughter.

"Because he's the only guy in the battalion whose English is good enough to talk to the media! Last night, he moved an American TV host to tears with his rampage on how there's no real difference between Americans and Ukrainians, and on how we even have passports of the same color, and on how what's happening to us may happen to Americans as well. So, just for you all to know—if you're listening to Matsarsky, you are the resistance."

Matsarsky wants to parry the jab but Kazarin breaks through again.

"Oh, now this guy is going to start telling tales in his soft, quiet voice. As if it's a late-night show and we don't want to wake anyone up," he giggles.

"So you don't like my voice?" Matsarsky pretends to be terribly offended. "Go and get yourself a new cohost then! When his war is over, no one will even want to talk to you without me. People will be telling you: Go away and get back with the real big guy. From this day forward, I'm sentenced to spend my days with Kazarin. We serve watch duties together, we accompany foreign journalists together, we sleep next to each other!"

"I must tell you, dear listeners, that Matsarsky snores," Kazarin laughs. "He's the nocturnal curse of our company's barracks. Anyway, let's cut to the chase. In Ukraine, military service has become a privilege. When it comes to the Territorial Defense Forces, there are more willing candidates than vacancies available. What we have now is really the people's patriotic war."

"When Kazarin and I went to the recruitment office on Friday, there was a truly enormous queue." Matsarsky clutches his head behind his microphone. "I feared the Russians would be destroyed before we had a chance to enlist. And everyone in the line was really hearty and supportive toward one another. And we were like, who is ready to be a commander? Who's got military experience? Luckily, there were guys who used to serve in Donbas."

"It's an incredible story," Kazarin says. "So, we got our weapons. And half an hour later, they gave us a mission to patrol streets behind military lines. It's the night, it's really cold. We stand on and on waiting for sunrise. As if there's the Siege of Gondor, and Frodo Baggins is about to toss the Ring into Mount Doom."

"We wanted the sunrise like it was our payday coming." Matsarsky keeps giggling.

"So the sun is finally here, we begin to relax a bit," Kazarin carries on. "And then a really poor old man comes out of a house nearby. And he brings hot water and several tea bags. And we see that this grandpa has got nothing in his life but his cat. And he brews tea for us and says, 'Soldier boys, please get yourselves warm, have a sip.' Oh, dear . . ."

Kazarin rubs his face.

"He was giving out everything he could," Matsarsky says, nodding. "And we've had a really stressful night, on high alert due to a possible Russian breakthrough. Everybody was really nervous."

"Then more and more people came out to bring us food," Kazarin says. "Meat dumplings, some enormously delicious soup. And this was happening everywhere, at many checkpoints all around us. During moments like that, you see what this is all for. This city is undefeatable. This city and this nation know where their defenders are."

"And we're meeting just incredible people in ranks." Matsarsky intercepts the microphone.

"It's really interesting to see what kind of people join the Territorial Defense." Kazarin leans back in his studio chair. "It's a sample of everything and everyone Ukraine is. All age categories starting from eighteen. In the force, we have people old enough to be my father. And I'm thirty-eight, as a matter of fact."

"And there are folks who could be your son," Matsarsky chips in. "And you're still thirty-eight."

"Exactly!" Kazarin says. "And daughters—we got our incredible Masha and Tamara, they are younger than their rifles. And I've never met people as motivated as those girls. Every morning, we muster up and decide who does what. And there's this scene. The unit leader says: 'Who's going to the checkpoints?' And they shout, 'We are!' 'Who's to check house roofs?'—'We volunteer!'—'Hold on, girls, we have another duty in mind for you.'"

"Yeah," Matsarsky says. "And then one of them sits somewhere out there and cries in the night. 'While you guys go out on patrol missions and get cold at checkpoints, I have to stay here and cook spaghetti. I'm so bitter.'"

"By the way, speaking of cooking." Kazarin lights up. "We have a guy who got a 'no' at the recruitment board. But he's a cook. A real professional restaurant chef. And he said he'd cook for us. And you know what? I don't want to get other companies and battalions angry, but ever since then, I have meals I couldn't dream about at home."

"Yeah, we have awesome food." Matsarsky beams with joy. "We really have a huge variety of people of all ages and professions. Last night, I took a few French journalists to a checkpoint. They were really interested. Several days ago, all the Territorial Defense members were regular civilians that had nothing to do with the military. And at the checkpoint, we had two guys. Both equally dressed, both equally unshaven, both hadn't changed their clothes for like several days, both equally serving their duty.

"So the French were asking them what they were before the war. One of those brutal dudes with weapons was like: 'I was an advisor to a minister. Now I also have a successful business.' And the other guy said: 'I worked as a warehouse worker.'

"All ethnic, religious, or social boundaries have disappeared. A blue-collar guy can stand next to a minister. Kazarin now can finally stand next to a decent human being."

The cohost breaks into loud laugher.

"While we still have time on air, I'd like to offer a highly sophisticated monologue on essential topics of the day," Kazarin says. "May I?"

"Does this mean I can leave the studio and finally get some tea?" Matsarsky says.

"Go ahead,"

"I'll go as far as switching my mic off to fully enjoy the moment."

"So, listen," Kazarin eagerly accepts the offer. "It's incredible to see the nation being so united and so enthusiastic right now. And here's the question I want to pose: What does Russia even hope for? How do people in the Kremlin see the future? We have witnessed Russia's blitzkrieg turning into blitz-cringe . . ."

"Wow," Matsarsky says, astonished. "What incredible wordplay, did you come up with that?"

"I'm sorry, dear listeners, we're having some radio interference that speaks in Matsarsky's voice." Kazarin waves his cohost away. "Let's just ignore it. So, the Kremlin may go on talking about its battlefield advances in Ukraine for as long as it wants. But the truth is that Russia has already lost. You want to know why?

"Moscow has never cared to study and analyze Ukraine, as distinct from what it did about the West, the Middle East, or Africa. They just thought there was nothing to study at all. 'Half of Ukraine is just like us, the other half is not, that's it.' So Putin ended up having zero understanding of what Ukraine is. He thought Ukrainians would greet his army with flower wreaths.

"Why is this important?

"Let's look back in history. In the days of old, medieval peasants anywhere in Europe didn't think much about who they were. And wars were, generally speaking, mostly about baron A fighting duke B. And peasants, unless the fighting parties were of alien religions or minority denominations, were generally indifferent about who they paid tribute to. But what changes after the eighteenth century?"

"National identities emerged!" Matsarsky pops up like a zealous grade-A student.

"Exactly," Kazarin eagerly gives him credit. "Nations realized themselves. A peasant began saying he's not just a local guy, but also Frenchman, or a Czech—or a Ukrainian. Here's his flag, his coat of arms, and his national anthem. Here's the flag he wants to live under, and here's the one he does not want. And also, there appeared mass armies and wars between nations, not just nobles.

"And so—here we go with guerrilla warfare behind lines. And now Russians are bombing Kharkiv and destroying Bucha and Irpin. And people living there don't say 'We don't care.' They have a very strong motivation for revenge. Partisan fighters begin pushing the occupation army around. The occupation army freaks out and launches punitive actions.

"But—because of that, more and more people join the resistance. It's an endless circle. In Vietnam, despite technological supremacy, the United States failed to get a victory. Because there was a psychotic Lieutenant Calley going nuts and burning a village to ashes, prompting even more Vietnamese to fight.

"So it makes little sense to fight nations in today's world. And there's the main Russian failure. They failed to understand that Ukrainians are a nation. And that they do not want to be part of Russia. Everything we see in the news, when unarmed people protest in front of Russian tanks, or when people throw Molotovs at tanks—it's a national resistance war.

"And no matter what Russians do about it, hatred toward the occupying power will only deepen. They are doomed to be constantly shot in the back. And they will inevitably fail sooner or later."

"They just don't have a large enough popular base in Ukraine to rely on." Matsarsky nods.

"And even if by a miracle they end up capturing the Ukrainian leadership and making it sign something," Kazarin carries on passionately, "such an agreement will not be worth the paper it's written on. The war will continue. Trying to force Ukraine into becoming a client state has only stripped some people here of their illusions."

Matsarsky smiles.

"I see Kazarin has really missed being on air all these days."

"Of course, I have!" his cohost shouts. "It was you who's been talking to all the global media, befriending all good-looking journalists, and collecting likes on social media. And making TV hosts cry."

"And I've been doing that because we need to give a shoutout to the world about the nightmare here in Ukraine," Matsarsky fights back. "We still have a few minutes on air, and then we'll have to get back to our unit. And in a bit more than an hour, I'll go live with CBC Canada. Because in all seriousness, we may sound funny and lively on this show, but on the ground, people here are dying as those animals shell Ukrainian cities."

"And I'm doing Sky News," Kazarin says.

"Matsarsky and I are just like Legolas and Gimli competing. 'I have forty-three!—And I have twenty-four, I'm going to catch up to you!' But yeah, in all seriousness, all the gratitude and support should be given to guys on the front line. They are stopping Russian armored columns coming at us.

"With every hour, guys fighting near Kharkiv are buying us just another quiet night in Kyiv, when we have only one or three, or four missiles incoming. Guys fighting in the south are buying quiet nights for Lviv. And there should be very special thanks to our air defense.

We're praying for you, guys. Thanks to you, civilians and the military feel safer now in Ukrainian cities."

Matsarsky nods and gives a really tired smile.

"We have just a couple of minutes left here, dear listeners, then we'll have to get going."

"Yes," Kazarin says.

"And just for the sake of a positive ending, here's a funny piece of news for you. In the Kyiv Zoo, a newborn lemur has been named Bayraktar. And moreover, over the last week, in the middle of this war, a total of three hundred ninety babies have been born in Kyiv. One hundred ninety-nine boys and one hundred ninety-one girls. No matter how hard Putin and the Russian leadership wanted to stop this, life goes on."

I met up with both of them again months later, during the Battle of Donbas, as hard-boiled old-timers of the force. They were still always together. And Anton Goloborodko, the TV host turned NCO, was also with them.

SIXTEEN

The outskirts of Irpin were silent.

Nothing but whirling wind whistling among metal fences twisted by shockwaves.

The neighborhood of single-family homesteads at the Irpin riverside had been turned into a mess of smoldering ruins and broken glass.

The Fora supermarket, which used to greet long strings of cars leaving and entering Irpin, was smashed to smithereens. Somebody, possibly workers who stayed there until they couldn't, boarded up what was left of the mall's entrance.

On the parking lot near the supermarket, a heap of eviscerated ambulances. A small church on the other side of the street was charred, its white siding riddled with shrapnel marks.

The road crossing's pavement was scarred with sprawly, flowerlike ruptures—mortar impact holes.

Just over three weeks of fighting have turned this thriving suburb in the woods into a doomsday scene.

Phone connection's dead.

Not a single soul walking around except for us, a handful of stray journos burdened by our sweaty field gear and a couple of Ukrainian soldiers with the Karpatska Sich.

It's something that we still call a volunteer battalion—a self-organized paramilitary force, the formation of which dates to the chaos of 2014. Back then, as one might remember, dozens of these bands of modern-day minutemen took up arms to supplement the regular military, which was in a woeful plight, to combat the Russian-led insurgency in Donbas.

The volunteer battalions were composed of a mixed bag of regular people, all proud, independent, combative, and welcoming of pretty much anyone willing to fight for Ukraine, regardless of health status or education or nationality.

Ukrainians, foreigners . . . marshaling on their own outside the system but coordinating their operations with the regular military.

In the years since, most of the volunteers were absorbed by the standing army or vanished in the haze of the war that was seemingly slowly fading away.

Well, now it's all back.

We're with a battalion that issued a call to arms with the February invasion and then headed to the front lines here in Irpin.

Again, calling their own shots, and safely ignoring some rules—such as those admitting us reporters to their lines despite a general ban from the command.

Fighters freak out every time the video guys with Narod Viysko ("The Army Nation"), a pro-paramilitary YouTube channel, try to get some good footage of the mess all around.

Using certain civilian-military diplomacy skills and even more of our foolish charm, we have teamed up to secretly sneak into Irpin with the Karpatska Sich guys.

"Don't even think about filming things the Russians can geolocate and get a bead on our shelters, hey," the fighters say.

Dudes, relax. We know the drill.

The unit was still guarding what's left of the sadly remembered bridge between Irpin and Kyiv City—a chaos of concrete rubble and rebar.

No one was fleeing Irpin across the ruins of the bridge anymore. The salvation lifeline had run its course.

Endless lines of smashed and abandoned cars stretched for hundreds of meters along the road, beginning at the gray abyss of the broken bridge and ending far away, closer to the city. They had been slowly devoured by advancing Russian forces.

Scorched car frames, the shattered glass, the tattered suitcases left behind in a hurry, the smell of decomposing garbage and sooty ash, all underneath the howling wind and the scudding skies.

Time and again, splashes of heavy thumping and echoes of intense shooting broke the silence over what's left of the Irpin bridge.

This was the last week of March 2022.

At that point, Russians were still holding on to Bucha and Hostomel, areas west of Kyiv City along the Zhytomyr Highway, as well as the northwestern part of Irpin.

Their second major attempt to regroup, concentrate, and break into Kyiv following the operational pause of March 8–10 got them very close to success.

It was in the small village of Moschun and in its tiny, twisting streets where the outcome of the Battle of Kyiv was essentially decided.

The fight was brutal. And those still living in the northwestern part of Kyiv could hear the exchange of artillery fire every night and see giant pillars of smoke rising from beyond the woods.

In the war's most famous episode, by March 12–13 the situation had become so dire that Ukraine's 72nd Mechanized requested permission to retreat from Moschun.

But General Zaluzhny had declined and vowed to bring in reinforcements. Leaving the town would mean Russians ultimately crossing the Irpin River and breaking into Kyiv's northwest and north via the city beltway and the Warsaw Highway running to Hostomel and Bucha.

Not the end of the battle, but still a major Russian success—the fight spilling into the capital city streets.

In a heroic effort that now feels like a man-made act of salvation blessed by the skies, Ukrainian army units reinforced with paramilitaries and Special Operations teams managed to repel the Russian push and drive the Russians out of Moschun by March 20–21.

Russians rolled back and lost their only foothold on the Kyiv side of the Irpin River, their best bet to break into the capital city. Nowhere else along the northwestern front had they managed to cross the Irpin— neither in the area of Demydiv, nor in the narrow corridor between

Kyiv City and Hostomel, or via the Irpin Highway, or in Stoyanka west of Kyiv.

Indeed, the Battle of Kyiv was ripe with bitter irony.

In the climactic moment of the biggest European war since 1945, a pretty mediocre local river running through woods and meadows became a truly formidable barrier to a force who called themselves the world's second greatest military power.

A traveler who decided to visit our parts would surely be stunned that such a humble river did so much to aid the outnumbered defenders of the Ukrainian capital.

Moreover, speaking of bitter irony, Ukraine's 72nd Mechanized and Russia's 155th Marines would meet again, many months after Moschun, in late 2022 and early 2023. In the Battle of Vuhledar in Donbas, Russia's Pacific Fleet marines would again sustain one of the most devastating defeats of this war.

By the beginning of the last week of March 2022, Russians had essentially made little progress toward capturing Kyiv.

They were still trying to advance into central Irpin from the north and the west, but to no avail.

Earlier, in mid-March, Russian forces had successfully crossed the Zhytomyr Highway, but there they stalled, moving farther south no more than a few kilometers.

What was supposed to be a rapid advance south bogged down along the highway between the towns of Makariv, Motyzhyn, Mriya, Petrushky, and Stoyanka, all west of the Kyiv City boundary.

It was already clear that bypassing Kyiv's western districts via Fastiv or Vasylkiv and cutting it off at the Odesa Highway in the south was absolutely unrealistic.

The Russian foothold east of Kyiv also got bogged down in the outskirts of Brovary and Boryspil, their resupply hanging by the fragile threads of highways running from Chernihiv and Sumy that were under constant assault from Ukrainian guerrilla groups.

Neither Sumy nor Chernihiv had surrendered; in almost total isolation, both cities were still fighting hard, drawing a large portion of Russian forces off Kyiv.

It was the battle's day thirty.

"Whoa, wow, wow, no!" soldiers protest as we reporters dash toward their emplacements set among the bridge ruins.

One of them jumps off an ammo box and starts waving us off with his rifle as if it's a stick in his hands.

"You guys better get out. The likes of you always bring bad luck."

The trials of working as a front-line war reporter.

This was a place of bad juju.

Weeks earlier, on March 6, Russian mortars hit this river crossing as evacuees streamed across, killing a mother and her two children, as well as their family friend, right in front of a crowd of journalists.

The day after, the *New York Times* ran a photo on the front page that showed their bodies on the ground, along with the Ukrainian soldiers who'd rushed to their aid, with no hope of rescue.

And then on March 13, also in the Irpin area, American filmmaker Brent Renaud was shot in the head and killed, presumably by Russians, while filming people fleeing the war zone. Two other journos were killed.

Ever since then, the Ukrainian military had effectively closed Irpin to the media—which is why those aggressive YouTube guys and I had to sneak into the city. All for the sake of a story.

Now try to explain to those guys in camouflage that we're not going to send the Russians their coordinates so they can raze this place to the ground.

"No, seriously, dudes, better just fuck off. Don't lure Russian mortars. Better go get some tea with our foreigners in the basement."

I cast a sad look on the gray car graveyard on the other side of the abyss stretching toward the nearest tower of apartment blocks in Irpin.

Russian checkpoints lie a couple of kilometers away, and a new fight seems to be brewing. The wind brings in the stifled rattle of gunfire and the roar of artillery far away.

The part of Irpin near the broken bridge used to be the separate settlement of Romanivka but was eventually absorbed by the growing city. Set on the beautiful riverside, it was a lovely esplanade perfect for walking and cycling.

The homesteads of Romanivka were bombed into oblivion by the Russians . . . but the grim picture of destruction was only a part of the story.

Beneath and among the damaged single-family houses, there was a fully outfitted and lively underworld hidden from view.

One of the Karpatska Sich units was manning an abandoned, opulent, relatively intact property (if we didn't mind the backyard smashed to bits) on Chaikovsky Street.

As a thunder-like rattle rolls down from somewhere among Irpin's not too distant apartment blocks, the warfighters wave hands and invite us to slip into their underworld.

The house has a huge cellar, with spiral stairs going down from the kitchen.

The owner, who fled the war, used the basement as his workshop and storeroom, and he kept it very clear and dry.

Soldiers putter around the abandoned house, passing mattresses and water bottles down the stairs, one after another.

"We need to arrange as many sleeping places as possible for tonight," a husky guy in full combat gear says as he comes up. "And please get your asses moving already before the shelling resumes again."

The platoon buzzes in at least four languages.

It's a mixture of Ukrainian, Russian, fluent and broken English. And from some evidently new recruits a Slavic language of which my Ukrainian ear can decipher little.

By the look of the clothes and gear they use, half of which was probably purchased at hunting stores or even the nearest H&M, this war band is even more motley than most.

Fighters come back from somewhere covered in dust and drop their helmets and rifles on sofas in the living room. While others lay down rows of mattresses in the basement, three of the four newcomers tiredly flop down in chairs in full combat gear—and begin stuffing themselves with tinned meat from the nearest food box.

It's always the same in war zones.

Be it Kyiv or Donbas, be it foreigners or Ukrainians, warfighters in trenches or among ruins have an unfailing knack for creating a perfect storm of tinned food, coffee, tea bags, plastic cups, both used and unused, moldy or fresh loafs of bread, piles of salt and sugar, spoons, forks, shopping bags, energy drink cans, sweets, and anything you can think of.

The newcomers keep murmuring to one another in a language that feels very Slavic but is still unrecognizable.

"We're from the Czech Republic," one of them tells me.

It's a miracle, the kind of people one can meet in war.

This Czech guy went under the codename Wi-Fi and did five years in the Czech military, and, unless my memory fails me, his wife was Ukrainian. So, a while ago, he came to Ukraine and joined the unit to fight, as simple as that.

Twitter gave big points to Wi-Fi's biceps after I photographed him holding his AK-74 high as he put the rifle's cleaning rod in place.

A certain famous female Ukrainian TV anchor happened to see the picture and publicly declared that the world's sexiest men alive were fighting for Ukraine!

In the house's shattered backyard, I come across a Scottish guy in his fifties named Stephen. Of all things, he was an olive farmer shuttling between Spain and Great Britain . . . and by some weird twist of fate, he ended up in Irpin with an AK in his hands.

And the night before, as Russians relentlessly shelled the unit's position, he came really close to becoming one of so many foreign volunteers who leave Ukraine shortly after arrival, terrified by their first experience on the battlefield.

Yet, Stephen, in his words, survived the night as his own personal test.

And now here he is, pacing the backyard among shattered glass, watching Ukrainian comrades feed abandoned rabbits in their hutches and showing off his shoulder patch.

"See? It reads, 'No one but us!'" he said proudly.

Passageways in this underworld among ruins lead into a dusty concrete cellar beneath a half-finished mansion.

Soldiers marked with blue elbow stripes walk in and out coming and going as radio sets buzz on their shoulders.

A curly mustachioed Ukrainian guy wearing United States Army ACUpat fatigues mounts a .50 caliber M2 Browning machine gun, resting on the cellar floor under the space's bare bulb light.

Wow, seriously? An M2, the legend of Korea and Vietnam, the one we all saw in old war movies, now in our war of 2022? The one designed by iconic John M. Browning? In the dust of this dim basement in Irpin?

That's some serious historic stuff going on there.

"All right, pals," the Ukrainian guy says as others gather around him, laying their weapons down to rest.

The lesson begins on the concrete floor next to the mattresses the volunteer fighters spend their nights on under Russian shelling.

"You better pay attention to what I tell you," the Ukrainian mustache continues, sweeping dust off the M2 Browning. "The other day, we knocked out a Russian vehicle with this thing. So, it's really old but gold. Believe me when I tell you, my little friends, .50 BMG caliber is the real deal. An M2 Browning can pump out nearly 400 rounds per minute, and it has the effective range of nearly up to 1,800 meters . . ."

A generous present from Italy, we learned later.

The instructor cracks open an ammo box full of rounds.

"Is there anyone who can translate what I'm saying? Our new foreigners seem to be not really getting into it. Hey, reporter, do you happen to speak English? Put your camera away and maybe make yourself useful over here."

Sure . . . sure.

Sometimes, you need be a yes guy when embedded with a war party. To gain reasonable trust and show yourself as "our kind of guy," who the soldiers can temporarily admit as part of their band.

It's always about the little things. Like having enough patience and paying enough attention to soldiers as they endlessly show you photographs of their loved ones and talk about how they miss their families, or breaking bread and sharing coffee with them, or listening to their demands and complaints on how shitty their commanding officers are.

You need to respect those little things—if you want to be accepted and get some material to pour onto paper later on. And at the same time, you must find the balance between being "our kind of guy" and slipping into being a shameful war tourist or something of the kind.

That's how a precious extra couple of hours with warfighters is earned.

Later, it's finally time to get going.

See you, guys.

We pack into an old Ford pickup marked PRESS, trying to fit our heavy bodies encased in armor and Kevlar into the bed of the truck.

Sounds of heavy fighting roll down from Irpin.

Stay safe, soldiers.

The way back home isn't far—the restricted war zone is literally a five-minute drive on a highway from the ill-fated bridge of Irpin to the nearest residential districts of Kyiv City.

At the entrance into the city, a little red-bearded guy dressed in the National Emergency Service uniform stops us at a checkpoint. The military couldn't care less, but this guys just jumps out of his skin from anger, seeing a PRESS car.

"Who let you in? Do you realize media representatives are banned from entering Irpin due to security concerns? Who let you in?"

Dude, you did. This morning. As we were crossing this checkpoint with the paramilitary, and the Karpatska Sich guys told you to get lost and stop wasting their time with your pointless questions.

"This is a strict disciplinary violation, and I'm going to report this to military authorities."

Yeah, you go ahead.

A writer and a couple of mid-ranking YouTube video makers that did their job without bringing any extra headache to the military are exactly who's going to be priority number one now as Russia launches their counterattacks—five kilometers away from this checkpoint.

The Army Nation guys drop me at a bus stop in our Kyiv neighborhood, just beyond the entry checkpoint.

The Novobilychi district in the very northwest of Kyiv was still a busy and important transportation hub, part of the city defense.

It's far from being the dark and menacing urban wasteland we witnessed a month ago when we first got back to Kyiv. It now looks like a very busy emergency response scene from a Hollywood movie.

Lots of yellow metropolitan buses still delivered a steady stream of evacuees from the war-affected outskirts. There were still a lot of police, the military, paramedics, rescue service workers rushing here and there.

Lots of trucks bringing medications, food, and warm clothes, lots of Territorial Defense troops sipping coffee at a small supermarket next to the entry checkpoint.

At a T-junction connecting the streets of Kyiv with the Irpin Highway, there was a grotesque but formidable fortress. A square-shaped foxhole constructed of super heavy concrete blocks, as if it was prepared to repel Saracens as they climbed their assault ladders.

At the moment, a bunch of Territorial Defense guys are getting warm and meditatively smoking cigarettes at a bonfire inside its concrete walls.

My iPhone rings.

"Salam alaykum," a familiar silk-soft voice says.

Yuriy Matsarsky, even in wartime, is inseparable from his love for the Middle East.

"Listen, I've got this dude in America, name's Lloyd. He says he's a United States Marine Corps vet, and he's already in Ukraine. He wants to enlist, so the guy's looking for recommendations on joining a decent combat unit. And also, on all that paperwork stuff. Can you please talk to him for me?"

Yes, sure . . . I rub my tired eyes.

"Send him my way, have him shoot me a message on What-sApp . . . we'll see what we can do for that marine of yours. I've just been with pretty interesting dudes in Irpin that welcome foreign volunteers."

"All right!" Matsarsky seems to be in an excellent mood, as always. "Oh, by the way, I saw on Facebook the other day that the International Legion was looking for a spokesperson. What do you think?"

"I don't know, man . . . ," I say. "Not sure if that's for me. Or if I'm qualified enough."

"What are you talking about?" Matsarsky protests immediately. "Of course, it's a job for you. You're going to be a real military service member, a decent human being—just like us."

To tell the truth, I did send my CV to the International Legion. For better or worse, they were not interested.

Anyway, let's get back to the poor apartment of ours, our ongoing wartime headquarters.

The old Soviet-time panel house's entrance hall looks out onto this rear front commotion.

What a time to witness.

For years, the normal thing was you'd spend a day with the military in Donbas, in trenches seven hundred kilometers away, and then slip out of your black sweaty armored vest and leave it in the deep of your hired driver's minivan.

And then an hour-long drive to the Kostyantynivka train station, a four twenty P.M. intercity bullet train to Kyiv, hot dogs and coffee shared with your photographer mate, and then a taxi that finally brings you home by midnight.

An ideal ending to yet another workweek in a war zone, the return to the safety and tranquility of Kyiv from the land of trench dirt and the smell of gunpowder. As always, the days after were about writing yet another war story that may (or may not, to my great disgust) end up on the front page.

It was that way for years, and it felt like it was going to go on forever.

Well, now the place you get your mediocre war stories is a ten-minute drive. And CNN and Euronews reporters in heavy armor sneak around your neighborhood trying to interview old women who haven't fled this place for one reason or another.

And the best thing you can do to entertain yourself in this situation is to take a silly selfie in your apartment house elevator mirror dressed in full field gear and hugging your helmet.

Just to have something to remember these crazy days on Instagram. Back to the laptop again for a quick headline check.

KYIV AUTHORITIES CANCEL A 24-HOUR CURFEW PREVIOUSLY SCHED-
ULED FOR SUNDAY, MARCH 27
RESTRICTIONS REMAIN IN PLACE FOR THE NORMAL NIGHTTIME DURA-
TION BETWEEN 8 P.M. AND 7 A.M.

Well, not bad news.

The stillness of nighttime curfews was still uncomfortable. Throughout the first weeks of the full-scale war, the Kyiv military-civilian administration declared "long curfews" on several occasions, locking up everyone at home for up to two straight days.

For those still living in the city, the first order of business was to stock up on food, fresh water, and other provisions necessary for waiting out a long curfew within four walls. And then there would come the totally chilling, mournful emptiness of the streets. That emptiness in broad daylight was the worst.

But again, just as during COVID-19, dog owners had a little bit of an excuse to go outside for a few minutes—and then strike up conversations with military patrols.

In other news:

Germany sends brand new Matador anti-tank weapons to Ukraine. The first batch of 2,650 pieces out of a total 5,100 worth 25 million euros is set to arrive today . . .

Reuters: United States sees Russia focusing on eastern Ukraine, as opposed to Kyiv.

The war was raging on across the whole of the country. On that day alone, there was a heavy missile attack on Lviv, with large oil terminals also burning in Dubno.

Also, continuing fierce Russian attempts to break through to Myko-laiv and Kryvy Rih, the enemy slowly taking over the city of Izium—the gateway into northern Donbas. Kharkiv was being shelled relentlessly day after day.

And worst of all, the tragedy of Mariupol was about to reach its final act. The city by the sea was all but lost, with Russian forces having locked it in a death grip.

Yet at the same time, there was a feeling that things had at last and irreversibly changed for the Russians in Ukraine's north, particularly at Kyiv.

In the last days of March, we saw constant Ukrainian counterattacks west and east, here and there.

On March 23, Ukrainian forces raised the flag over Makariv, a key town some thirty kilometers west of the capital along the Zhytomyr Highway. In western Irpin, more incremental Ukrainian progress, with local police units resuming service in a non-occupied part of the city on March 23.

The day after saw steady Ukrainian progress east of Kyiv along the H-07 Highway, with Ukrainian forces retaking the town of Lukiyakivka and proceeding farther east.

As early as March 18, Maxar published satellite images of Russian earthen berms northeast of Kyiv, particularly near the key transportation hub of Borodyanka, as well as the Antonov Airport near Hostomel.

The Russians were digging in.

And due to fierce Ukrainian assaults, they had to largely switch to defending their supply lines. Which, along with their logistical problems and the degraded state of their forces after so many days of fierce fighting, was seriously diminishing their offensive capabilities.

Moreover, the same was happening in the Chernihiv and Sumy oblasts, as well as the outskirts of Kharkiv. Between March 23 and 26, Ukraine's 93rd Mechanized Brigade successfully counterattacked and forced Russia's 4th Guards Tank Division units from the city of Trostyanets and later proceeded farther toward the Russian border.

Ukraine was clearly getting the upper hand over the severely degraded Russian forces in the north.

After March 25, the Ukrainian media began circulating rumors of Russian forces getting trapped in a cauldron southwest of Kyiv, somewhere around the Irpin-Bucha-Hostomel triangle.

There were even indications of a possible Ukrainian rush to Ivankiv, a key logistics hub and the gateway into Kyiv Oblast from the Chornobyl Exclusion Zone.

Four weeks into the battle just below our windows, many of us here in Kyiv could feel it in the air that the ravaging beast was growing weaker. Driven out of its hole, it was still lashing out and roaring, but it was also spluttering hard with its own blood.

Long gone was the sense of dark fatalism that stalked us all in the early days of the invasion.

One could feel that the pendulum had swung in the other direction.

It was clear that Russia taking Kyiv was out of the question.

It was over.

More and more, sunlight was breaking through the gray clouds hovering over Kyiv.

And getting warmer every day. Spring was finally coming to the city, after so many nights of cold fear.

It was the kind of fresh spring weather when one cracks open the windows for the first time to let in the sun and the warm breeze.

And still, the sound of artillery.

In the final days of the Battle of Kyiv, Ukrainian artillery almost never stopped pounding the Russian lines. Ukrainian guns were placed in the woods not far away from our neighborhood.

So, day and night, a heavy roar reverberated and echoed within our neighborhood's panel apartment blocks.

Sometimes, the rounds were quite distinguishable, something really heavy that shook the air and made our windows rattle.

Quite possibly, 203-millimeter 2S7 Pion cannons with Ukraine's 43rd Artillery Brigade. There are just some twenty of these in the Ukrainian military. These monsters of unimaginable power gained/secured/attained their fame during this time and in many ways saved Kyiv.

Sometimes, the distant barrage would merge into long rumbling batteries, like fresh springtime thunder.

I cracked my bedroom's window open and put my iPhone on the sill to record the roar. The chattering of kids running around a playground below, the gentle wind, and the thumping of heavy guns.

Ivan peeps into my bedroom.

"Good lord, our guys are just exterminating those Russians," he says. "Stoyanka must be in shambles now. How is it even possible to survive under such a barrage?"

Ivan proceeds to take a huge pack of pirogi and a couple of beers from our wartime stash.

Life is good, huh?

It must be acknowledged that we two did a pretty good job surviving the first month of war.

Two more heavy booms followed by the roar of air alert sirens coming from districts deeper in the city. Recording off. My humble contribution in documenting history in the making.

We all know where this is all headed. Hopefully.

Laptop open, time for another story.

UKRAINE REACHES BREAKING POINT IN RUSSIA'S WAR

Yeah, a bit of a bold statement.

Around this time, during an online event hosted by the Atlantic Council, retired United States European Command commander Philip M. Breedlove told me I was being extremely optimistic to say that Russia might have to consider leaving the Kyiv area in the following weeks to avoid a devastating defeat.

But hey, this war is filled with surprises to the max. A month before, the whole world was burying us alive.

Why not dream big now that our military has the momentum?

Back to the story draft.

> Russia's all-out war in Ukraine has subverted a lot of prophecies—doomsday omens and bright hopes alike.
>
> It has now been a month of this new reality since Russia's attacks began early in the morning on February 24, 2022.
>
> Yes, the Kremlin really did launch a World War II–level military offensive against Ukraine. Their invasion is full of war crimes and barbarities and lacks an obvious rationale.

No, Ukraine didn't turn out to be frail and didn't kneel down before the invading army.

Instead, after a month of hostilities, tangible results indicate that Ukraine has sustained the war's first major blow. It defeated the Kremlin's initial, most dangerous plan of a quick, shock-and-awe invasion.

Now, the war is entering a new phase—a grueling longer-term war of attrition, and a new, difficult test for the Ukrainian military and the nation . . .

It's a weirdly incredible feeling to write all this stuff in the same room from which one imagined the coming of apocalypse such a short time ago.

It's like having a rigorous MRT doctor tell you that the end is near and that you should hurry to see the sea before it's too late (because heaven is all about talking about the sea) . . . and then, five weeks later, you're still enjoying the sunshine and hope is still very much alive, and it's winning.

All life is a mystery.

According to the latest reports, Ukrainian forces, following a series of advances, took nearly 80 to 85 percent of the Irpin city territory and also gained a foothold in the key town of Makariv some thirty kilometers west of Kyiv.

Fresh Ukrainian progress against the towns of Borodyanka and Ivankiv, key supply points on the roads to Belarus, might further deteriorate the position of the Russian troops northwest of Kyiv, which reportedly includes two undermanned infantry brigades.

In general, the new phase of war sees Russia forced to halt its costly attempts to advance and Ukraine saving and expanding its full combat potential.

The key factor now is Ukraine's ability to keep pressure on the Russian military for as long as possible. As such, Western suffocation of the Russian economy is vital.

Vast defense assistance in all regards possible—from simple firearms and munitions to anti-tank and, even more important, air defense systems, both short-range man-portable and stationary medium-range.

To achieve victory, the next big mission is to eliminate the Russian presence in the air.

Done.

I told you—even if the worst was to come, nothing was predestined.

Unless we had all given up before the battle had even begun.

Ivan peeps into the room again, tastefully sipping beer from the bottle.

"I don't know about you," he says as our windows rattle from artillery thumping, "but I'm going to get a very wonderful sleep on my couch as our guys do their thing."

Suddenly, lights are out.

I check my phone for alerts.

No electricity in northwest Kyiv due to hostilities. The authorities vow to get the problem fixed—as soon as repair workers can make it to the war zone.

Weirdly enough, throughout the battle of Kyiv, I think we only had a couple of days of electricity blackouts in our neighborhood. And the power supply would always get restored literally within hours—all thanks to the heroes of this battle who did not wear camouflage.

So many heroes in this war, and this one is tired after my trip to the front to visit the actual heroes.

Anyway, best not to draw down my batteries. Time to follow Ivan and get some sleep.

SEVENTEEN

A nother day of this routine.

Another cup of morning coffee being brewed to the sound of rolling thunder.

There's a group of Ukrainian Humvees beneath our kitchen windows.

A small group of United States-provided armored cars waving blue-yellow banners slowly dashes through the narrow lanes of our neigh-borhood and heads toward the Irpin checkpoint.

Last night was relatively calm, at least not as insane as the previous one. Mostly, nothing but the roar of distant guns blazing, and the night wind bringing echoes of machine gun bursts rattling.

I can even state that we've had a very good sleep. I even took the liberty of a lingering lie-in in the morning sun—for the first time in so many weeks of war. Shame on my lazy ass.

Nothing really fresh in the news.

Except for the power being back on, which is just awesome. Frozen meat (and also beer) remain a vital part of our fortress apartment's wartime provision stash, so Ivan was worried about the integrity of our fridge.

A message from Natalia.

"Hey, sweetie . . . how was the trip to Irpin?"

She misses me painfully. Me, likewise, her.

"Good, pretty good. We didn't make it to the actual combat zone but saw plenty and talked to a lot of our guys. Even after some sleep I'm still tired from running around with my field gear on."

"How's it in Kyiv? I feel like crying all the time. This war has only made me realized how much I love the city. I really want to come back . . . what do you think?"

"Well . . . the Russians are still close, just several kilometers from my place . . . and they're still pounding the city. Ivan and I were at what's left of the Retroville mall, that big one in the Vynogradar district. It's just a nightmare—obliterated. The entire neighborhood surrounding it—all the windows shattered."

"I saw that in the news, yeah . . . and that apartment block on Bohatyrska Street you reported from. So many families tossed into chaos in the very dead of night because of the shelling."

"Yeah . . . so, you better stay with your parents for the moment. Things might change for the better soon. At least here in Kyiv. Anyway . . . how are your mom and dad?"

"They're pretty good . . . The town is still carrying on in its usual quiet way, except for all the newcomers who've come from the cities, including Kyiv. They pay insane money to wait out the war here. Dad, of course, is glued to the news. But he's also getting our kitchen garden ready to plant potatoes, as they always do this time of year. He's pleased you have his knife in Kyiv, even though it's really a cheap piece from AliExpress . . ."

"Wait, what? I thought that was a precious present to bless my trip to war."

"Well, it was! In a way . . . I'm so glad that we're going through this together. Really. It's hard to believe we got together only last December, just a couple of months before this nightmare."

"I hope my mom isn't too much trouble. She's . . . very irrational now. She tests my patience every day. She's still in shock and in denial of what's happening. She wants to get back home, to the Russian-occupied zone . . . and I'm afraid, knowing how stubborn she is, she'll actually do it."

"Please don't worry about her. My mom is pretty good at calming her down. She's going to stay with us here—she'll get a job at the local pension service department. My parents are glad they can help a war refugee from Donbas, especially as it's your mom."

"All right . . . I hope she'll stay with you at least until we have a clearer understanding of where things are headed. We're in the middle of a fucking war, and everything is pretty messed up. At this point, who knows what our future may look like."

"Did you see that at least five thousand people have been killed in Mariupol so far?"

"Yeah . . ."

We talked for a bit longer, good and bad news.

Wartime stuff, and, really, it's all bad, cruel, senseless. This did not have to happen. I pictured Natalia in her yard, phone to ear, the garden plot ready for the seed potatoes. That's what we should be thinking of, what we have been robbed of. Everyday life. Now it was all extraordinary, and in a bad way.

If I hadn't met Natalia, if we didn't have each other, it would be so much worse, I think.

I tell her this and we both choked up and then said our goodbyes.

I'm a bit jumpy.

Ivan doesn't seem to be around, probably off on another secret mission. My editor signed off on my latest and I apparently have some time on my hands.

A lull in the shelling moves me to the window and low and behold it is a beautiful day.

Let's maybe try to recall how great it is to take a ride through a sunny city. To try to pretend we're back in our lives before the darkest day.

The gloves, the sport glasses, the tactical backpack, the bicycle de-mothballed after months caged up on the balcony, the streets of Kyiv.

War or no war, a bicycle freak like me simply can't miss the beginning of the cycling season. And believe me, there were quite a few bicyclists roving among the concrete blocks and endless checkpoints of the war-weary city.

Who knows what's coming our way—with our dire fuel crisis, when getting twenty liters of gas is a huge achievement, there was a good chance that Kyiv might turn into a new Amsterdam—blissfully carless, but not by choice.

Riding on . . . Peremohy Avenue, the wide backbone of the west bank of Kyiv, still not as busy as usual, but nonetheless exceedingly slow and painful because of the checkpoints set up every several hundred meters.

What's great is the soldiers manning the checkpoints couldn't care less about cyclists cutting to the front of the long lines of cars slowly crawling forward.

"Ride on, don't impede the traffic," a national guardsman says, waving me past a roadblock next to the Polytechnic Institute Park.

The city had changed again.

It felt like those streets and buildings had discarded the veil of gray sorrow and doom and breathed in the first deep breath of hope.

The rusty crosses of anti-tank hedgehogs were still everywhere, as were hulking concrete blocks and abandoned, shot-through vehicles amid broken glass and ash. But Kyiv was slowly getting back to its true self.

As I ride on, I begin to sense the chilly air of swan lakes in Nyvky Park not far from the United States embassy. The giant variegated figure of a giraffe at the Kyiv Zoo seems lively again, even though no one is queuing up to spend a day watching our animals.

And finally, Podil—the sanctum sanctorum of Kyiv pubs and coffee shops.

I finally hit the brakes at Kontraktova Square, hard by the area's tram terminal. Still, almost no one walking or driving around, except for the rare pedestrian sneaking into local groceries.

A door to the business center where we rented our office space appears to be open.

The fifth floor, the elevator doesn't work. I could use the exercise.

Luckily, I happen to have keys to the *Kyiv Independent* office with me.

The empty and silent office looks just the same. Dirty mugs on desks, reams of paper, stacks of magazines, crackers. Trash cans not emptied, our coffee machine on and ready to brew a fresh pot.

The office frozen in time as we left it that night, just hours before the catastrophe of February 24, 2022.

I'll be totally honest with you—back before the day of all days, I thought the *KI* would simply cease to exist. In the hell of a full-scale war, I was almost sure we'd lose one another trying to save our own lives . . . who would think about running a media outlet when you could almost feel the cold metal of a pistol at your forehead?

But . . . our guys did it.

Our North America team—Americans, Canadians, and expat Ukrainians—carried the load as we lost connection to the internet and kept the website updated. We in Ukraine all found safe places to work 24/7 from wherever we could: bomb shelters, distant towns in the Carpathian Mountains, or in small villages just over the Polish border.

As it turned out, a small team of Ukrainians and foreigners with laptops would become Ukraine's leading voice in the ocean of media buzz during the biggest European war since 1945.

That's dedication and commitment. And people who actively sided with the right side of history in the darkest moment, regardless of nationality.

And of course, it was about readers—the number of ordinary people from around the world willing to support the paper skyrocketed into many thousands in the early days of war. Almost immediately, our Patreon membership shot to number one in Ukrainian media, by a very long margin.

It's been only a little more than a month since we all left this office. But it feels like it happened a lifetime ago, and I'm inside a time capsule from an epoch long forgotten.

Truly, I never believed we'd ever get back to the old office again. I thought Vladimir Putin's twisted face on TV screens and the first blasts of Russian missile attacks that night signaled the end.

We would all try to play an honorable role in the defining drama of our time, and then be pushed offstage.

And those few among our friends and colleagues who managed to outlast the hell of war would have to look for another life somewhere else. I thought we'd lose our home and our way of life, at least for a very long time.

The downfall of the world as we know it.

But all life is a mystery.

Millions of men and women in this country, from top officials to the military and regular people like us, made a moral choice.

While the larger world debated whether Kyiv would fall within forty-eight or seventy-two hours, so many in this country decided to do what was right.

The Battle of Kyiv taught me one thing—in the darkest moments, always act according to your highest moral principles. No matter how hard and scary that might be.

It will be hard, but at the end of the day, it will always be the only right decision.

The seemingly easiest way is always wrong. Deals with the devil made out of weakness and a desire to sweep trouble under the rug never end well.

When the time came, our comedian-turned-president, a leader whose popularity was in freefall, declined to escape what seemed like certain death and leave Kyiv. His legendary phrase "I need ammo, not a ride" is most probably a media myth.

But the moment he videoed himself and his administration in front of the Bankova Street government building on February 25, he was reborn as the most prominent war leader of this young century—not a failed president in exile good for little more than meaningless public statements and the occasional angry interview, issued from the safety of a foreign state.

And the soldiers of the 72nd Mechanized, and from so many other units, fought fiercely and died bravely at Moschun because they had faith and real hope of saving the city.

And regular people of Kyiv, untrained civilians from all walks of life, snapped up Kalashnikov rifles and prepared Molotov cocktails, ready to fight and die in the streets of Obolon.

As for myself, returning to Kyiv to fulfill my role as a journalist in one of the most dramatic episodes of modern history was the best decision of my life.

We didn't give up and we didn't think about personal consequences. We had faith and hope in something larger.

Because of this, history made a sudden U-turn.

I pick up a book from my newsroom office desk. I thought I'd never see this volume again.

The white cover shows an old black-and-white photo of British troops guiding a Mark VI tank trying to overcome a muddy trench. The Battle of Cambrai, between late November and early December 1917.

John Keegan, *The First World War.*

An edition in Russian.

Even during those days in late March 2022, when there was new hope in the air, no one seriously had any illusions of what might come next.

But good lord, in the worst of our expectations, could we even imagine—the slaughter of Mariupol, the blood-soaked fields of death of Bakhmut, the insanely endless stalemate of trench warfare, the destruction of the Kakhovka dam, or a winter in the dark and cold amid Russian missile barrages?

The Battle of Kyiv was just the beginning, but we could see the way forward. The most defining victory had been achieved, and the nation took a step away from the brink of the abyss.

Even in this small and mediocre newsroom office. Within the next few weeks, the space would be noisy and busy again, our little band gladly reuniting in these premises to see one another's smiling faces at desks behind laptops once more.

It's the unspeakable miracle of small, heartwarming things that one begins to really appreciate at the brink.

The fight continues and would continue, for how long no one knew. But right now, I want to get out into the sunshine and absorb my favorite city neighborhood.

And I owe you that tour I promised a while back.

Podil is the historic area we venture into if we want a decent beer-and-meat pub or an even better coffee place.

I don't really get this, but almost every corner of this district of shop windows, god-awful tram routes, and early nineteenth century revenue houses is so iconic that there's a saying that "Kyiv is not possible without Podil."

People sometimes call it "the little Prague." And that's fair, given the amount of abominable graffiti Kyiv and the Czech capital are both infested with.

Podil is a flat lowland that descends from the hills of Old Kyiv to the Dnipro riverside. After Mongolians overran ancient Kyiv and left it in ruins, local life gradually moved downhill to Podil—which essentially became the city center for the next seven hundred years, until the early nineteenth century.

It was always the place for small merchants, craftsmanship, and trade fairs.

Merchants would come to the Kyiv port from lands up the Dnipro River and strike deals with local tradespeople. Kontraktova Square, the heart of Podil, was called that simply because merchants made trading contracts there at the riverside.

As centuries passed, Podil became the center around which Kyiv, the perished capital of an ancient kingdom, slowly resurrected itself as a classy, modern eastern European city.

One can still see many traces of the seventeenth century in today's Podil. From that period date several wonderful Cossack Baroque churches and many more houses, the stone walls of which are painted white and roofs green.

That was a time when kingdoms and princedoms fought fiercely and serially replaced one another as rulers of Kyiv: Lithuanians and Poles, Ukrainian Cossacks and Russian tsars, then Russian emperors.

And then Kyiv had to radically change its face once more. Following the great fire of 1811, it literally rose again from the ashes, only now as a classy nineteenth-century city—and this is what Podil in many ways looks like today.

If you ever get a chance to visit Kyiv, Podil is the place to go to.

Begin by descending from the hills of Old Kyiv crowned by the large statue of Prince Volodymyr the Great and go down to the Dnipro embarkment at Poshtova Square, which shines so bright in the night.

Or go down from St. Andrew's Church on the hills along the legendary Andriivskyi Descent—the home of writers, theater actors, and painters—right to Kontraktova Square.

And then proceed to wherever your eye beckons, because Podil is a place where one can find interesting things in every direction. From the circular main hall of Kyiv Mohyla Academy—one of the oldest universities of Eastern Europe—to the Zhovten Theater—which is almost as old as the very notion of sound films—or the green boulevard of Val that once served as the northern defensive wall of Kyiv.

Podil is especially great during the warm months on a sunny morning, when one can have a cup of drip coffee on a terrace.

A day like today, though coffee will be hard to come by.

Or in the evening, when one can have some high-quality craft beer at a pub and then take a walk across Podil to a subway station, catching the St. Andrew's Church shining from the hills of Old Kyiv.

For some mystical reason, this district of often unremarkable shop windows and crooked streets all enwrapped by a cacophony of church bells and tram squeals is utterly magnetic to me.

Throughout March 2022, when Podil was cold, empty, and strewn with rusty anti-tank crosses, it was still delivering its vibe. And this legend was so critically close to being rubbed out under a Russian soldier's boot.

I suddenly stop by a shop window on Kosyantynivska Street.

The warm light and mild music issuing from behind closed roller shutters. That's the Titka Klara, a mediocre pastry bakery . . . open again and expecting customers.

I can't describe the pleasure of being able to just quietly sit at a bakery and sip unimpressive Americano from a paper cup—in a beloved city that has prevailed.

Ivan drives his Daewoo Lanos through the deepening twilight along Velyka Zhytomyrska Street.

It's wet and cold outside tonight, and there are not many streetlights in downtown Kyiv, so traffic signals splash bright and large through thin mist.

We're out for a little party that we at the *Kyiv Independent* humbly think we deserve.

So, four of us journalists and Ivan, who has launched a skyrocketing career in media as our driver, decided to get together and commit a bit of lawbreaking.

It's March 29, 2022.

The radio in Ivan's car once again interrupts its music program for the roar of a broadcast air raid siren.

The same chilling howl echoes outside in the streets.

"Attention, attention!" a sonorous male voice flows from the broadcast. "A missile strike threat has been announced in Kyiv. Make sure to take cover and stay in a safe shelter until the all-clear signal."

Fucking Russians and their missiles. That was the fifth air threat alert in Kyiv since last night.

Never mind. It's the new normal now for us all.

I keep scrolling newsfeeds and read news aloud as Ivan drives on toward downtown Kyiv.

> Amid a new round of anemic talks between Kyiv and Moscow in Istanbul, the Russian Defense Ministry announced a decision to "radically reduce military activities" at Kyiv and Chernihiv . . .

In the last days of March, Ukrainian counterattacks were unfolding in full swing—and the Russians were retreating. By March 27–28, Ukrainian forces had retaken the whole of Irpin and were pushing the enemy off the Zhytomyr Highway from the south.

East of Kyiv, Ukrainian forces were quickly advancing along the H-07 Highway and retaking towns and villages farther east of Brovary and Boryspil.

Quite rationally, the Russians decided to withdraw from the Kyiv region before it was too late to avert a disastrous defeat. To put a good face on their humiliation, they presented the move as a "goodwill gesture."

This would be the first of many such gestures and already they elicited nothing but tired smiles.

"Mmmkay," Ivan only murmurs to express his reaction to the news. "Fuckers got their asses kicked, then."

It's hard to express how mundane and ordinary our feelings were about the first indications that Ukraine had achieved its first and most important victory in Russia's full-scale war.

Ivan parks the car not far away from Sofiivska Square. And we head to the Buena Vista bar—its kaleidoscopic colors shining bright right next to a police roadblock.

A police guy regulates traffic at the entrance.

The bar roars with Latin music and is absolutely brimming with joyful clients—and at least half of them are foreigners enjoying the finest cocktails and iced whiskey. And yes, a lot of familiar journalist faces.

Welcome to the underworld of wartime Kyiv, a place where you can forget about war and the blanket ban on alcohol sales—if you're not too short on money. The authorities don't seem to mind, at all.

"Heeeeeeey!" Our *Kyiv Independent* guys wave at us from stools ringing a small table.

Three of us were in Kyiv throughout the battle: Igor Kossov, our Ukrainian-American, Anna Myroniuk, our investigative reporter, and yours truly. And as the initial shock of war dissipated, more and more of our guys were returning home from evacuation.

Everyone missed the good old town of ours.

Our political editor, Oleksiy Sorokin, had just returned after a month in Chernivtsi, to his absolute joy.

"Finally, oh finally," Anna screams through the Latin music. "The media veterans of Kyiv are all in the same room. Why did it take so long?"

"I think we were all a bit busy." Oleksiy smiles. "You know, Russians at the city gates and all."

Ivan returns to our table with a load of cold lagers.

"Hey, let's raise our glasses for our new team member, Ivan," Anna says.

I join in: "Without your ride, your patience, and your ability to find the treasure of a full tank of gas, there wouldn't be so many stories from Kyiv. And thank you for what you did to help my mom."

Yeah, that was a moving moment.

Anna's mom managed to flee Russian-occupied Bucha in mid-March, during yet another Ukrainian attempt to evacuate women and children into Kyiv.

Her bus column made it through Russian checkpoints and the front line. With Ivan driving, we met her in the outskirts of Kyiv, and mother and daughter hugged each other in tears after weeks in the hell of Bucha.

"I'm so glad I made it home," Oleksiy says. "Staying in Chernivtsi and watching what was happening to Kyiv sucked. I'll never leave the city again . . . Anyway, I think we've been doing a pretty good job in wartime. We are the Ukrainian voice in this war."

"Amen. And cheers."

"Yeah . . . ," Igor says. "Getting back to Kyiv to cover the war was so right. If I had stayed away, I would never be able to forgive myself."

I sip my beer and look around the bar.

Damn, half of the world's top media outlets are hanging out here.

"I think given all the recent developments, we have every reason to celebrate." I raise my glass. "Who could have thought that things would go this way . . . that Kyiv would kick Russia's ass so hard. It's not the end of the war by a long shot—let's see what happens next. But damn—it's history. Russians are leaving Kyiv defeated."

"So, cheers to all those who are driving history this way," Igor says.

"And also . . . to those who record it," I continue. "How many of our colleagues have been killed and injured lately . . . five, six of them? Ukrainians, foreigners. All those guys shot dead and smashed in shelling while doing our job. And Maks Levin, the photographer . . . you know, he's gone missing for like two weeks already. I really hope he's alive in Russian captivity somewhere."

Smiles quickly fade from our faces.

Ukrainian police will find Maks Levin's body two days later in the forest southwest of Kyiv. Russians shot the internationally acclaimed news photographer and his mate Oleksiy Chernyshev in the head from a short distance and set the latter's body on fire in their car.

"Guys, let see one another more often here in Kyiv," Anna says. "How about we meet up every Friday, just like now, shall we?"

"Yeah . . . why not," "After all, we're still a family-type newsroom. I don't think there have been many news organizations that literally survived their capital city under siege and looked after one another at the same time."

Nope. And we all fall silent and grin at one another.

Anyway, it's time to get going.

There's a lot of work to do to prepare for yet another day in wartime.

As customers leave the illegal party little by little, Ivan and I decide to get more of the Prohibition vibe and reach out to the bartender to buy two bottles of mediocre Scotch whiskey—at an insanely inflated price.

If only we could have known that as soon as the next day, the Kyiv administration would lift the booze ban in the city "due to the improving security situation."

Good news for this night, however, is that as of yesterday, authorities rescheduled the beginning of the regular nighttime curfew from eight P.M. to nine P.M.

One more hour to go.

We all dive back into the dark city to make it to the shelter of our homes.

But the lines of military checkpoints and empty avenues don't feel creepy anymore.

Our city is getting back to life.

EIGHTEEN

In 2023, I started noticing pro-Russian propagandists aggressively sowing a conspiracy theory regarding the end of the Battle of Kyiv, a theory that seemed especially aimed at an American audience.

It went like this: Ukraine and Russia were close to a deal in Istanbul to end the war—but the Biden administration, as evil warmongers, prevented that from happening so that their "proxy war on Russia" could continue.

Well, let me tell you what really happened and why the Istanbul "peace talks" didn't stand the slightest chance, with or without the West.

It is true that toward the end of March, the Zelensky administration was still trying to get a deal, talk to Putin, and find a workable compromise with Russia.

Russia's disastrous position at the time probably gave new impetus to diplomacy. And the Zelensky administration and the president himself were publicly voicing a number of possible concessions: Ukraine's neutrality, the nonnuclear status (as if Kyiv ever had a chance to get nukes again, uh-huh). Even occupied Crimea was suggested as a subject for talks between Kyiv and Moscow—the status quo of Russia keeping Crimea and Ukraine officially not recognizing this would continue for fifteen years.

Yes—Ukraine might agree on a guaranteed peace through concessions, but not if the precondition for these concessions amounted to little more than a brief cease-fire, during which Russia would only stoke up hostilities and perpetrate further land grabs.

So, Ukraine also demanded a full cease-fire, international security guarantees (yeah, good luck with that!), and the Russian withdrawal from all territories occupied since February 24.

But, of course, for the Kremlin, this war was never about NATO, or nuclear weapons, or any security concerns—but about the conquest of Ukraine's territory and its subordination.

The whole of Ukraine or as much of its territory as possible.

Given Russia's initial ambitions, forcing them to acknowledge the preinvasion borders of February 24, with Kyiv "assuming obligations" to "never attack Russia with NATO" would be a total failure—this was not what Putin unleashed this war for.

They were withdrawing from the Kyiv axis because of a military defeat. Within a matter of days, by April 1, they had completely pulled back what was left of the main strike force as Ukrainian artillery pounded them on their way out.

On March 30–31, Ukrainian drone surveillance operators reported zero hostile targets in Bucha. Then Hostomel . . . Vorzel . . . Ivankiv. On April 3, Ukrainian troops reinstalled the national flag over the Chornobyl Nuclear Power Plant.

Russia's military presence surrounding Kyiv was wrapped up in a snap, as quickly as it had poured down in late February. It happened so fast that few in Ukraine really believed it was true.

And since Russia had to give up on Kyiv, it made no sense to continue wasting its severely degraded power on Chenihiv and Sumy as well. They left from the whole of northern Ukraine, effectively giving up close to 40 percent of Ukraine's territory taken after February 24.

But fierce fighting and devastating assaults were continuing everywhere Russia was able to advance farther—Mariupol, Izium, the outskirts of Kryvy Rih. Taking as much Ukrainian land as possible.

Human ferocity and thirst for power know no bounds.

Even after Kyiv, Russia was ready to accept nothing but territorial grabs and Ukraine as a puppet quasi-state. The rest was just hot talk. And Ukraine would never agree to simply cease to exist as a nation.

It was zero-sum game with no middle ground between life and death.

Exact figures remain to be established in the future. But as of April 15, 2022, Oryx had verified and documented Russian losses of some 500 tanks, close to 800 infantry fighting vehicles and personnel carriers, over 800 trucks, over 150 artillery pieces, over 50 rocket systems, and over 50 aircraft and helicopters.

All the result of an extremely overconfident, delusional attempt to play out a blitzkrieg rush that led to Russian battlefield losses not seen since World War II.

The defeat was so costly and staggering that Russia greatly narrowed its megalomanic war goals and switched the focus to Donbas. And this new stage would turn into an unprecedented nightmare, leaving the entire region devastated, depopulated, cast back decades in time with little hope on the horizon.

The hot talk would go on and on.

And then the fog of war evaporated.

We journalists saw firsthand what the Russian army left behind in Kyiv Oblast. At the first chance, we followed the Ukrainian military or the police as they entered the bloodland.

What we saw exceeded our worst expectations.

The Zhytomyr Highway, after the thirty-six-day battle, transmogrified into a giant cemetery of tanks and incinerated wreckage.

Russian Kamaz trucks and T-72 tanks—clusters of dozens of them almost everywhere—many burnt to the color of rust. Many smashed literally into pieces, many with their turrets ripped off.

And civilian cars riddled with bullets and shell fragments, with the cyanotic remains of those who were unable to escape lying on the asphalt. Gas stations and roadside malls we all knew so well reduced to ashes, all stores brutally plundered if not burned to the ground.

Those scenes rolled out to the horizon as far as the eye could see—through thick fog and absolute, chilling silence. As if the coldest abyss of Dante's inferno was frozen in time and made available for a camera.

Roads among the forests northwest of Kyiv were graveyards of tanks and infantry fighting vehicles. Countless remains of what had been Russian armored columns rammed into the ground by Ukrainian artillery.

Borodyanka, the key transportation point from Chornobyl to Kyiv, was in shambles. In early March, someone hiding between the town's nine-story apartment complexes fired an RPG rocket on a Russian truck column on the march.

In retaliation, a Russian bomber obliterated every last one of the buildings, with all of the residents still inside their apartments.

Local women told us about those trapped under the rubble screaming and groaning for hours as the Russians stood by and refused to authorize rescue efforts.

And then, every single night, local men, armed with whatever was at hand, would emerge from their daytime hiding places and attack Russians across the town.

In many other towns, such as Motyzhyn, west of Kyiv, there were pits of death filled with the bodies of executed citizens barely covered with thin layers of sand. Local officials, activists, those who had signed up for the Territorial Defense Forces and never managed to muster ahead of advancing Russians.

In the aftermath of Russia's month-long occupation, over thirteen hundred civilian bodies were recovered and identified, and some three hundred more people were missing. The Ukrainian police would continue to discover new pits of death across the region for many months after the battle.

And those funeral crosses.

So many handmade crosses of scrap lumber erected over improvised graves, next to houses, over parking lots, in the woods, near churches. Wherever survivors could quickly bury their loved ones (or sometimes just people next door) and leave their names handwritten on wooden boards.

Dozens of them in places so commonplace, so usual and familiar, now embraced by the venom of gruesome death.

Try to imagine seeing a grave hastily dug in the parking lot of the Walmart in Carrefour—the one that you've driven to millions of times, the one that's part of your life's everyday errands, the one at which you'd never expect to see anything other than your neighbors messing around with shopping carts at their car trunk.

Such a rapid intrusion of mass death into the beautiful routine of everyone's life is one of the most unspeakably horrifying things one can witness.

The Antonov Airport, the place this all began . . . a giant moonscape of impact craters and trenches dug in the clay soil. And scores of destroyed Russian helicopters scattered across the runway.

A large concrete pad among hangars was literally a mishmash of ruined Russian armored vehicles, trucks, and ammo boxes.

And the world's greatest cargo aircraft, Antonov An-225 Mriya, moored in a crushed hangar, with its charred fore-body torn off as if chopped with a giant axe.

Goodbye, Mriya. Thank you for your service.

We reporters tried to walk carefully among the debris next to the aircraft. And in that terrible blend of twisted metal and charred artillery shells, many didn't notice a horrifying detail—a blackened human torso that used to belong to a nameless Russian soldier.

His comrades left that body part behind as they were leaving the Hostomel Airport. Likely because they failed to notice it, too, in the twisted mess of their armored vehicles trashed by Ukrainian artillery.

Bucha was cold, gray, and utterly silent when we arrived.

It's hard to describe the sense of that place from those days. Nothing but rot and mournful stillness. As if the evil that was done there still reigned over the town.

Also, the inexplicable sense of disgusting abomination. As if troops of doom left the very air of this place poisoned with the miasma of dark grief.

Russians left behind crude scribblings and graffiti and marking everything they touched with the letter "V." To this day, one can still come across a fence on the main street of Bucha: "Those entering the no-go zone shall be executed. V."

And bodies of the dead. In basements, in backyards, in improvised graves. Dead faces appearing from the dark as Ukrainian policemen broke through doors into abandoned premises.

The worst thing was charred and mutilated bodies.

Two males and two females, one of them possibly a teen girl. They lay on the ground, not completely burned, with their mouths open and their hands twisted.

They had been dead for quite a while. They'd probably been hiding in a basement somewhere nearby, and Russians gunned them down, gathered their bodies at a playground and set them on fire.

In Hostomel, I remember discovering another handwritten message on a garage wall in Russian, spelled with a grammatical error in the original: "We're liberating Ukraine from Nazism."

At the Andrew the Apostle Church, the white temple that rises high over Bucha—the mass grave that we knew existed from mobile videos and satellite images.

Ukrainian coroners dressed in white one-piece hazmat suits and face masks carefully removed layers of wet clayish soil and put the unearthed bodies on simple wooden doors, under the cold drizzle.

And then a tow truck hoisted the cadavers up one by one, hour by hour. Time and again, the rain intensified. And the coroners would hastily cover the grave with plastic sheeting stained by a mixture of dried gore and rainwater.

A total of sixty-seven bodies unearthed from the pit's several layers.

"My theory is that there was a very brutal Russian commander in charge of Bucha," Kyiv Oblast chief of police Andriy Nebytov told me and several other reporters that day near the ill-fated church, standing in front of a row of microphones. "And they unleashed hell in this place."

The police chief gave a short briefing to the media in the pouring rain next to the death pit.

I remember a guy named Mykola Mosyarevych whom I met at the Continent apartment complex, which used to be one of the finest in Bucha.

He was a young and fit guy in his thirties . . . a likely target for the Russians as a potential guerrilla fighter or a Territorial Defense member.

He spent the whole month in a basement, seeing little to no daylight.

He had survived thanks to his neighbors and the silent permissiveness of certain Russian soldiers, who once allowed them to get some food from a destroyed ATB supermarket nearby.

On the day I came to Bucha, he was sitting at a basketball court at his damaged home, staring down at a pair of ripped Russian fatigues marked with the orange-and-black-striped Saint George ribbon—the notorious symbol of war and love for destruction.

He was shedding tears. And he couldn't stop repeating: "I just don't understand. I don't understand. I don't understand why they would want to do all this to us."

We all asked similar questions. There were no answers commensurate with the awful reality.

Fragments of thought of little use to this traumatized man who had lost everything: insane lust for power, years of aggressive propaganda celebrating a hateful thirst for revenge, and an unbelievable sense of impunity. A weak would-be emperor grasping at illusion. Deep down, fear.

I walk alone with my camera through what was left of the ill-fated Russian armored column on Vokzalna Street.

The horrific pictures of the scene made headlines around the world.

A couple dozen BMP-3s and BTRs were moving toward Irpin to attack Ukrainian positions at the Giraffe shopping mall and then onward toward Kyiv.

The battle's most critical hours in late February . . . defenders of Bucha later told us journalists that Russian troops riding the armor were moving carelessly and singing patriotic songs.

They considered themselves undisputed victors rightfully taking what was theirs in glory.

The strike was classic.

The war party's leading and trailing vehicles were destroyed first. The column stops. Russian fighting vehicles scramble like bumper cars trying to maneuver among the damaged machines, find a way out, and save themselves—one could see that from the battle's destroyed remains.

Vokzalna Street is a narrow place. It was a trap.

And then there came a devastating Ukrainian artillery strike, likely leaving no vehicle in one piece.

The result was a Death Valley of eviscerated armor.

The layer of ash on the ground was so thick it scrunched underfoot like snow.

And this cemetery used to be a leafy green lane, part of my favorite bicycle route via Irpin to Bucha and Hostomel.

"Hey, man, check this out!"

A company of Ukrainian emergency service workers hangs out among the debris. They draw the attention of one of their own, who appears to be quite sensitive to the hellscape scattered all around.

"Boo!"

They kick a Russian soldier's ripped-off foot in a boot toward the guy.

"Oh, seriously, fuck you, guys," he cringes, making them all laugh.

In some three weeks, Ukrainian workers will get all the rubble cleared away. And they'll put down fresh pavement on the road, leaving little trace of that Death Valley of scorched Russian armor.

And later, the son of Warren Buffett will donate funds so that Ukrainian authorities can completely renovate the entire street, construct new, Scandinavian-style single-family houses crowned with green lawns and short fences.

Not a single living soul will recognize this place as that very hellscape from pictures in the news from Ukraine. And people on the internet will leave tens of thousands of likes and comments under tweets comparing the Vokzalna Street during the Russian occupation with what it was turned into.

A Western photographer who had also been there later said Bucha was a "place cursed forever" after the massacre.

Well, hell no.

Believe me when I tell you that springtime soon came, too.

And endless lines of cars, thousands of those who had fled the doom, poured back to their little hometown literally days after the liberation.

And young moms got back to the green streets with their strollers blazing in the sun.

Life went on as it should.

Time will absorb all the horror and grief into oblivion—as it did with so many wars and battles that had visited this land before.

EPILOGUE

Any season in Kyiv is good to feel.

But late spring is awesome, especially if one has the chance to enjoy a moment of tranquility and sunshine at Mariinsky Park. It's one of Kyiv's most famous parks, dating back to the nineteenth century and stretching between the city's government quarter, the Dnipro riverside, and the Arsenalna subway station.

It's a tiny forest of effervescence in the middle of the city. And this May it's as full of green, sunshine, and birdsong as ever before.

Kyiv is back big-time as a peaceful, bustling city.

Streets are noisy and busy again. Roadblocks and anti-tank barriers have disappeared without a trace, almost all of them. Maidan Square shows off lovely rows of tulips in red, yellow, and pink.

Rumors even have it that they will turn on the square's fountains this May, despite wartime limitations. Kids rush around park paths next to crowds of hipsters riding their e-scooters.

Kyiv embraces the fragrance of chestnut blossoms, which today smell like freedom. Yet another springtime in the grand old city.

Natalia is back in town again, for the first time since the apocalypse day of late February. This is literally our first real wartime date, and we agreed to meet up at Mariinsky Park.

So here I am, spread-eagled on a park bench, enjoying the warm sunshine beaming through the green, and gnawing my ice cream.

My loved one is a bit late.

The heart shrinks a little.

Tomorrow is a big day. I'm leaving for yet another front-line assignment. Now it's Donbas. Ukraine's 79th Airborne Brigade is waiting to get me and my photographer embedded with a combat unit holding the line on the banks of the Siversky Donets River near Lyman.

Ivan will pick me up early in the morning. We're set to rendezvous with the photographer in Dnipro, and then head to a rented apartment in Slovyansk.

And then we dive into the artillery fire and the dirt of trenches again.

There's always this obscure feeling of anxiety when I leave Kyiv for war. So, before that, I want to take a deep breath of chestnut blossom and sunshine.

The colossal Battle of Donbas that unfolded following the Russian failure at Kyiv had been going on for nearly a month.

And it was creating devastation comparable to that of World War II, without exaggeration.

A grim picture in the news.

Russian forces stand some twenty kilometers away from Slovyansk, the symbolic heart of Donbas where a Russian-led insurgency ignited the regional war back in 2014. Immense hordes supplemented by absurdly gargantuan artillery power slowly devour the region from the north and the east.

The bloody drama of Mariupol is coming to an end.

The city is flattened after some eighty days under siege. An estimated twenty thousand to twenty-five thousand civilians dead. The last Ukrainian garrison trapped at the Azovstal steelworks fights with its last ounces of strength—and begs for its slowly dying wounded amid the ruins to be evacuated. Serhiy Volynsky, a marine commander at the Azovstal, posts his bone-tired, bearded face on Facebook via Starlink and sends a desperate message to the world: "What do I hope for? A MIRACLE!"

The city of Popasna has been reduced to dust. The all-eviscerating wall of Russian artillery fire draws closer to Severodonetsk, Lyman, Slovyansk, Bakhmut.

With all that, it's good to plan something pleasant for when I return. You always need an unfinished bullet point in a to-do list, a thin thread between that hell and home.

Natalia and I will go see a jazz band play Frank Sinatra songs on a rooftop at sunset. Yes, these beautiful and very popular shows are up and running once more. Or we'll go see a movie at a theater in Podil—but God forbid it's Marvel-universe comics again.

We owe so unspeakably much to those who have shielded this city from this insanely absurd yet terribly bloodletting war.

Tens of thousands of lives, combatants and civilians, cut down in that giant meat grinder ravaging far to the east.

I keep scrolling through pictures of the Battle of Kyiv on my iPhone.

A photo from March 18 pops up on the screen.

A Russian name tag reading "Lubsandabayev B.N." One of the patches I photographed on the battlefield of Rusaniv during a body exchange.

I'd wondered off and on about that name for weeks after that day.

We naturally despise the enemy. We see a faceless death army that commits horrific things no one would ever want to see. We mourn our dead who we loved, the people who had left friends, lovers, thoughts, dreams, and lives to live.

But what about that name I saw next to eviscerated Russian BMP-2s?

What's really behind those charred Russian BMPs and frayed patches? Do I want to know?

Natalia is taking her time, and I have my MacBook with me.

The internet is forever, and Google knows everything.

"Lubsandabayev B.N."

Yep, here we go.

Bair Lubsandabayev, senior lieutenant.

The 1st platoon, the 4th company, the 21st Guards Motor Rifle Brigade. Based in Totskoye, near Orenburg.

Age: twenty-four.

A mugshot shows the face of a young Asian man.

Born in Tsagatui, a town of just seven hundred in Buryatia. It's a very distant region in Russia's Far East near the Baikal Lake. I guess one needs to be into geography to find those places on a map without googling.

Bair, an ethnic Buryat, obviously.

Google Street View shows a poor village of log houses and dusty, unpaved streets. And lonesome hills on the horizon. A place lost in the steppe some 30 kilometers from the Mongolian border.

I wonder if the guy was a real, natural-born Buddhist. That would be an interesting topic for conversation.

Whoa, the guy was really into sports.

Volleyball, soccer, tourism. There's a short article in some military propaganda publication mentioning his name as part of the 21st brigade in Orenburg Oblast.

His mother, Ariuna, is a schoolteacher—in their hometown. And he also had a sister, name's Ayana.

The father's name is probably Nikolai.

Their lives and destinies are wide open on social media. Just regular people living their quiet lives in a country far away.

What can I say.

You could have just stayed home, Bair.

You could have had a family. You could have worked to make life in your poor village better. You could have been the town's successful mayor, I don't know. Or you could have become a decent soccer coach and trained local kids. Not a bad way to spend one's life, Bair, don't you think?

But you met your death near a Ukrainian town seven thousand kilometers away from home—in an idiotic war for the sake of just one delusional old man's monstrous act of megalomania.

And for nothing more than that.

What's even worse is that your mindless obedience helped inflict the death upon so many of the best people Ukraine had.

And this is one of the most unspeakably painful things about this war.

So many Ukrainian soldiers and officers could have gone on breathing, listening to music, continuing with their careers, enjoying cold beer in the evening, holding the hands of their girlfriends and boyfriends, and hugging their kids.

But no.

They sacrificed their lives to stop the army of those proudly preventing a maniac's lowest instincts from coming into their homes to desolate, slay, and oppress.

And they can't get anything in return for their ultimate sacrifice.

It's over for them, too.

As epochs come and go over the old battlefields and soldiers' graves, they will stay in the dark of nonexistence—forever.

ACKNOWLEDGMENTS

My endless gratitude goes out to the men and women of Ukraine's Defense Forces—heroic and self-sacrificing—who managed to alter the course of history and thanks to whom we are alive and able to see the way out through the dark.

Every day of Ukrainian freedom was the greatest gift given by those wearing blue, yellow, and green sleeve patches.

A NOTE ON THE AUTHOR

Illia Ponomarenko is a Ukrainian journalist known as a former defense and security reporter at the *Kyiv Post* and subsequently a cofounder of the *Kyiv Independent*. He has covered the war in eastern Ukraine since the conflict's earliest days, as well as Russia's full-scale invasion of Ukraine since 2022. He has also had deployments to Palestine and the Democratic Republic of the Congo as an embedded reporter with UN peacekeeping forces. Ponomarenko received the Alfred Friendly Press Partners fellowship and was selected to work as *USA Today*'s guest reporter at the United States Department of Defense. He lives in Bucha, outside Kyiv.